COURSE IN DIVINITY AND GENERAL COLLECTANEA

OF ITEMS BY AND ABOUT

MARY BAKER EDDY

DISCOVERER AND FOUNDER OF CHRISTIAN SCIENCE
AND AUTHOR OF ITS TEXTBOOK
SCIENCE AND HEALTH WITH KEY TO THE SCRIPTURES

NOTES ON MARY BAKER EDDY'S

COURSE IN DIVINITY

Recorded by Lida Fitzpatrick, C.S.D., and Others

WATCHES, PRAYERS, ARGUMENTS

GIVEN TO STUDENTS BY MARY BAKER EDDY

ITEMS FROM GILBERT CARPENTER'S

COLLECTANEA

NOT ALREADY INCLUDED IN THE ABOVE

INSTRUCTION IN METAPHYSICS

FROM MARY BAKER EDDY

Recorded by Dr. Alfred E. Baker, M.D., C.S.D.
TOGETHER WITH SOME NOTES ON
METAPHYSICAL WORK

Compiled by
Richard Oakes

Acknowledgments

Healing Unlimited, as publisher of this work, is deeply indebted to the efforts of Gilbert Congdon Carpenter, Sr., C.S.B., and his son, Gilbert C. Carpenter, Jr., C.S.B., for their perseverance and loyalty to the cause of Christian Science and to Mary Baker Eddy in preserving this sacred history and making it available for posterity's sake. Also, a forever debt of gratitude goes out to Richard Oakes for his courage in originally publishing this material in what has affectionately become known as the "Blue Book," and later on, in the publishing of subsequent volumes, the "Red," "Green," "Yellow," and "Brown" books. Lastly, Ralph Geradi and Jerry Lupo of the Rare Book Company in Plainfield, New Jersey, spent years keeping this vital material in the public domain, even when threatened with legal action from the centralized Christian Science church. History records their faithfulness for their stand for the truth. This book is still available from Jerry as well.

NOTE: All original spellings as they appear in the book have been left intact for searching purposes in the digital versions—e.g. "wilful," "Saviour," etc. Names have been included in brackets [ ] after initials in many instances, to help in the identification of a particular student. The last line of each page may not end at the right side of the page; so that the exact wording for each page may be identical to the original in order to find words from existing concordances.

The print and electronic (digital) versions of this book are available from:

Healing Unlimited
www.ChristianScience.org
heal@ChristianScience.org
(800) 962-1464

Printed in the United States of America and other countries.

ISBN: 1-893107-56-6 Paperback edition
ISBN: 1-893107-57-4 Hardcover edition
ISBN: 1-893107-38-8 Adobe® ebookReader
ISBN: 1-893107-40-X Adobe® Acrobat™ PDF

FOREWORD

Readers of the pages which follow may find it interesting to look at the *Church Manual* of The First Church of Christ, Scientist, by Mary Baker Eddy—to the pages (67-9) where she specifies the arrangements for the call of workers to her home. It is indicated that some of them would be taught 'the course in Divinity' and would be required to pay for their instruction in the event of their leaving her before the term of service was completed. Several of the students in her home took notes of what was referred to as the Divinity Course, and they and many others kept notes of other unrelated items of instruction given in the home, together with the text of specific work they were required to do, or of 'watches' they were required to keep. It is the aim of this compilation to preserve as much of this as possible.

Students' notes have for a long time had an unverified circulation among Christian Scientists; and it was in the hope of preserving at least one version of the Divinity Course in the form in which it was taken down by the original hearer that Gilbert Carpenter Jr. privately printed the Lida Fitzpatrick notes in 1933 and entrusted two copies to the Congressional Library in Washington. This version, probably the fullest and most authentic obtained, was granted a copyright in 1933 in the name of one claiming ownership, but the copyright expired unrenewed.

In 1950 Mr. Carpenter further gathered together a miscellaneous collection of *Watches, Prayers, Arguments* given by Mrs. Eddy either verbally or in writing to members of her household. Some of these were given direct to his father while the latter served Mrs. Eddy as assistant secretary in 1905-6; in the case of others the original recipient is often not known.

Adam Dickey, in his *Memoirs of Mary Baker Eddy*, gives some interesting details which show the extensive part which the 'watches' played in the household. He writes: 'The most important work in connection with our Leader's home was that done by the mental workers, who were there because of their experience in the field as practitioners and of their ability to handle the claims of evil as they presented themselves. This work was done under the direct supervision of our Leader, and through her secretary she informed the other workers just what phases of error she felt should be given special attention. Her secretary, at her request, prepared what was denominated a "watch". This consisted of typewritten sheets of paper containing in numerical order the names or description of the phases of error that Mrs. Eddy wished them to handle.'

Among those who were closely associated with Mrs. Eddy and who kept notes was Dr. Alfred E. Baker, M.D., C.S.D., particularly during his residence in Concord between the years 1898 and 1902. It was he who was chosen to be teacher of the course in Obstetrics when the Board of Education was called into being in 1898 under the auspices of the previously closed Massachusetts Metaphysical College. As such he was a very frequent visitor to Mrs. Eddy's home, Pleasant View. The notes he took at this time he treasured to such an extent that he hired a professional copyist to print them into two notebooks specially bound in soft leather. The ink used was a waterproof variety and the paper a special India stock. The first book contained the notes for the Obstetrics course, prepared under Mrs. Eddy's supervision; the second contained items of instruction in metaphysics and notes on metaphysical work done while in association with Mrs. Eddy. Since this second book covers much the same ground as the Carpenter compilation of *Watches, Prayers, Arguments,* it has been decided to include all the relevant material at the end of this volume. Evidently it is not confined to items given to himself, for the reader will find extracts from a letter written by Mrs. Eddy to a student in 1885 and other passages passed to him through other students. Where he duplicates items included in the Carpenter compilation, these have been omitted from one or the other, according to which version was the fuller or where the item seemed better placed.

Mr. Gilbert Carpenter Sr. records an interesting story regarding the origin of one of the items in the Baker notes. 'As was Mrs. Eddy's custom,' he writes, 'she kept a pad and pencil near her bed. What she called *Instruction* was written in bed in the wee small hours of the morning. After it was completed she directed Calvin Frye to hitch up the horse, drive to Christian Science Hall and deliver what she had written to Dr. Baker, with the statement that Mrs. Eddy wanted him to have it immediately. Dr. Baker said that Mr. Frye called him from his bed to give it to him. He also stated that he knows of no instruction by Mrs. Eddy that is exactly like it. He considered it a masterpiece.' This *Instruction* presumably refers to the item given here on page 269.

The compiler of this volume records his great appreciation of the energy and devotion with which Gilbert Carpenter Jr. collected and edited not only *Watches, Prayers, Arguments* and the Divinity Course, but also the earlier *Collectanea of Items by and about Mary Baker*

Eddy. In particular I add my gratitude for his assistance and encouragement enabling me to reproduce the available material in this way. A full account of our association appears in the foreword to Essays and Other Footprints. During my last visit to Mr. Carpenter I went through Collectanea with him item by item, so that I could classify and rearrange the work as now found in this volume. Although no longer printed as a separate book, 'Collectanea, Revised Edition' can be found here in its entirety, its three chapters being renumbered VI, VII, VIII for the purpose of inclusion in a book to which it really belongs. The exceptions are Items A and D of the original Chapter 1, which have been dovetailed with the similar items of the present volume's Chapters IV and V.

In making the rearrangements I was also guided by consideration of the possible universal application of what was presented. Some statements which relate to specific persons and events seem to need a great deal of context before they can begin to meet the above test and these are not included here. Context or date is included where possible, but since this is the exception rather than the rule, much has been left in these pages which is but a string of isolated comments. Their value, and the wisdom of sensing the correct context, are matters left to the reader. It might well be borne in mind that a student can hear and record only what he or she is capable of hearing (understanding). Hence the value of 'translation' into the 'original language, which is Mind'. Whatever the Revelator of Christian Science may have said or written on the subject is of vital importance, whereas a human estimate of Mrs. Eddy's personality is spiritually worthless.

In view of the oft-repeated warnings and instructions given by Mrs. Eddy, it is obvious, for example, that where persons were mentioned in the 'watches' it was their function or job that was involved, never a personality. The 'watcher' in such cases was called upon to 'watch' for the correct functioning of the various phases of Mind-activity, realizing that one Mind governs, whether the occasion was called the articles written by a Journal editor, or a Christian Science lecture, or a dish prepared by a cook, or one's duty to the Discoverer of Christian Science. Indeed, Mrs. Eddy's instructions were specific on the point of personality, even when she mentioned individuals and individual conditions. Once in a call to a trusted student to help an official she made it plain that the former was not dealing with a person 'out there', but with his own ability to see what Mind was expressing to him in a certain situation; for she added succinctly: 'It is only God Himself that you are communing with, and your answer comes from divine Love who saith, "Ask and ye shall receive. Seek and ye shall find." '

In his foreword to the Carpenter edition of *Watches, Prayers, Arguments,* Gilbert Carpenter Jr. quotes a letter which Mrs. Eddy once wrote to one of the Board of Directors on the subject of personality. She said: 'Naming persons in prayer is the fight between beasts. Overcoming ... evil and lies with good and Truth in your prayers is *Christian Science.*' And in a letter dated December 5, 1906, she wrote: 'Please remove your thoughts utterly away from *me*.... Only break the law of the lie. You and the Committee on Business keep *me* out of your thoughts.' And later: 'Again I have to write, *Do not think of me.* Your tender thought reaches me—*costs me much.*'

There is much valuable information and comment in the prefaces which Mr. Carpenter added to his compilation of *Watches, Prayers, Arguments* and the Divinity Course. The main passages are accordingly added below by request, excluding those points already touched on, or where there is duplication between the two prefaces.

London, England

R. F. OAKES

INTRODUCTION BY GILBERT CARPENTER JR. TO NOTES ON THE COURSE IN DIVINITY

In the *Christian Science Sentinel* for August 17, 1935, is an 'Item of Interest' from the Christian Science Board of Directors in which they state that these notes recorded in Mrs. Eddy's home by Lida Fitzpatrick, Laura E. Sargent, George H. Kinter, and possibly others, should not be accepted as genuine, or as giving accurate statements by our Leader. They state, 'It is neither fair nor loyal to our Leader to attribute to her anything that is not authenticated in a dependable way. Writings said to be hers which did not come directly from her and which do not accord with her printed works in substance and phraseology, may well be regarded as apocryphal, if not downright forgeries.'

In defence of these notes let it be said that the writer of this introduction has discussed the accuracy of the statements attributed to Mrs. Eddy with the following students: Miss Minnie Adelaide Still, Mrs. Caroline Foss Gyger, Calvin C. Hill, and Gilbert C. Carpenter. Miss Still served Mrs. Eddy as her personal maid from early in 1907 until she passed on in 1910. Mrs. Gyger was her maid from April to August 1906. Mr. Hill served her in many capacities over a long period of years. Mr. Carpenter was her Associate Secretary for the period of one year from 1905 to 1906.

These students are unanimous in declaring the accuracy of the expression and thought in these notes. Those who served in the home declare that they have heard our Leader give just such cryptic pronouncements, day after day. They also declare that she was most insistent on accuracy in quoting, or repeating, whatever they heard her say, or whatever they read in the Bible, or in her writings. For any inaccuracy in quotation they received a severe rebuke. Therefore, we can deduce that whatever these students recorded was set down with the greatest concern for accuracy. Mr. Hill has shown the writer a copy of these notes which he has in his possession, and although not as full as those preserved by Mrs. Fitzpatrick, correspond to them. Mr. Hill received his copy as a gift from Mrs. Laura E. Sargent, Mrs. Eddy's maid and helper for so many years.

The Christian world accepts as infallible, statements which were made by our Lord and Master, which were not recorded for from thirty to sixty years after he made them. The statements recorded by Mrs. Eddy's students were written down within a few moments after they were made, a fact which should weigh on the side of proving their accuracy and correctness....

Mrs. Eddy did not make the mistake of trying to teach the course in Divinity, when she knew that God alone could do that. She could not make the explanation to the students, however, because, when students are told in advance that certain things are provided to develop spiritual sense, the good effect is often lost, since part of the development comes from struggling with problems without knowing why. Therefore, Mrs. Eddy lovingly and patiently gave out that which would prepare students to receive the course in Divinity, and she was divinely guided to put such preparation in the wisest possible way. At the same time she referred to the preparation as the course itself, waiting on God to reveal to students that which she could not tell them, because divine wisdom did not permit her to.

How does man develop spiritual sense? By use. Before he can use it he must know he has it, and begin to lose faith in the adequacy and satisfactory nature of the false sense. Thus, when a problem is placed before the student, the solution of which defies his trained human mind, the despair he feels over the inadequacy of the human mind to supply the solution helps to drive him to the use of the divine Mind, which of necessity involves the use and development of spiritual sense.

An example of this was the building of The Mother Church. Mrs. Eddy laid down arbitrary provisions and requirements which made the human mind feel that such requirements could not possibly be fulfilled. The result was that those in charge worked on the problem from the standpoint of demonstration with more determination than perhaps they would have otherwise. To some degree they relinquished the human mind, because they felt it to be inadequate to perform the tasks successfully according to the demands of their Leader. In this wise way did Mrs. Eddy ensure the building of the church being a spiritual development for those engaged in the work, as well as the result of a scientific demonstration of divine Mind, rather than a product of mortal mind, or material sense.

It can be affirmed that whatever our Leader declared, or gave her students to do, that seemed to be beyond their human performance and understanding, was an effort to force them to the use and development of spiritual sense, which would include preparation for the course in Divinity, since, as has been stated, this course is received wholly by spiritual sense.

The deduction is, that the cryptic statements our Leader gave the students in her home in connection with the course in Divinity, were for the purpose of putting before them that which they could not comprehend without spiritual sense. Thus such statements were not given them for purposes of instruction, but development. This was also true of the tasks she gave them to do. Once she gave her personal maid the task of altering a waist. The student said she could not do it, because she had not been trained in that sort of work. Mrs. Eddy did not comment and gave the task to Pauline Mann; but the sadness of her face indicated that she had offered it to this student that she might demonstrate spiritual ability from divine Mind, which she could have done, and thus performed the task successfully. Mrs. Eddy saw it as a lost opportunity for this student. At another time, she gave this same student the task of cutting off to the elbows the sleeves of a suit of underwear and then refused to let her measure her forearm. This might seem strange unless one saw as her purpose to force the student to do it by reflecting divine intelligence, which effort would be correct and mean the development of spiritual sense. Had she permitted her to measure her arm, the impulse to demonstrate would not have been fostered.

If a student today selects a cryptic statement from among these household notes and seeks to discover its true meaning through the listening ear—listening for God's voice—instead of seeking to discredit the statement given by our Leader simply because he does not understand it humanly, he will be enabled to perceive the divine purpose back of these statements. Too, he will learn how they can be used by an advanced student without breaking the Manual, and will prove them to be of the same value to him that they were to those who heard them directly from our Leader's lips....

...On page 181 of the first edition of *Science and Health* she writes, 'The literal meaning of the Scripture is not its highest sense; its spiritual signification is what explains God and man.' The same holds true for all the vast material that has been preserved from our Leader's lips and pen that is not to be found in her authorized published writings.

FOREWORD BY GILBERT CARPENTER JR. TO 'WATCHES, PRAYERS, ARGUMENTS'

In the home of Mary Baker Eddy, the Discoverer and Founder of Christian Science, those whom she called mental workers were instructed to sit quietly in their rooms and watch and pray, usually for an hour at a time. These periods she called *watches*, after the Master's query, 'Could ye not watch with me one hour?'

It was her custom to furnish these workers with written texts or outlines of thoughts which she expected them to amplify. Calvin Frye, her Secretary, would pass these papers around to each worker. When there was a special need, the amount of such work was increased. Gilbert C. Carpenter relates how, in 1905, the workers watched for three days and nights, without going to bed or removing their clothes, being permitted fifteen minute rest periods from time to time. When the work was done successfully, Mrs. Eddy told them so, and the home returned to its normal schedule of three main watches per day in which everyone, including Mrs. Eddy, participated. Each worker had an additional hour in which he worked alone. Mr. Carpenter, for instance, had what was called the midnight watch, watching from 12 to 1 A.M.

Mr. Carpenter states that only Mrs. Eddy knew what the circumstances were that required three days of watching. She directed the lines of work that were taken up, but she did not disclose what the problem was, not even when it was handled....

The compiler of these watches would have it understood that his purpose was in no sense a sentimental attempt to 'memorial' something from the past. It is his conviction and hope that God guided him to collect these watches in order that the vital spiritual work for Christian Science and the world, which Mrs. Eddy conducted in her home and among her students, may be renewed and continued. If such work was needed and efficacious in her day, is it not still needed? And will not a vast amount of good be done if loyal students, who are ready and fitted to carry on such work, take it up with a consecration and dedication that augurs of success and merits God's approval and blessing? ...

One attempt to discount the value of these watches to present-day workers who are ready for them is made by those who contend that their use would violate Mrs. Eddy's own By-law in the Manual, which forbids the use of formulas. Yet this very By-law states: 'Sometimes she may strengthen the faith by a written text as no one else can.' And what are the watches in this book but Mrs. Eddy's own written texts? Furthermore, if a student felt that it was not fitting to use the exact statements which our Leader formulated, by having them to read, he has the priceless privilege of learning just what were the weapons of her warfare which were found efficacious to the pulling down of strongholds; thus will he be helped in formulating his own.

A novice may study the music of a master with no intention of copying it. In his own efforts to write music, he is helped by a study of the compositions of great composers. A study of the flight of a seagull helped the Wright brothers to construct a plane that would fly, but in doing so they were not limited by nor confined to a bird's use of his wings.

The world may never know the loss it sustained when it no longer had Mrs. Eddy at the head of her household of mental workers, directing them day and night to pour into human consciousness a volume of scientific thought that aided greatly in counteracting and neutralizing the error in human consciousness, and opening the way for Truth to enter and govern. In this group she was the chief worker who set the pace for all. Students found it not only possible but easy on the whole to sit and work for one hour, where she worked at the same time and took the lead, when they could not have done the same thing in their own homes for more than a short time. One is reminded of a bicycle race where speeds of fifty miles an hour are achieved by having a motorcycle cleaving the air ahead, and the bicyclist pacing behind.

In calling on students to watch faithfully with her, Mrs. Eddy put them on their honor that they would spend the hour in no other way, nor cut it short because it became wearisome. She indicated that the success of her church and mission was largely dependent on such work. In fact she wrote to Hannah Larminie that if such watches had not been kept in Boston, the Cause would have been lost. She said to her, 'This Cause must be carried by silent argument just the same as you carry it physically. This is the great duty for Christians that they must do, or be accountable to God for leaving it undone.'

In reading these watches one wonders at Mrs. Eddy's insistence on students handling the weather. Gilbert C. Carpenter reports that she kept Laura Sargent working on the weather much of the time, even while she had other students working on specific problems that needed attention.... If a student should become fixed in the notion that the entire mission of Science is to heal mankind, it would help him to read these watches, so that he might learn that in Mrs. Eddy's eyes it was no misuse of Truth to apply it to the weather and other general discords. The task of the working Scientist must include correcting the sense of weather, if it violates the law of harmony, as well as to work on whatever else comes to his notice in the world that calls for divine help. On page 427 of the textbook we read: 'Immortal Mind, governing all, must be acknowledged as supreme in the physical realm, so-called, as well as in the spiritual.' . . .

The following extracts from the diary kept by Calvin Frye tell an interesting story: 'August 6, 1900. When Mrs. Eddy was out on the swing this morning, she told me to go and tell Joseph Mann for him and me to constantly hold the thought, the sun will not appear for three days and three nights, and there will be a constant rain; the clouds will be continually replenished. It is a very hot sunny day. Suddenly at 10 o'clock tonight a severe thunder shower came up with almost a cyclone. Mother told me to tell Joseph, there is no cyclone. We united in that thought and in less than five minutes the wind (which was filled with water like mist) came down to a gentle breeze. Mother then told me to tell Joseph, no thunder and lightning, but continuous gentle rain. In a few moments the thunder died away in the distance and there was a steady gentle rain. Today, Aug. 7, there has been a gentle rain most of the day without thunder.'…

Another point to be noted in these pages is Mrs. Eddy's frequent use of the names of various poisons, and her insistence that students use a terminology that included such names. On May 26, 1903, she said to her household: 'If you take up arsenic you will hit it in most of the cases in 1903.'

Mrs. Eddy was past mistress of the art of formulating arresting as well as scientific terminology that would challenge thought, when perhaps it had become jaded in its use of familiar arguments. A declaration loses its incisiveness through much use; and since the efficacy of Science is in proportion to the extent that thought is mentalized as well as spiritualized, the use of certain material terms in connection with that which is obviously mental, becomes a help in resolving things into thoughts, and so aiding one in reaching that vantage where one admits that, even in the human realm, when one tells the truth about the lie, all is mind. For instance, when one takes material poison and suffers ill effects, mortal mind, not matter, causes such effects.

Thus the lesson Mrs. Eddy was bringing home to her students concerning mental causation became more potent when she called upon them to handle certain poisons like arsenic and mercury, when it was evident that she was referring to no possibility of such poisons having been taken or being present materially. Thus she was referring to mesmeric poison operating exactly as the hypnotist operates when he causes a burn to appear with a piece of ice.

On August 9, 1900, she wrote to the Board of Directors, 'The one devil, evil, takes thought by drugs as well as siege. The drugs are morphine, opium, hashish, arsenic, rhus-radicant, strychnine. There is a need of awakening before it is too late.'

There is no doubt but that the effect of all mortal suggestions on the advancing student is like poison in the mental realm. Is it strange, therefore, that Mrs. Eddy should find this out and instruct students to work accordingly?

Among other things Mrs. Eddy had her students handle electricity. On July 13, 1904, when Lewis Strang was asked to interview a student as a prospective maid for her, she wrote: 'Ask her, have you always been well and strong in belief before coming into Christian Science? How do you handle belief of nerves, M.A.M., electricity?'

Electricity functions by a discharge from the positive to the negative pole. From this phenomenon we learn the nature of animal magnetism in its claim to be contagious, and to dart from one mortal thought to another. Hence our defence must lie in acknowledging this claim and then refuting it with the truth of being.

Once Mrs. Eddy asked a student the question: 'Do you understand the handling of electrical poisoning? It is mental thought transference with malice behind it—with an intent to harm. Mortal mind sends its messages without wires. It is aggressive mental suggestion maliciously directed.'

When Mrs. Eddy detected that the mental workers were not basing their prayers on a true and scientific realization of the nothingness of the error which they were taking up, she would stop their work on the basis that something was out of tune. At times she told them to drop the argument entirely and to hold with God. At other times she would tell them to stop denying the error and to affirm the truth without reference to the negative side. Such instructions were given according to the immediate need, and in no sense were they general rules.

When she found the students making error real, she had to stop their work and direct their thoughts to the right side only. When she found them repeating arguments like parrots without a spark of spirit in them, or with a strained anxiety that carried little faith in God, she had to rebuke them.

How do we account for the fact that at times she formulated prayers which had about them the aroma of old theology? Her mission was to call students to rise from the old personal sense of God to a scientific definition of Him. In this effort there is a danger that one's scientific sense become so impersonal and cold, that one ceases to feel the Father's presence as a palpable sense of divine Love watching over one at all times and under all circumstances. Proof of this contention may be found in the beautiful definition of God which Mrs. Eddy gave to the class of 1898, as recorded on page 90 of Irving C. Tomlinson's book, *Twelve Years with Mary Baker Eddy*.

The male and female of prayer may be said to be the scientific exercise of power through scientific declaration, *inseparable* from a loving, humble acknowledgment of Him as ever present and the one source of all power and intelligence. Mrs. Eddy watched to see that the students kept a proper balance in their mental ministrations. If she found prayer becoming too masculine—too coldly scientific she would outline a fervent prayer of acknowledgment and petition to the loving Father-Mother forever near.

When she found students using the repetition of mere words without the spirit, she declared that they were chattering the letter of Science like mocking-birds. She explained that the apathy, the lack of love and Christian vigor came of seeking only the letter of Truth and stopping there, because it costs so much more to gain the spirit thereof.

A formula is a superstitious belief in the efficacy of the repetition of mere words—like chanting some magic recipe, illustrated by the witches in the play, Macbeth. Even the watches in this book could be used as formulas, unless, as one works and prays, he seeks to have God govern his thought. A formula is a human remedy in the mental realm, as medicine is in the physical realm, since it is based on a belief that a set phraseology has the power to heal disease, when the scientific fact to be realized is that there is no disease to heal.

Arguments in Science are like the match one uses to light the gas in the stove. It is the gas that bakes the cake. Arguments become a formula when one tries to heal by their means, as if one tried to bake the cake with the match. Mrs. Eddy watched the students, lest they sink to the level of believing that their declarations were what accomplished the work. On page 454 of the textbook, we read, 'Remember that the letter and mental arguments are only human auxiliaries to aid in bringing thought into accord with the spirit of Truth and Love, which heals the sick and the sinning'.

An airplane taxies on the ground to gain the speed necessary to rise where it may soar unfettered. The repeating and declaring of arguments—even those furnished by our Leader—becomes the use of formulas unless, as one uses them, he carries in mind the goal of Science, where one's thoughts blend with God and soar in the illimitable realm of Mind.

Mrs. Eddy furnished the tools of scientific thought and work, but she told her students always to go to God for the wisdom to use these tools correctly, as well as for the love to put into them the unction necessary. Only as God directs our thought and work can we be sure that we are not using a formula.

No student should approach any problem—even though he uses Mrs. Eddy's exact phraseology—without seeking God's wisdom to direct him and God's love to inspire him, since God alone can guide one to treat a case scientifically and enable him to put into it the divine love that heals. To apply mere words, statements, or arguments to a case, mechanically, without the spirit or the directing wisdom of God, breaks the letter and the spirit of the By-law in the Manual forbidding the use of formulas.

There are those who contend that, when Pleasant View as Mrs. Eddy's earthly home, ceased to be her platform of scientific activity because she had left our midst, the watches which she issued to students should have been likewise destroyed, since they were adapted solely for use at the time she issued them.... Mrs. Eddy's earthly home, called Pleasant View, or Chestnut Hill, is not important to students today, but her sense of home that she established is, namely, a place where one seeks to establish divine Mind as supreme in all that he does, even in the most commonplace and menial tasks, and to continue this effort until he has made divine Mind his permanent Mind, and all belief in a so-called human mind has been ruled out. A student who seeks to fulfil this purpose may declare that he has been to Pleasant View in proportion as he fulfils the purposes of Pleasant View. By seeking to do everything from the standpoint of divine Mind, he makes his own home a Pleasant View, and if using Mrs. Eddy's *Watches* will help him in this direction, he should have them and use them eagerly every day. What can be more helpful to the student who is ready for the privilege, than to learn from Mrs. Eddy's *Watches* how to occupy his time?...

Note for British readers:

In the following pages where dates are given in figures, the month number comes first in accordance with American practice.

CONTENTS

CHAPTER ONE

NOTES ON THE COURSE IN DIVINITY

given by MARY BAKER EDDY, the Discoverer and Founder of Christian Science, and Author of its Textbook, *Science and Health with Key to the Scriptures,* at Her Home, PLEASANT VIEW, Concord, New Hampshire, during the Years Nineteen Hundred Three, Nineteen Hundred Four, and Nineteen Hundred Seven

Recorded by
LIDA FITZPATRICK, C.S.D.
AND OTHERS

May 13, 1903. Is there any darkness in light? No.

Is there any evil in good? No.

What tells you there is? Belief; my false sense.

Have you a false sense? No. THERE.

Is there any belief? No. Then KNOW it.

Sight, hearing, memory, action cannot be lost; they are eternal, of God; eyes do not see, it is Mind; then if I have lost my sight God has lost His; if I have lost my hearing God has lost His.

You do not have to sleep; Mind is always active; cessation of thought is not what is needed, but the ever-presence.

Have you a nose? No.

Then can nose have any secretion or constriction? No.

Then ran nose have catarrh? No. There, it is done.

All we have to meet is sin; it is sin to believe a lie and we know it; now you know what to do with sin A sin to believe you have a nose, catarrh, when you know you haven't it.

My suffering (Mrs. Eddy's) is from believing other people's thoughts affect me; I say, Mary, it is not other people's sin, it is your own thought; nothing can MAKE you sin, you do it yourself. There is no prenatal belief that can make you believe it, there is nothing but God and His idea. The devil tempted Jesus; said, come down and I will give you all you see; and the devil had not an acre of ground to give; and has nothing to give you. Jesus did not stop to argue with a lie (argument of error); did not say, now Mr. Devil

I will argue with you about it; he said, 'Get thee behind me, Satan'. He 'spake the word and it was done'. Shut it all out. You do not have to argue; KNOW. KNOW God and His idea, and not argue about sin.

It was years before I argued.

In teaching a class I tell some joke to start the thought moving; God tells me to. There must be action; that chair cannot come unless it is moved; I get the thought started. A lady in Lynn was so angry at me she would not speak to me after healing her daughter, because she said I spoke disrespectfully to her dying daughter; the physicians had said there was only a little piece of her lung left and she was dying. I was called and there were Spiritualists around; I tried to reach her thought, but no, could not get at it; so I said, 'Get up out of that bed!' Then I called to those in the other room, 'Bring her clothes'. The girl got up and was well; never even coughed again; is living yet for all I know; I have never heard otherwise; but her mother has never spoken to me since.

I speak sharply sometimes, but the thought must MOVE.

What is a demonstration? Proof

Well, the proof already is. I never say I have had a demonstration, for it was always done.

A year is a short time for a Divinity Class.

May 14,1903. 'EATING my flesh', etc. That word 'eating' has been so misunderstood; as in olden times the plucking out of an eye, etc., taken literally; when we depend upon those things we are against God. When we are asleep we are not the image and likeness of God, for God never sleeps; mortal sense says, you take away eating, sleeping and these things and you take away everything. Now you must look always to Spirit—not matter—for EVERYTHING.

May 18, 1903. I know what is coming. I dare not tell you what I know; you are young yet, and now is the time to experiment. You will know some day.

We are told the world will be destroyed. How? By malice. By cyclones, electricity and be burned up. What is a cyclone? It is a condition of mortal mind—malice; what burns up? Malice. We are told, like Mt. Pelee, there is an internal fire (malice) that will finally burst forth and destroy the world. It is all malice, and our textbook tells us, Christian Scientists will hold such things in check. God never made them and they can be overcome just the same as sickness. It is all within.

Now when there is the claim that the weather is sultry, handle it and you will see a breeze spring up; if it is cold, handle it; it is all in Mind ever the same, harmonious. God did not make sultry weather, etc.; then if we through belief have made it we must unmake it. When it looks like thunder and lightning, handle it; there is no sultry atmosphere to cause thunder and lightning. When I first came to Concord (before hypnotism and mesmerism joined hands to work upon me) there was no snow the first winter at all, and no thunderstorms the first year. When sultry I would close my eyes for a moment, then open them and the leaves would all be stirring; a breeze had sprung up. We make our own atmosphere. These things are easier to handle than sickness. I used to handle them until I forgot about it. Lately I have attended to the work and only kept above the effects. When Clara was here I would speak about the thunderstorms and she would work alone and they would all disappear. You can do this, and if you are not at first successful do not get discouraged; keep on trying. When you have the first indication—forestall it.

May 20, 1903. Know that a shock only makes us go higher. Death is fear, and one awakes to find that experience (fear) did not kill him. Now let us know when mortal mind shocks us we can use it to go up higher and so know it cannot catch us there. (This was said after a shock during a drive.)

May 21, 1903. The true Science—divine Science—will be lost sight of again unless we arouse ourselves. This demonstrating to make matter build up is not Science. The building up of churches, the writing of articles and the speaking in public is the old way of building up a cause. The way I brought this Cause into sight was through HEALING: and now these other things would come in and hide it just as was done in the time of Jesus. Now this Cause must be saved and I pray God to be spared for this work. If there is not work done in the line of Spirit—not matter—or overcoming the material way (I have always stood for God alone), if I were not here to still stand, the Catholics and Spiritualists would wipe every Christian Scientist out. Now you see what we have to do for the world; be a transparency for SPIRIT. Things must turn and overturn, until He whose right it is shall reign.

We must show the difference between the healing of Christian Science and quackery.

Healing is demonstration, nothing else is. When I first heard them speak of demonstration I asked—who? I thought someone had been healed. I lectured one time where the Spiritualists tried to break up the meeting; they would jump up and contradict without being asked. A lady in the audience (with whom I boarded)—and the audience was large —was taken with one of her attacks of gallstones; fell on the floor in excruciating pain; I said to the Spiritualists present, 'Now is your time to prove what your God will do for you; heal this woman.' They jumped about and did what they could, but she grew worse and worse. I stepped down from the platform, stood beside her a moment and the pain left; she arose and sat in her chair and was *healed*. This went broadcast, and through the healing this Science was brought to notice. It is lost sight of and must be regained. I have left the word 'chemicalization' out of the book (S. & H.) and substituted 'chemistry'. Chemicalization denotes a fight, while chemistry denotes the neutralizing process, as Spirit destroying the claim of matter.

May 23, 1903. 'He that *endureth* unto the end shall be *saved*.' Jesus endured; after he disappeared from their view he endured. The Lord delayed his coming so the disciples went back to their nets. He endured; he showed the same nail prints and the same body after as before, showing it was the same Jesus. And so shall we be saved if we endure.

May 25, 1903. If you do not understand what words *mean* they are without power. One was saying, 'The law of the spirit of Truth (life) in Christ Jesus hath made me free from the law of sin and death'. I asked, what is the word? The answer was, 'diphtheria'; was asleep mentally; then I said, what is the word? The *spirit* of Truth (life). Then he saw it meant KNOWING it; the spirit of it, and the relief was experienced at once. That is the work—knowing what this Science *means*, and so get out of the sense of *apathy*. Jesus said, 'Can ye not watch with me one hour?' And they were asleep. Now WATCH, You may sit in your chair all day and say over beautiful words and it does not amount to anything; it is the SPIRIT that is needed.

Our blessed Master did not have the Science of it, that is, did not give the premise, the conclusion and the logical reasoning as this is; he had the spirit of it and gave it to the disciples. You cannot enter eternity until you have broken the law (or sense) of time. There is no collapse, neither is there any relapse.

May 26, 1903. If you take up arsenic you will hit it in most of the cases in 1903. 'If ye drink any deadly thing it *shall not hurt you*'; there you have the promise.

A man could not furnish milk because of not having water. Mrs. Eddy took it up and the next day when he came, said he had two feet of water in his cellar and no rain. Rain is good. Clara could bring the clouds and the rain. Just realize harmony; then there will be no tornado and no thunder and lightning.

May 26, 1903. Mother's Lesson on Rain.

The gentle clouds and the gentle rain fall upon the just and the unjust; no electricity, no thunder and no lightning, no cyclone, no tornado, no destruction, for the dear Father's face looks out from the cloud in love and in harmony. No malice, and no hatred—or there is nothing to interfere with His government in Love. There shall be the gentle and beautiful rain upon the earth to water the whole face of the earth.

May 27, 1903. Handle the thought of reversal. You can do it. The reign of harmony is; you can make it rain; it can water the earth. Is there a devil that can reverse God's government? No. Then have faith as a grain of mustard seed. You can.

May 28, 1903. Do not take up, there is no thunder and lightning; know that God governs the elements and there is nothing destructive or harmful. God sends the rain that watereth the earth. Human will cannot come in and govern.

You would not argue diphtheria if the case was consumption; neither do you argue thunder and lightning when it is sin (malice). If thunder and lightning come then know forces are of God and not destructive. If too much rain realize harmony; if drought—no drought. S. & H. 102: 9 (268th edition).

May 29, 1903. Anything that comes from the body is human will; that which comes not from the body and can only do good is the Divine. I (Mrs. Eddy) am only a windowpane through which the light comes. You are helping yourselves more than you help me, for I am *helping* you; the Discoverer has to discover the way to meet these things; you will not have that to do; you are *learning* NOW how to meet them; I have had to discover it.

May 30, 1903. The circumcision of the flesh—the letter—is what the Jews held to; the circumcision of the heart which takes out of matter, is what Jesus taught. What they were putting into matter Jesus (and Paul) was taking out. There was a nice quiet rain an night and Mrs. Eddy said we brought the rain; this broke the thought of drought.

May 31, 1903. Now drop arguing and hold to God. I used to do my healing with—'God is All.'

I never argued until I began teaching students and I had to meet the thought where it stood. Now hold the allness of God, then there is nothing else; if error says arsenic, can't sleep, can't eat—can; there is only one God. I have been made the way-shower. The devil said to Jesus, 'Others he saved, himself he cannot save'. 'Come down from the cross.' 'He will send angels to bear thee up', etc. What did Jesus say? 'Get thee behind me, *Satan*.' It says now, 'Come down from the cross'. 'You have said you do not have to eat or steep to nourish the body; come down and prove it.' Jesus told Satan to get behind; he was not ready for that proof yet; when he was he made it.

So will this be; I can eat, I can sleep; when I am ready for that demonstration it will be made. If the students that have passed on had understood this they would have been here today.

Another error which students do not understand is, 'Your old beliefs have returned'; meet it by knowing the beliefs are destroyed, rooted up, there is nothing of them to come back, is how I should meet it. Could you believe a corn could come back to a perfectly smooth toe? No.

About twelve or more years ago I (Mrs. Eddy) was working for the world, busy, when a claim came; I did not take time to pay attention to it, but one day a student said she had just met the claim of the sting of death for a patient. I said, 'Jesus hath taken away the sting of death'; as I said it the claim all left me.

June 1, 1903. You do not have to wait for your patient to tell you all about what to meet; you should see it and meet it. Break the law that AFTER the treatment is given the patient is worse. Break law that you are worse every hour. You are better every hour; so is everyone in the house.

June 2, 1903. Arouse yourselves and throw off this spell cast upon you. 'Choose you this day whom ye will serve', God or evil suggestions. It is not of any use to talk to a drunken man; RISE.

June 3, 1903. After a battle there is a thunderstorm; electricity is made up of zinc and copper—poisons. I have to take that up for myself; now realize there is no electricity but that which God governs; no vital force but God; only the gentle rain can come; no cyclones.

June 4, 1903. God does not come and go; it is the dream that does that; God *stands*; and we are one with Him; we cannot be shaken.

June 5, 1903. You must have the balance on the right side; a row of ciphers without the numeral '1' is nothing; now have your '1' with God; there is *no* evil; God is All. There is nothing (cipher) that can weigh against God.

June 12, 1903. In working for the weather, never say: there is no wind, there is no lightning, no rain, etc., for if you do it will act like mesmerism; it will break out in some other phase; but know the elements are in God's hands (His fists), they are not destructive, but governed by harmony, and express harmony. God gave us dominion over the earth, but it is His dominion; the loving Father gives us what is for us and nothing else can; He is Love and Love controls the elements and all things.

Someone said to Mrs. Eddy, 'I love you'. She said, 'Don't love me (person) but LOVE, then you will include me and all, but if you love some person you are shutting out Love; if you were to love a person you would probably love me more than any one else, but if you loved person you would have the result of it. Oh! the infinitude of *divine* Science.'

If I say to you, 'There is no thunder and lightning', then I say, 'Do not say there is no thunder and lightning but know they cannot be destructive', am I inconsistent? No. If I say to a dyspeptic, 'You have no stomach', then say, 'Eat food and it does you good', am I inconsistent? No. Absolute Science you cannot prove yet; that is, if you try to work that there is no thunder and lightning you will get into trouble for it keeps coming, and others believe it purifies the atmosphere. So you can see it has no power to harm, is not destructive, can only be harmonious. The dyspeptic, if you tell him to eat and the food does him good, will brighten up and be healed; when, if you declared no stomach, no food, you could not prove it yet. S. & H. 442: 23 (268th edition).

We can know that God governs all harmoniously.

June 14, 1903. 'Owe no man anything but to love one another.' I (Mrs. Eddy) have all the way in Christian Science, when I wanted to do anything, 'sat down and counted the cost'.

Do not be too cheerful, too quick to laugh; this is earnest, sober, vigilant work. I used to be so *full* of laughter, my mother missed it so much after I was married and went away—'that dear child's bright laugh has gone out of the house', she said.

God looks out from the clouds; He is Love and we are His reflection; we have love in our hearts because He is Love and we reflect Him, and we have no clouds.

Why is it a student will be so brave in the work in one direction and not in another? Because there is not enough love in the heart; it should be EVER-present, always ready. If a mother has a beautiful child which she loves, and another deformed, weakly one, can she not love that one, too? If she doesn't she has not the mother-love. Love not person, but *love*; it is always present for all occasions.

June 19, 1903. 'Lovest thou me?' Yes. 'Feed my sheep.' Can you separate the Principle from its idea? No. Can you love the

Principle and not its idea? No. Can you love the idea and not the Principle? No. Jesus was teaching this all the way along. It is the same today—that is the handle.

The Babylonish woman in the Apocalypse has thrown wormwood into the waters to turn trusting thoughts to hatred against me, the idea; handle this and you will find your patients healed. Love and its idea are ONE.

You would declare you love me, when underneath is the hatred nagging; kill it and go on loving.

Mrs. Eddy said a woman to whom she had been kind, was stricken down with disease, but she did not know it until one day a man told her she was dead. *Dead,* she said, DEAD? He said, well she was dying when I was there and I suppose she is dead by this time; the next day she was around the house at her work, well, and remained so; she said the family never knew what healed the woman.

Another woman who was ill, used to watch for Mrs. Eddy's carriage to pass; finally the woman said Mrs. Eddy had healed her by just riding past the house.

When Mrs. Eddy drove by a house and saw a woman on the porch holding a baby bundled up, she knew what that meant—sick baby, wanted her to heal it.

A mother used to send her boy out where Mrs. Eddy would drive by; he was idiotic; his chin would drop down and his eyes had no expression. One day she saw him with gloves on going to church.

June 21, 1903. We can feel encouraged in the overcoming of error, but do not feel satisfied until you 'awake in His likeness'. Every spiritualized thought is that much in this direction.

July 8, 1903. 'Peace be still. PEACE I leave with you, my peace I give unto you; you are in the arms of Love which shields you from everything.' These words must be accompanied by the spirit of them.

This was to show how to handle a case when many minds were at work on a case; which would be like wild beasts fighting, locking horns. The realization of peace is needed at such times; will unlock the horns; will stop the discord. The higher one senses harmony, the more sensitive he is to discord; the same in music. 'The greatest wrong is but the supposititious opposite of the highest right.' S. & H.

July 12, 1903. When we detect error as unreal, and God as All, we will be immortal.

July 15, 1903. If worse after treatment begins, take up, no reversal. If do not help declare, I *can* help.

July 18, 1903. Theosophists profess to make a law that will hold good for six months; they do not sit up nights to work. Now break these laws; then when that is accomplished and you go out from here you are ready for the next that is to be met, and when the need is to come here you will come back again; but if you do not meet it and go out from here you are not ready for the next and so cannot come back. This is the divinity. In healing a patient do not try to regenerate the whole; be like a carpenter, strengthen the weak places first, and while doing so the patient will be helped mentally; you cannot take the whole structure until you have reached that point. I am now doing the work of meeting the sin of the world.

July 29, 1903. Break the so-called laws which say you cannot heal, you cannot help the patient; the patient will relapse, etc.; work at it every day until they are destroyed; not wait until you have it to meet with the patient, but work every day just as hard as though the patient were dying, until you have the mastery; then they will never have dominion over your work. Look to God, whose only law is harmony.

July 31, 1903. The drunkenness produced by belief in wine is not to be compared with the drunkenness in thought—mental darkness. 'Drunken, but not with wine.' Isaiah 51: 21.

Keep awake by loving more; love the idea of God and you will love God; you can only love God as far as you love His idea, and love will be *expressed*. What would you think of one who says he loves but never expresses it? Love does express itself; it *heals*; if you do not heal you have not enough love. Prove your love. Love is God and expresses itself.

August 1, 1903. Do not treat the weather as though a storm could go around and let our neighbor have it. When I take it up I face the clouds and see God's face, Love, shining right through; then the clouds scatter and there is no storm to break upon anyone.

August 3, 1903. There is a great struggle before us, and it is for Life. What is our Life? 'Hid with Christ in God.' Then all there is of man is what is left after animal magnetism has gotten through with him; now measure your height.

August 7, 1903. It is not enough to smile and look pleasant when talking to the devil; speak with authority, stamp your foot if necessary and command it to come out of him as Jesus did. The smile and pleasantness will be all right when you are out of the flesh, but in the flesh you must *strive*.

Mesmerism will smile and be pleasant and all the while doing some mischief.

Good is All. Evil is not mind, has no intelligence, is powerless and falls by its own weight.

August 11, 1903. Humility is the door, honesty is the way and spirituality is the summit.

Oh! If we could only see ourselves in God, 'In Him we live and move and have our being', we would have no other consciousness.

August 18, 1903. The world is to us as we see it. The five senses (material) are lies and can only repeat lies; now rise above them to Spirit—the real; that is where health is and freedom from limitation; the lies will disperse as we have seen the clouds disappear; there is no such thing; God is All; you do not have to delve into matter, the body, to know how things are. Spirit shows us things as they are.

Keep your thought up there; this will heal; it is all that is necessary. When you are 'on the housetop, do not go down into the house to take anything out'.

August 19, 1903. Mr. K. asked, 'When you reach a place where you have done everything you know to do or what to do, desiring, striving for divine guidance and it does not seem to come, and discouragement comes in and causes you to doubt your ability to grasp it, what do you do?' Mrs. Eddy replied, 'Shut out the senses and take side with God; if it comes to you that you do not know which is the side with God, turn to Him ALONE, shutting out everything else; this is the way.'

We must learn that we do not depend upon material food for health and life; Spirit—not matter—sustains us and we must prove it. It is not necessary to eat as much as we do even now.

Mrs. Eddy was called to a case of fever where two physicians present, said the man could not live; he had refused to eat *anything* for a week; as she went to his door he was saying, 'This tastes good and that tastes good', and he did not have any food in the room. Mrs. Eddy said, 'With that consciousness he can live without eating'. The physicians laughed at it. 'Well, then he can eat', she said, and instantly he was in his right mind, recognized someone in the room and called for something to eat; they brought him a bountiful supply and he ate it all; dressed himself, went out in the yard and was entirely well. Mrs. Eddy did not think about the physical, just 'God is All', and shut out what the physicians had said and everything else from the sense side. She at first demonstrated health in the flesh; now she is demonstrating health outside of the flesh, she said.

August 28, 1903. The students who are called here do not come to this house for glory; when they come here they come to the cross. The first step is willingness to leave all; then the cross; *then* 'Enter thou into the joy of thy Lord'. You cannot gain the crown except by 'taking up the cross and following'.

September 8, 1903. We are all drunk without wine, in the senses; sleep is one of its phases, and Spirit will compel us, sometime, to give it up; false gods, etc., must go; cannot enter the kingdom; each has this work to do.

The teaching should be more in the line of showing the student how to overcome the evil, than by cramming with the letter, smoothing over, making things pleasant and taking the money. There must always be the *cross* before the crown; the cross cannot be smoothed over. It is the plucking out of the eye and cutting off the hand. A student of S. & H., who has the spirit, when he goes to a patient, does not know the letter to gabble over, and is better off than to be filled with the letter and not the spirit.

Each one must work out of matter, for it is wrong in every way, from the hair on the head to the toe. If I were teaching a class now, and there was one in it would get angry if I rebuked her before the others,—her pride would not let her receive it,—1 would tell her to walk out of the class; such a one would not be ready to help others out of the same difficulty.

There is no power in evil; the reverse is true, God is the power. He is infinite; then your work is the Christ power against nothingness; hold there, *know* it and there is nothing else, *know* it is with power and what else is there? Nothing; then the work is done; God did it.

September 9, 1903. If you have a patient who does not respond, would you say, I have done the best I could, and give up? No; it is the opportunity to rise higher and meet the demand.

September 12, 1903. Science does not ameliorate error, it *destroys* it.

September 13, 1903. Charity is good and peaceful, but it must not cover iniquity; just as long as you compromise with error, just so long will the error stick to you. In teaching students I have always uncovered the error to them; that is what should be done, and not all the pleasant things said only. 'He that covereth iniquity (his sins) shall not prosper.'

The error that is holding them must be uncovered to students so they can overcome it.

September 15, 1903, The weather expresses our concept of it, and can be handled the same as any claim, if you do not hold it as something apart from you, governed by some other power or almanac, etc. God governs all; this is the way Jesus stilled the tempest. There is no person and no persons that have any control over us; that belief is all illusion; God is All; we must prove this, We learn through suffering as the Scripture reads, 'Thy *rod* and thy staff they comfort me'. 'Whom the Lord loveth he chasteneth, and scourgeth every son whom he receiveth' (Hebrews 12: 6). Am not I an example?

September 24, 1903. 'When you are on the housetop, don't go down to take anything out of the house.' I am a great way out of the house (body) and it will not do for me to go down into the house (argument); I gain more by holding to God; if you are in the house you will have to heal others (argue) and so get out of the house; one who has suffered sickness or discord, I have always found more tractable in Science than one who has always been well. Do we have to be sick to work out? Not if you can get out without; health in matter must be given up for health in God. If one is a tenant and is satisfied he will remain there; the owner may want him out of the tenement and so takes out the windows, boards up the doors and makes it so uncomfortable for him he finally gets out. God is the owner; if one is comfortable in the material tenement, he must be made uncomfortable in it to get out; but if he gets out without being made uncomfortable (sick, etc.) all right. I have never seen one who did. The Bible continually speaks of tribulation. If you are well, heal the sick and so get out of the material tenement (matter), and learn health in God; do not court sickness but get out of material belief. I have come so far through tribulation.

Do not think you are out because comfortable; do not *think* you are out when you are not. A pup; I may work out an example on the blackboard wrong, and think he is right; the teacher is out of it and sees the mistake; then the pupil must be made to see it in order to get out. Spirit is the way; it will take you out.

September 25 and 26, 1903. You must watch, as Jesus said, if you would not have the house broken open; you think you are watching, but are you when the house is broken open? What would be thought of a watchman who let the place watched be burglarized? Would he be the right kind of a watchman? That is just why I named our paper, *Sentinel* and on it, 'Watch'.

Now how should we watch? A guard who was watching on the side of the Union soldiers in time of the war, was walking up and down while on duty, when he suddenly *felt* the approach of the enemy—danger; so he began to sing, 'Jesus, lover of my soul, Let me to thy bosom fly', etc., and the verse that did the work was, 'Other refuge have I none, Hangs my helpless soul on thee', etc.; he gave up to God. He afterward talked with the man who said he approached with his gun to his shoulder to shoot the guard, and he said his arm fell and the rifle with it; he could not shoot. That was watching; we must *feel* the danger and lift our thought to God; He will save us.

If we do not feel the danger and go right on as though everything were all right, declaring you are all right, you can not die, etc., when the seeming is all wrong, you will not be watching with God.

When we *feel* the danger then we earnestly turn to God.

When one is drunk without wine-mesmerism, apathy—he will talk with a thick tongue something like a drunken man; I can always tell it; they must arouse out of such a sense. I (Mrs. Eddy) was in a street car once when a drunken man came in and sat down. I said mentally, 'You are a fool and don't know it'. I kept thinking that and nothing else; in a few moments that man was perfectly sober; it had roused his dormant sense to the situation, and when he saw, that was the end of it. Keep awake—watch; the right kind of watching.

October 1, 1903. Do not tell anyone he can't die, can't be sick, until you can prove it to him. I (Mrs. Eddy) used to look away from the patient sometimes until I would get the thought, and the patient would vanish right out of my thought, and when I would look back at him, he would be *well.* I never told them they could not die, until I could see it; then when I spoke it was *done.* But we must keep at it, declaring it to ourselves until we can see it.

It used to be easy healing sickness -anything, a man all cut to pieces. But now we are meeting sin. I would rather have a man with his head cut off, to heal, than sin. In S. & H. I wrote, 'Sin will make deadly thrusts', etc., and 'Christian Scientists will hold crime in check', etc., and I knew no more than a babe what it meant when I wrote it; now I do.

December, 1903. Mrs. L. repeated lesson given while I was away as follows: When you can, rise above corporeality, see out of the flesh, then you can commune with those who have passed on; not corporeally as in spiritualism, but in Mind.

December 7, 1903. What we most need is wisdom.

We must take advantage of time, not time of us. There is a time to do everything; a time to speak to students; a time to speak to the world; and we must have wisdom and know when to speak and act. Jesus said, 'Can ye not discern the signs of the times?'

When a student is wrong, if it is not deep sin, I (Mrs. Eddy) walk with them a way to help them out; even when they are working right against me sometimes; walk with them a way and open their eyes to the error; then when they see, the error is gone. Not go at them denouncing them, pouncing upon them.

I love; one will ask, whom do you love? I answer, I love. What do you love? I love.

If you love, you can raise the dead. Love will heal death; that is the way I have raised the dead, by Love. Love that is above the human.

God is Father and Mother—one; the Christ reflects the male and female Principle—one—not two.

The end of the belief in male and female as two, will be when woman stops child-bearing.

The monthly period left me the moment I came to Christian Science and I have never seen anything of the claim since. Change of life is an error. Life never changes and the giving up of an error cannot cause suffering. Sexuality and sensuality of any kind are not of God; now go to work and prove it.[1]

December 9, 1903. The earth is spiritual—not material; a compound idea (S. & H.). Matter is a subjective state of mortal mind—a thought projected.

In teaching I bring out the facts clearly; get down to the bottom of things and not mix them up by comparisons; the distinct line between matter and Spirit must be drawn.

What moves your arm? Mind. What mind? Mortal mind. Is there a mortal mind? No. Then you have come back to—nothingness. God does not know anything about the moving of your hand. If you can control your hand, move it out and back, can you not control the clouds also? Yes. I am now speaking from the material sense. In immortal Mind there are no clouds and no storms. When

[1]The following may be found in some versions of these notes: In a booklet entitled *Fragment of a Lost Gospel,* published by the Oxford University Press, giving account of sayings of Jesus that are regarded as authentic by scholars, we find the following: 'When Salome asked when those things about which she questioned should be made known, the Lord said, "When ye trample upon the garment of shame, when the two become one and the male with the female, neither male nor female".' The meaning being that Christ's kingdom on earth would not be manifested until man bad returned to the state of innocence in which sexual ideas and relations had no place. 'When Salome asked how long death would prevail, the Lord said, "So long as ye women bear children, for I have come to destroy the works of the female".' Logia of Jesus, *Christian Science Journal, Vol.* 25, 'Jesus was asked, "When shall the dominion of death cease?" Jesus saith, "As long as (material) birth continues, for I came to destroy the works of birth." See Matt. 5: 17 and S. & 11. 69.'

the workmen could not finish their work if it rained (and it did not rain for three weeks) and my neighbor could not furnish milk because his well was dry, and the next morning he found three or four feet of water in his well and it had not rained and he asked if we were witches or prophets here, I did not depend on clouds or storms but upon the higher power.

The material senses are lies; the spiritual sense is the real.

The spiritual sense *destroys* the material.

When you move with human will and think through human will, that is not Christian Science; it is working with the objective instead of the subjective.

The question was asked, 'How did I heal, the other day, when I felt so helpless to do for someone who saw so far above me?' The answer was, 'Through that helplessness you let Truth in and it was Christian Science which healed the case, not your own exertion'.

You are under no law but God's law.

When I first came to Christian Science I was lifted right out of the belief of sickness into the belief of perfect health; since then I am working out of that belief in health into the Science of health, and it would have been easier if I had never been in that belief, just as it is with one who sings by ear, which is not the science of music and afterward learns the science of music; it would have been easier to have commenced right in the first place than to have to unlearn and learn over again.

December 15, 1903. The preachers speak of Jesus as though he were always so placid, never ruffled, while really he was very stern; the Scriptures speak of him as saying to his disciples, 'Get thee behind me, Satan'; and just before he ascended he called them 'fools'. I used to be very amiable before coming into Christian Science; was a peacemaker at home when arguments about temperance, politics and philosophy would arise; but now I am *stern.*

December 17, 1903. My students will place themselves in conditions which to carry through would strike at their life; then they will throw it all on to me; then I have to give the master stroke.

It was not the material cross that killed Jesus, but it was the desertion of his students that killed him. This is the reason he gave up quicker than the malefactors with him, knowing the loss that desertion meant to the Cause which was so dear to him; but he did not lose it and he came back and proved that he had not. God was with him.

December 22, 1903. The whole of error from the beginning to the end is summed up in one word—talking serpent. In the South they have copperhead, the moccasin and a variety of snakes, The moccasin the Southern people fear the most.

A lady in the South told me something which I will give to illustrate my point: The moccasin will not harm one while that one is asleep; will even try to keep him asleep —charm him, but as soon as that one awakes, then he strikes with his fangs. This lady always carried a dirk with her; she was on the beach one day and lay down and fell asleep; she awakened and saw a moccasin lying right beside her; she quietly reached into her pocket, took her dirk and killed the serpent before it had a chance to attack her. This is the nature of error; it will strike us when we have awakened to see its unreality and we cannot meet it by fighting it, because it (the devil) is larger and more powerful than you are (I should hope so); then we overcome it by seeing its nothingness; then there is nothing to fight; it is killed. We have wakened and the serpent would strike us; it will get the better of us if we fight it because it is more powerful than we are; so if we argue about it and fight it—this would be the beastly way—we will not gain the victory over it; but we must rise above it and so see its nothingness. When Moses saw the rod turn into a serpent he ran before it, but he was commanded to handle it, and when he did (saw its nothingness) it became a staff in his hand upon which to lean. I (Mrs. Eddy) am meeting the serpent in its phases. There is not one belief of sickness that comes from my individuality. I now have to overcome that which says I feel other people's thoughts; that if it cannot touch you it will work through someone and reach you; this is the theosophical line of work. We are not to fight as beasts but to handle-see the nothingness-and so kill error.

December 24, 1903. Let us take 'heart' as a token of our Xmas; the great heart of Christ; it is the palpitating presence encircling the universe; it is the only intelligence, and that is what? Love. Could there be anything greater?

December 26,1903. Did God give you dominion over the earth? Yes. He gave you dominion over all. Then you can control the weather.

Your body is of the earth earthy according to the Scripture; you have dominion over that; then you have over the weather.

M.D.'s say the lungs, bowels, etc., have dominion over you; theosophists say the earth currents have dominion over you; one is just as far from Science as the other. You have dominion over all. Elijah made a cloud to come; he made it rain; if he could make it rain, he could make it snow. You can do the same; you can produce a sweat (until there is no need for one); you can do the same with rain or snow.

You are not a Christian Scientist until you do control the weather.

I cannot produce sickness. I experimented one time; a student went into another room and I argued sickness for him as hard as I could; he said he kept feeling better and better. Then he argued for me and I began to feel pain right away. I am working now to overcome sin and not feel others' thoughts. You can see by the above I cannot be a malpractitioner. I feel others' thoughts mentally but I am trying to work out of that; do not want to feel them.

December 27, 1903. My brother George was not a religious man and it troubled my father who was religious; when George was on his dying bed my father asked him to accept Christ. George said, during the intervals of labored breathing, 'I have always done as near right as I knew how, the rest I leave with God'. George awakened in heaven and my father awakened disappointed after passing on.

December 28, 1903. Now stop the negations in treating and hold to the Truth. If you have disease in your thought, you will transmit it; you say your patient is healed; but he is not if you are holding disease in thought, and it will appear in some other form; you do not want to hold with the witness but against.

Jesus read the minds of his students; he saw their sins, but did not believe it was their mind, and this did the healing.

January 2, 1904. *1* never knew anything about relapse until I had a student who was a malpractitioner; look at the weather how it snows then stops, snows and stops—relapse. What is the belief in earth currents, astrals and planetary effects, polarity? Theosophy. The belief is that they work through nerves, nerve centers. What are nerves? Mortal mind. And there is no mortal mind. When you yield to weather as having power—dominion—you yield to nerves; when you yield to nerves you yield to mortal mind—hypnotism; then you cannot heal.

Now have the faith of a little child and prove your dominion over all. (A little child will say—my mamma can do so and so.) Love is the remedy, and what is Love? It is *giving*, not getting. Love *gives*. Students who are getting from the book (S. & H.) and from me, when they are put to the test are wanting. Why? Because they have taken it of me instead of God; now what I have given take in usury; use it, and more will be given; like the one who had a talent given him and did not use it, lost it; but to the one who did make use of it more was given. 'Unto every one that hath shall be given, and he shall have abundance; but unto him that hath not shall be taken away that which he hath.'

January 3, 1904. I love. What do you love? I don't know; I *love*. Do you love all? Yes; all or nothing.

How have I gained what I have? By being honest; being faithful over a few things; and I will make you ruler over many; then, 'Enter thou into the joy of thy Lord'. These are the steps.

Lida, God loves you. He loves you much. He loves you dearly. You have suffered affliction. 'Whom the Lord loveth he chasteneth.' Now you return that love by giving out to others, bringing rest and peace to the world, and yourself.

January 5, 1904. 'The wrath of man shall be made to praise God.' Malpractice is the wrath of man, and it is being made to praise God by driving you out of the tenement (belief in body); if it doesn't drive you out, it will kill you in it

The negation will not do the work, i.e. arguing no disease, etc.; it is the Truth that does the work; standing on the right side; keeping the two commandments: 'Have no other gods before me', and, 'There is no life, truth, intelligence nor substance in matter'.

The moment you are pleasant with or in error, that moment you can do nothing with it. There must be *authority*. It is not seeking but *striving* that enables us to conquer.

January 8, 1904. Jesus said, 'Watch and pray.' The watching comes first. You must watch, see the enemy before it comes and strikes; destroy before it approaches.

One present said, 'God will raise up someone who will be faithful, as John was at the cross'. Answer, 'How do you know? Look within and see who that one should be. It is opium, ether . . . etc., that would cause you to suggest it should be someone else.'

January 12, 1904. *Is* anyone sick? No. Would you tell your patient he is sick? No. Am I suffering from other people's sins, or my own? No. Would you tell your patient there is sin? No. Was Jesus crucified? Yes, according to belief. Did Jesus die? Belief said he did, but belief is a lie. Is there death any more than sickness ? No. Now go and prove it.

You cannot be made to believe you cannot heal; you do heal. There are a few laws to be broken; then we will be free.

January 17, 1904. Learn what *watching* means.

Nothing material belongs to Spirit; all materiality must be given up to get into heaven, there is no other way; you cannot take any of it with you. I have watched all these years for you and the world; do you think any one else in the world would have done as I have, held on through everything and not given up? I left everything, father (mother had gone), brother, relatives, everything; and because I held to this my relatives would not speak to me; said I had disgraced them; would ride along in their carriage and I would be on the sidewalk and they would not speak to me. All these have I given up and I work on without a cent for it except from books —although I always advocate, 'The laborer is worthy of his hire'. Now you watch; be always on duty—on guard.

If we were to pass on right here now in this room, we would waken right here, and nothing would be changed any more than you see it now.

January 23, 1904. All is Mind. If you do not heal, it is because you have not reached the realization in your treatment—or reversal. S. & H. 412: 16 to 18 and 22, 23, 'To prevent disease or to cure it, the power of the divine Spirit must *break* this dream of the material senses.... Conform the argument so as to destroy the *evidence* of disease.' Also 417: 16 and 17, 'When you silence the witness against your plea, you destroy the evidence, for the disease disappears.'

January 29, 1904. Is it necessary that one eat and sleep? No. Then do not talk about eating and sleeping being a normal condition. Know that we depend upon *God* for everything, and then the emerging gently will take care of itself. Leave that with God. A musician would not call a discord a chord, one time any more than another; neither must we mix Spirit and matter. What is this body you see? A belief of mortal mind. Are there any clouds? No. Any weather? No. Atmosphere? No; simply beliefs. Then haven't you dominion over the weather and clouds (beliefs) as you have over the body? Yes. Now prove it.

Wrongs are done to me, and yet I turn right around and do them a kindness; not because I intend to do so but I cannot help it; do it without thinking.

January 31, 1904. I used to heal with a word; I have seen a man yellow because of disease, and the next moment I looked at him and his color was right; was healed.

I knew no more how it was done than a baby; only it was done every time. I never failed; almost always in one treatment; never more than three. Now God is showing me how, and I am showing you.

All we have to do is one thing; keep the First Commandment, 'thou shalt have none other gods before (beside) me'—infinite Mind and that is infinite Love. There is no evil mind; that sweeps away error; there is infinite Mind—good. Infinity is all. There is no other intelligence, life or love. Now work out your problem from this standpoint. If we do not keep the First we cannot keep the Second—'to love one another'. If ye love not man (your brother) whom you have seen how can you love God whom you have not seen? You only love God as far as you love man.

February 8, 1904. When I say you are not doing a thing and you contradict, you say you are, when there is no manifestation of it; you *think* you are but belief is talking the louder and the patient feels the belief instead of the Truth and feels worse. You go right on arguing as fast as you can and think you are doing something; the way to do at such a time is to turn from the mesmerism to God, knowing He is All and there is nothing else. The above described condition of mesmerism is lack of faith in your treatment, and in what I tell you. Know that the treatment is with power, for all power is God.

February 16, 1904. The Bible would seem to contradict itself, but it does not when you know what it means. 'Answer not a fool according to his folly.' 'Answer a fool according to his folly.' They say my book (S. & H.) contradicts itself, but it does not when you understand it.

The Bible says, 'Honor thy father and thy mother that thy days may be long', etc.; then when it says, Luke 14: 26, 'If any man come to me, and hate not his father and mother, and wife, and children, and brethren, and sisters, yea, and his own life also, he cannot be my disciple'. This would look like a direct contradiction of the words just quoted but is not; after we have honored our father and mother, then comes the next step—forsaking the flesh for Christ.

We must be Christian Scientists and do as we say we believe or else be hypocrites. We *say* Spirit is All and then when we have to take our choice between Spirit and the flesh we cry, the flesh, the flesh. God is coming very near to us; is making demands upon us. Mr. Frye made his choice twenty-one years ago and since then has been having his experiences, and if he should pass now would waken to glorified being. Those who choose the flesh will yet have all the experience to go through. What is the result of forsaking all for Spirit? Dominion over the earth.

February 20, 1904. God is Love, and Love is infinite; realize this and you are safe from harm; nothing can touch you.

February 21, 1904. God is testing us. Jesus illustrated by the parable about the 'owner', etc.; the servants said, 'My lord delayeth his coming; let us eat, drink and be merry', etc. I pray that my faith may be strengthened by this testing.

February 22, 1904 In the year twenty-one hundred I think will be the end. Then Christian Scientists will have held crime in check as the book (S & H.) says.

At that time either the world will be saved through universal salvation, or those who now are working against us will burn up as the physical scientists say the world will be burned up, by *volcanic action;* we know what they call volcanic action is mortal mind destroying itself. All must learn they cannot sin and escape punishment, as they think they can. Those who have worked against this Cause and those who are then doing so will all be burned together. Those who work out now will be saved; the others will be hundreds of years; all the woes Jeremiah predicted will come to pass. God is making demands upon us, (Do not mention this prophecy.)

Do not let self-justification cloud over the Principle of right doing.

February 24, 1904. Do not work *against* error, but *feel* the Love that dissolves it.

February 26, 1904. If you can do a thing right once, you can every time. Honesty and sincerity God cares for.

When I was doing the healing I went right along performing the remarkable cures; but I, evidently, had not overcome the latent fear altogether, and God has called me to do that. When that is accomplished, I will perform those miracles again and will not have the suffering to go through again.

Have God in your thought and *no devil.* You and all must have some belief of a devil or the works would show, all God.

February 27, 1904. Repeated through Mrs. L.:

Disease is not in matter, it is a dream; it is in thought. You do not tabernacle in the body, but in Mind, Spirit. Action is harmonious and governs all things harmoniously until you know it through harmonious action. There is no body and you know it.

February 15, 1907. Not arrange things and then go to God, but go to God first. (Then followed the reading of Luke 24: 1 to 16 about the resurrection.) These things are occurring again. My words seem as 'idle tales' to you; but I speak truth.

February 17, 1907. There are no lies. All is Mind and governs. What is matter? Nothing. Mortal mind is matter; it cannot talk. Then hold to Mind, and the rest will take care of itself—the rest is nothing; this (material) is all nothing.

Life is divine, immortal, and there is no other life. That is all the Life there is and is ours.

February 23, 1907. Stand with God and you will stand with Mother; stand with Mother and you will stand with God.

February 26, 1907. There is but one way through, and only one way through; and that is to unself.

It is my unselfed love that has made a success of this Cause for the world.

Can you get rid of a lie and not get rid of it? No. Is it a lie that there is life, substance and intelligence in matter? Yes. Then unself it. Everyone must do this. There is too much looking out for self instead of others. This is the trouble with the teaching of today, and why there is so much erroneous teaching being done; not unselfed enough.

You cannot *teach* Christian Science in that way. You can say over the words, but unless you prove it you are not *teaching* (imparting). Prove it in healing the sick and casting out sin.

I pray and watch in the little details; someone must, as good is expressed in the minutiae of things.

February 28, 1907. Mrs. Eddy told of a colored minister that preached from the text-where the sheep were placed on one side and the goats on the other. At the conclusion of the sermon he said, 'Bless the Lord; he knew where the wool grows.' (Sheep and wool of colored people.)[2]

March 7, 1907. What is the one evil? Animal magnetism? Yes. Is it person? No. Is it anything? No. Then we cannot be harmed by it. That is what I mean by the one evil.

March 8, 1907. God gives us the victory. His plan is made long before we know anything about it; then we have to carry it out.

[2]George Kinter recorded in 1907 regarding Mrs. Eddy in his statement for Next Friends' Suit: When I went South as a young bride my gallant husband, Major Glover, took me into the Episcopal church; but I was unacquainted with that service and longed for the simple worship of my New England home, the Congregational. So I asked George, as I always addressed him, to take me over to the colored people's meeting in the woods. But he demurred. When I insisted, either upon going, or that he should tell me the reason for his objection, he said, 'Why, Mary, it is scarcely a fit place for you. They sometimes get the "power" and become very boisterous. You are delicate and nervous, and I don't want you to go.' But I finally prevailed upon him to take me, and when the old colored preacher discovered white folks in his audience, he decided to take a different text, and started in with a new sermon, 'And the shepherd divided the sheep from the goats. Now, my brethren, you all wants to know if you was sheep, or if white folks is the goats, and I calculate to explanation of this fact to you today so you will never forget it, even if you live forever. Jess let me ask you one question. Who's got de wool on der heads? Don't that settle the whole question? It sure do, and we will now take up the collection, not omitting the folks what come in carriages.'

The human heart requires many scourgings sometimes before it falls in line, but it must come. We can help one another and can help ourselves, but God gives the victory. When I used to preach in a hall, I would go there sometimes and the door would be locked; could not get in. Others would be inside in the front seats, laughing and talking. I would have to get a policeman to let me in; then in the room where I would stay until time to go out to speak, there would be cigar stumps lying around.

Then when I had a Church I said, we will not have By-laws; see how I had to give that up? I finally said, there will have to be laws to put a stop to this (mortal mind) work. Then I wrote the *Manual.* I never had a Church until I had the *Manual.* See how God led me! I wrote the *Manual* as I did S. & H.

We must not feel too much encouraged over a victory, for everything in mortal mind must be overcome. If you fail in one iota, like an example in mathematics, every figure right but one, the example is incorrect; so it is with our problem. All little things must be overcome. Then we rise above substance matter; and that includes sin, sickness, death.

I used to be a very timid person; did not want to meet people, etc. After I came into Christian Science I overcame timidity, and when I appeared before the audience in Chicago, a man spoke of my carriage as I walked on the stage, etc. What was it? I had overcome timidity. Before going out on the platform I would shut out timidity entirely, and when I went out would not remember that there was an audience there. We must overcome all little things as well as large,

March 9, 1907. What is a way-shower? There is a human and a divine meaning. A way-shower is that which shows the way; it must be some *thing* or some *one.* Jesus was the Way-shower, the Christ with him, and if he had not been, where would we be? He showed the way as the masculine idea of Principle, then woman took it up at that point—the ascending thought in the scale—and is showing the way, thus representing the male and female Principle (the male and female of God's creating).

Is there anything in the world of more importance than holding up the hands of the way-shower? No. If they had all done that with Jesus, we would be in the millennium. We must become unselfed.

Can you heal a disease by holding it or its symptoms before you ? No. Then hold to the opposite (absolute Science) which does the healing.

March 10, 1907. From the beginning and all the way along, I got my leading from God, through the Bible. Right in the beginning I got-'Write it in a book and it shall be for all time'.

Today He is speaking to me again, Isaiah 16: 14. 'But now the Lord hath spoken, saying, Within *three years,* as the years of an hireling, and the glory of Moab shall be contemned, with all that great multitude; and the remnant shall be very small and feeble.'

I am sure this will be fulfilled, but don't tell anyone about it.

(Calvin A. Frye's note: While Mrs. Eddy was troubled today at the lawsuit just instituted by her next friends (Glover & Baker) she prayed God for direction and opened her Bible to Is. 16:12, 13, 14. This gave her renewed courage.)

March 12, 1907. Do you believe what the book says about chemicalization, that, 'The higher Truth lifts her voice, the louder will error scream', etc. (Page 97)? Yes. I was just thinking how I am being abused (Glover case and newspaper articles) and I could feel the tears starting to come, when suddenly I thought of two cases of healing I had, and then joy took the place of sorrow. One of them was one of the worst cripples I ever saw. I was walking along the street—I walked because I hadn't a cent to ride—and I saw this cripple, with one knee drawn up to his chin; his chin resting on his knee. The other limb was drawn the other way, up his back. I came up to him and read on a piece of paper pinned on his shoulder: help this poor cripple. I had no money to give him so I whispered in his ear, 'God loves you'. And he got up perfectly straight and well. He ran into the house (told the name of the people—Allen I think) and asked, 'Who is that woman?' pointing to Mrs. Glover (afterward Mrs. Eddy). The lady told him, 'It is Mrs. Glover'. 'No, it isn't, it's an angel', he said. Then he told what had been done for him.

The other case was: I was at a house (told the name and place) and the woman came running into the room as white as ashes, and said, a cripple was at the door and he looked so dreadful she slammed the door in his face. I went to the window, and there was—well, it was too dreadful to describe; his feet did not touch the earth at all; he walked with crutches. I gave him through the window all I had in my pocket—a dollar bill—and he took it in his teeth. He went to the next house and frightened the woman there, but she did not slam the door in his face. He asked her to let him lie down a few minutes; she let him go into a bedroom and lie down. He fell sound asleep, and when he wakened up was perfectly well. Sometime afterward the woman, who was kind to him, was in a store (I think) and this man came rushing up to her and said, 'Yes, you are the one, but where is the other woman?' Then he told her he was the one who was healed by me. The papers are writing up my history; the history of my ancestry; writing lies. My history is a holy one.

When I went where the people were not good it produced a chemical. While I was writing S. & H. I moved to eight places. I would no sooner settle down and begin to write, than it would produce such a chemical I would have to go to some other place.

In writing my history they can say nothing against me, so they begin to tell lies. It will do the same by *you*. Your truth produces the chemical until all is worked out.

March 13, 1907. God talks to me through this book (the Bible) as a person talks to another, and has for forty years.

March 14, 1907.'Mrs. L. E. S. [Laura E. Sargent, C.S.D.] repeated:

The true sense of love is to love God—good, then we love all, for God is All. That love is unlimited and flows out freely to all, and all feel it, The human sense of love narrows itself down to a concept, or a person, and shuts out others; that is not love. Really we do not love person; it is the good we love. This true sense of Love brings freedom and an enlarged sense of things. *Miscellaneous Writings* 312: 1.

March 15, 1907. We must be resurrected from the dead; dead in trespasses and sin; the belief of life in the body, of matter, of life, substance and intelligence in matter, the proclivities of the parents manifested through a belief in heredity, etc.; we must be resurrected from all this, for what does Paul say? 'Except ye have part in the resurrection my preaching is vain.'

March 16, 1907. The hour is—the acme of hate against Love, and Love alone can meet it. God *demands* God. Truth destroys error.

March 17, 1907. In balancing a pencil on the finger, if you put anything on one side you take from the other. God is infinite, All, and has no opposite. Then the way to do is, to hold with God; if not what have we? Nothing. We must give up *all* for Christ, Truth; and not say, I have bought a farm, or a yoke of oxen, or married a wife and cannot come. One and one are two; you cannot deviate from it one iota and have a correct answer; neither can you deviate from the law of God, or take the opposite of what the Scriptures say and have a correct result. Error cannot get into the kingdom, so we must divest ourselves of it. We must hold with God alone.

I used to say before going before an audience: Now, dear God, here I am, use me; I *am* absent from the body and present with Thee in consciousness. Love uses me in its own good way. I would lift myself right out of the material sense of self and audience and let God use me.

Mrs. L. E. S. [Laura E. Sargent, C.S.D.] repeated:

All there is of us, is what there is of us under the fire of mesmerism. Meaning, what we manifest under the fire of mesmerism is what we are—what we have attained—the test.

March 20, 1907. My revelations for 40 years have come through the Scriptures; study them yourselves.

March 22, 1907. Stop denying error and place all the balance on the right side; the side of God. You can negative error without individualizing it so much. 'Answer not a fool according to his folly lest he be wise in his own conceit', and 'Answer a fool according to his folly', said Solomon. These are exactly two opposites; yet they each have their time. The time is now, 'Answer a fool not according to his folly'—leaving out the 'folly'. Suppose you balance a pencil on your finger, what you put on one side takes from the other; if you argue no pain, no catarrh, etc., you are putting weight on the side of error. Take the side with God, and put *all* of the balance *there.* This is what is needed. Hold with your Leader and with God.

In the time of Paul was the talk about the crucifixion; if he had left out the crucifixion he would have had all in the balance with God, but he did not. Kept talking about the crucifixion. Now let us have God without the 'crucifixion', and the resurrection of the dead, not dead and the body buried in that sense, but resurrected to the living man of God,—the spiritualized sense.

Hold with your Leader and with God.

March 24, 1907. I have no child. The kingdom of heaven is in our midst. Heaven is harmony, and harmony is peace, love, joy. We must see health and our relations in the spiritual.

March 27, 1907. The disciples followed Jesus up to a certain point, and then deserted him, and darkness followed. Follow the way-shower and you will follow the divine idea; turn away from the way-shower and you turn away from the divine idea; like turning away from the windowpane, you turn away from the light. It is not my personality you are following, or that you love. You are being turned from the person to the idea. When this is accomplished, then you wilt be free—in health—to go on and do for the world.

Spoke of a certain student as so good that she forgot to do anything for him. If I let you alone you may know it is all right. Isn't that natural? Yes. 'God is the only power', said a student. Yes, that is true, but wisdom would bid you be wise in working to that demonstration; and meet the things of the hour.

March 29, 1907. Before coming to Christian Science from the time of the belief that I came into the world, I was troubled with sleeplessness; after coming to Science I could drop to sleep at any time. I must yet come out of *that* belief. Eating, drinking, sleeping, being clothed, are only a human concept; these and the belief of life, substance and intelligence in matter, must all be given up for the immortal. The Christ takes us out of the discord of not eating, sleeping, etc., and gives us the pleasurable side of it; takes us out of the pain and gives us the pleasure, then replaces *that* with the spiritual. Life is immortal, eternal. There is but one Mind. All is Mind, there is no matter. We must give up *all* for Christ and Christian Science. We must come to see we do not depend upon eating, sleeping, etc., for life and health, but depend on Mind. The spiritual cannot be touched.

Jesus did not make the demonstration over death, but yielded to it—because of the desertion of his disciples. If they had stood by him we should now be in the millennium.

That demonstration must be made or the world will again be left in darkness. The students must hold up the hands of the wayshower. They will say *you* have no need,—but *you* can see the need.

Laura E. [Sargent] repeated:

All there is of personality is the fear of it or the love of it.

March 31, 1907. EASTER—RESURRECTION. We must be resurrected; must put off the old man and put on the new.

If you dress for Easter, your clothes are all in keeping—are clean. You do not put on some clean ones and some soiled ones. Neither can you put on part of the new man and part of the old; you must put on the whole of the new man-the spiritual idea.

If you put a new patch on an old garment, you still have the old garment. There is a time when you take off your old garments before you put on the new. Now if we patch up this body, try to make a better eye, a better limb, etc., we are not putting on the new.

We want to say: eye, you cannot talk to me, I have put you off. Rise to the spiritual sense, then your body will respond; then take no thought what you eat, your clothes, etc., for your heavenly Father knoweth ye have need of these things. This is the resurrection. The resurrection is not to be resurrected from matter—dust. There never was any life in matter to be resurrected. The resurrection is seeing the real man that was never in matter; he never was sick to be made well. That is the way I did the healing. I never saw the material man before me, but the real man, perfect, and this healed instantaneously, and no relapse. This is the way Jesus healed, as in S. & H. it reads, 'Jesus beheld the perfect man', etc. This is the resurrection.

April 1, 1907. When I was introducing this work and they would throw stones at me through the window—and never touch me—and said there was dynamite under the building where I was to speak, I went right along, and I screamed Truth all the louder; if they screamed, I screamed all the louder, until they stopped.

April 5, 1907. '1 am the way.' What is that way? Infinite Principle. What is infinite Principle? Truth, Life, Love. Can a lie affect Truth, Life, Love? No. Then hold your thought in Truth, Life, Love; while doing so can you be touched? No. Then hold there. This will destroy all evil. This is the period in which it must be done.

I live with the Bible; I have not another thing on earth to be one with but the Bible and *Science and Health.* I, the Bible, and S. & H., the trinity, three in one.

April 6, 1907. It is all summed up in a few words. Love, Life, Truth, God, is all there is.

April 8, 1907. In healing you either have to know the allness of God, where there is no sickness, as I used to do, or else you must know what the disease is and argue it down. The same way with healing sin; you heal it with knowing there is no sin, for God is All, or you must know what the sin is and heal it that way. In healing sickness it is fear back of it; destroy the fear and the case comes right up out of it. In healing sin, hate is back of it (meaning hatred to Truth); so you must destroy the hate, and keep at it and keep at it until it is destroyed.

It is not of any use to want to die to get out of this constant struggle; for if you should do so, you would still have to keep at it until accomplished, and even more so because you would have to overcome not having done it when you could—a lost opportunity.

Lida, you have done beautifully since you have been here; have helped me *so much.*

April 9, 1907. When we *realize* the allness of God, that He is Life, Truth, Love, omnipotent, omnipresent, infinite Principle, all will be accomplished.

You have a belief about God—I have a belief about God.

April 11, 1907. The laws which Christian Scientists are under are God's laws, unchangeable, unbroken, for ever. To abide in these laws is not to be touched by any supposed laws—such as theosophists claim they can make—a law that people shall love and that they shall hate. 'My times are in thy hands', said Jesus. He also said, 'The works that I do shall ye do, and greater works because I go to the Father', and, 'I and the Father are one'. Materially that has been made doctrinal; but in its spiritual sense it means one with the divine Principle, God, the only I. Not materially through the personality of Jesus, asking in his name, but spiritually—*yes;* the oneness with the Father; the true individuality. As you rise to spiritually understand that, you lose your sense as an 'I' in matter, and gain your true selfhood in Spirit. This brings the divine health, which is not dependent on the body, but is of the Father, forever the same.

I remember reading novels was a great pastime with me when I was young. And now I recall something I read when I was between sixteen and twenty, which was written by Charlotte Brontë and was as follows—'The ties which link the happy may be dear, but those which bind the wretched are tenderness unutterable'.

April 18, 1907. The way-shower must explore the way. You learn that way by that experience. You are learning now from my experience. Old age is just as much of a claim to be overcome as cancer or any other belief. You have not come to it yet, but you will.

Overcome the belief in it *now;* you have it to do sometime.

When I let my thought down, I can hear the mental arguments of error, or the devil (there is no devil); it cannot hide from me when I want to know what it is doing.

I can lift my thought right above it and shut it all out, or I can find out what it is doing.

If there was an assassin which could overpower you, it would be better for you to know what he was doing, so as to be better prepared to meet it.

If the work had been done in the time of Jesus, it would not have to be done now; but the disciples did not do their part; they were not obedient to him; they questioned what he was doing; did not understand, and it was not done. So it must be done now.

We can enter into immortality here on earth, and now, and overcome death. We must do it. 'Bear ye one another's burdens and so fulfil the law of Christ.'

April 20, 1907. After reading from the Gospel of St. John, said, this talk from the Bible is as plain as though the person, John, were present, speaking to us, because Truth is *im*personal.

There are no personalities for God is *im*personal and to personalize ourselves, to say *I*, etc., is to selfishize ourselves. To personalize others is to selfishize others. This is not Christian Science.

The neighbor is one with the Father; so are we; all one in Spirit. The 'I' is one, infinite. The one who sees this and abides in it, becomes unselfed and is then ready to do for his neighbor—is a Christian Scientist. 'Inasmuch as ye have done it unto one of the least of these my brethren, ye have done it unto me', said Jesus. 'Bear ye one another's burdens and so fulfil the law of Christ.'

When you rebuke sin, you cannot be nice to the sinner. Jesus said, 'Get thee behind me, Satan', and called them *fools*, hypocrites. He did not palaver and smile and be nice to them.

May 3, 1907. We must rise above the religion of the Hebrew, the Greek, the Catholic and the Protestant, to Christian Science; you only know as far as you demonstrate, as far as you prove. It is not Science to be too thin nor too fleshy; either is a state of fear, for flesh manifests mind.

May 5, 1907. Mr. G. H. K. [George H. Kinter] repeated from Mrs. E.:

The way I would teach a child to learn the Bible would be to teach her to love it, and then she would go to the Bible to read it for her own entertainment. I would also tell her the Bible in story fashion; it will stick to the memory in that way, and she will become interested to look it up for herself. I would preferably confine myself to the New Testament for a child; but the Old is good, too.

May 7, 1907. There is one thing needed all over the field and which is only supplied here, and might not be supplied in the field in centuries; that is, to have but one God, divine Principle and its *demonstration.* (There is nothing can prevent it.) To have one God,—father, mother, wife, children, lands, can have no claim upon you.

The sense of death everyone wants to get rid of, and can only be done by realizing the sense of Life. You may die a thousand deaths until you realize this, for it is the only way.

Mrs. L. S. [Laura Sargent] repeated:

Food and sleep belong to sensualism and we must learn to do without them—not depend upon them. Mind is All.

May 8, 1907. Mrs. L. S. [Laura Sargent] repeated a prayer given to the early students:

O Love! Give me higher, holier, purer, self-abnegated motives and desires, and spiritual inspiration.

May 9, 1907. Matthew 26. History repeats itself, but in different forms; now without the crucifixion.

May 12, 1907. Handle the weather just as you do any belief of mortal mind.

May 14, 1907. I ask myself: In my life-work am I just? Yes. Am I honest? Yes, if I am just. Am I of good report? No, because I am thus. Am I right? Yes, as far as I live up to my highest sense of right.

God has worked through one in this age because He could. The light will come through the window because it will let it, while the wall will not; it would shine through the wall if it could. God is no respecter of persons. Then would you say the wall can let in the light the same as the window? No. Then does one person let in as much light as another? No. Can the one who lets in the light see what is best for the others better than one who does not? Yes. That is the trouble with those outside (the wall); they think they can run things just as well and a little better than I can (the windowpane). How do you know I am a windowpane for the light to shine through? By the works.

May 16, 1907. If you are a Christian Scientist and can speak the Word and it is *done,* all right; but if you have to argue, be very careful *what* you argue.

May 19, 1907. Mrs. L. S. [Laura Sargent] repeated:
You can heal ignorant sin, but wilful sin must be suffered out.

May 24, 1907. There are three things to keep before us continually: 'to have one God—one Mind; 'to love our neighbor as ourselves' and 'do unto others as we would have others do unto us'. To have one Mind means for all to work alike;—not you work in your work and I in my work, but work *together.* It is time for us today to be Christian Scientists and keep these points before us, by asking ourselves these questions every time before doing anything.

May 25,1907. God is All. To have God is to have all-harmony. Discord comes from looking away from all, thinking there is something else. You heal disease by knowing there is none. You heal sin in the same way. The prodigal goes into a far country thinking there is something there. I go after them thinking they have gone after something, and so it goes. But we must look to the spiritual as Paul says—II Corinthians 4: 17, 18, 'For our light affliction which is but for a moment, worketh for us a far more exceeding and eternal weight of glory; While we look not at the things which are seen, but the things which are not seen; for the things which are seen are temporal; but the things which are not seen are eternal.'

May 26, 1907. DIVINITY LESSON, Reading in the Bible about loaves and fishes, spoke of fishes as floating around, not gathered, and the going out after them to bring them in as the spiritual meaning.

Have you a throat? No. Have you a nose? No. Do you see? No; not through eyes. Do you hear through ears? No. Do you have to eat food? No. Does food sustain you? No. Does food hurt you? No;

it only says so. Can food talk? No. What is it that does talk materially? Nothing.

What I am reaching is the spiritual; the material fights it and I fight the material; it will do it to you; the more spiritual the thought, the more will you be fought. That which takes the place of God and creates men and women, and sees everything material, will fight the spiritual. We must see everything spiritual.

To sense I am on the cross. Am I? No. What makes me on the cross? The belief that I am there. If I am I would have to come down. What would come down from the cross? The belief of being on the cross. What would kill? The belief of being killed. See me (and others) all right, as a spiritual idea, and not on the cross; then you will see me as I am.

If Jesus had fully understood himself as wholly spiritual—not on the cross-he would not have died; but would have remained and administered to others.

If I tell the truth of a he have I lied? Yes. If I tell a lie about the truth have I lied? Yes. We cannot talk aloud Christian Science nor spiritually, for talk is material. I sometimes think argument hinders the work by materializing the thought. Hold to the spiritual.

Knowing you do not depend upon the action of bowels or stomach, eyes to see, ears to hear and sleep for rest, will rest you more than sleep. I have demonstrated this.

Has God accomplished much through me for the world? Yes. How have I made it possible? By giving up *all* for Christ.

Father, sister, etc.; when my father told me if I disgraced the family with Christian Science, I should never darken his door again; and my sister would not speak to me; I gave them all up. I am now being punished by the fruits (the Glover case now in court) of my marriage. Only as you give up all for Christ can you be Christian Scientists. If the wife comes to Christian Science she should show the husband so he will help her to do this work and give up all. If a husband comes to Christian Science he should show his wife so she will let him do his duty to this Cause. We are all working together with one aim—the Cause. I am not breaking up families; I am all the time praying for harmony. I only show them what Christian Science is and leave them to make their own decision. We cannot go up the mountain carrying our baggage; we must be free.

May 27, 1907. Hold to the omnipotence of God, Truth; evil is not a power; it is the opposite; and by opposite I mean that which is *unlike,* in quality, quantity and nature.

May 30, 1907. God's laws are eternal; they cannot be reversed; they *stand.* In your work you declare the Truth about things; know those declarations *cannot* be reversed. I have for forty years stood with God through all this effort to reverse my work. If I had allowed the devil to reverse my work where would it have been? No. I have stood and carried this Cause in spite of it and all of you can do the same.

Are the laws of health to be relied upon? No. They are material. Are the laws of husbands, wives, sons, etc., to be relied upon? No. Jesus said, 'Who are my mother and brethren? They which do the will of my Father.' This does not do to give out, for the world is not ready for it. The papers are already after me on this subject, because I am tearing down their idols by giving the interpretation of Jesus' words on this subject. He said, 'Take up the cross and follow me'. People want to come without taking up the cross. This cannot be accomplished; we have to give up *all* for Christ, family ties and all.

When I have made a storm disappear I did not argue,—'there are no clouds'; I said, 'God's face is there and I see it'; and the storm would break and disappear.

God is infinite; is there anything else? No. He is the only lawgiver. Hold to it. There is but one law and that is the law of Love, Life.

June 2, 1907. The passage from sense to Soul is the one which interests us all and in which we must each take part. In this passage from sense to Soul we have to give up everything for Christ. Cannot carry our baggage with us (our material sense of things), father, mother, wife, children, all things.

God took away everything from me, I had nothing to cling to materially; but I can see some progress spiritually.

I did not understand S. & H. when I wrote it. I would write just as fast as I could; I would have to do so; could not help it. The desire to write would begin in the morning at about a certain time, and leave in the afternoon. I would not stop for dinner when I was writing, and the people where I was boarding used to wonder at it, and would sometimes bring my dinner to me on a tray and set it beside me; but I would not stop.

When we seem to be surrounded by materiality, rise above it for you were never in it, and this will take you out of the belief.

When Christian Scientists come to Pleasant View, I demand of them that they leave their belongings and take up the cross. You cannot win the crown without bearing the cross.

The question was asked—What is the 'second death'? The death of every sin you possess. What is the first death? Coming into the belief of life, substance, intelligence, etc., in matter. (The first death is dying to Spirit, or rather coming into the belief in matter. The second death is dying to matter. Dying into matter and dying out of it.)

Mrs. Sargent quoted Mrs. Eddy as saying, 'When we go to heaven the book will be there' (Revelation 20: 12).

Also while sitting at the dinner table one day Mrs. E. said, 'If I should pass on sitting here in this chair now, I would awaken right here in this chair; nothing would be changed'. Mrs. Sargent asked, 'Would we be right here also? She said, I do not know; that has not been proved yet'. After a Scientist had passed Mrs. E. said, 'She is so much better off; she would not come back here'. Mrs. Sargent said, 'What do you mean by that when S. & H. says that death causes no change? Mrs. E. answered, 'If you were working out a problem on the blackboard and kept making a mistake, after you had corrected your mistake you would be that much freer to go on with your problem; so it is in waking from the dream (mistake) of death'.

Mrs. Sargent told of two sisters who knew nothing of Christian Science; one was passing while sitting in her chair and said to the other one, 'Don't you see them?'—named father, mother, sister and others; the other one said, 'No; why? She said, 'Can't you hear what sister is saying to you? 'No.' 'She is saying for you not to hold me here but let me go; why this is nothing at all'—and she was gone.

So there is no need of passing through death; the problem of life can be worked out and the interval of death can be bridged over as S. & H. says.

CHAPTER TWO

WATCHES

Given by Mary Baker Eddy to Students

WATCH—Learn what watching means. I have watched all these years for you and the world. Now you watch; be always on duty—on guard.

WATCH—Don't see *things.*

WATCH—Stick to the truth of being.

WATCH—Take it in your watch:

No pain.
No nerves.
No neuralgia.
No fear.

WATCH—Better for Mrs. Eddy's teaching.

Truth heals.
It cannot hurt.
It cannot be reversed in its effect.
Love governs all.

WATCH— Every effort of the leader of this gang blesses us, makes our way easier, gives us better health and a shorter way to heaven.

WATCH—Can't hurt anyone by telling the truth and no one can hurt me by lying.

WATCH— More mental work for the field must be done.

WATCH—Nothing can reverse the Truth, for Truth is All.

WATCH—No surplus electricity.

All is governed by divine Mind, etc.

WATCH— Impersonal evil cannot use me as an avenue through which to express any discord; there is no evil. This hourly declaration will keep me invulnerable from error.

WATCH—God loves all of us in this house. God governs us.

All things are working together for our good.

WATCH—Electro-magnetism conveys nothing to nerve centers, and there is no telegraphy over the nerves of the body.

WATCH—M.A.M., you cannot make me believe that I cannot heal, nor can you prevent me from healing.

(Three times a day if not more.)

WATCH—A lying argument has just the opposite effect.

The wrath of man shall praise Him, and we rise because of it, i.e. by overcoming it.

WATCH—Let your minds go out every two hours:

All is peace, good will, Love, etc.

Say nothing of error.

Confine your thoughts to the right side.

WATCH— No fear of mortal mind. It has no power over us.

We have full confidence in divine Mind, for it is All; there is none other.

WATCH—M.A.M. *rages* and Christian Scientists should be *strong* and meet this secret influence with counteracting mental work.

WATCH—Truth reverses every argument of error and brings out just the opposite results.

WATCH—Hold steadfastly to God.

Do as *you would be done by,* and God will bless you in it.

WATCH—No fear.

No sleeplessness.

No suffering from mortal mind turned on us, for there is *no mortal mind.*

No suffering from the World article.

One Mind, etc.

WATCH—Know and realize:

Good is omnipotent.

Evil is impotent.

There is but one Mind.

There is no mortal mind.

WATCH—No unconscious mind. It is all conscious and I govern my thoughts.

No poison can get in here.

One God, one power only, and it is good and not evil.

WATCH—I am the image and likeness of God. No mortal or mortal opposer of Truth can confine this image in any mortal body to mar or molest it, for divine Mind holds it intact, forever free from mortal touch.

WATCH—When we are better, we are not made worse. When we help others, it does not hurt us, The good we do does us good. God is Life. God is never death. We can no more lose life than we can lose God.

WATCH—There are no *lies,* nothing is *real* but the *Truth.*
There is no loss of sight.
It cannot be lost.
Hold this point and demonstrate it.

WATCH—Love controls the weather.
No electricity of mortal mind.
No thunder; no high winds to blow.
Divine Mind governs all.

WATCH—No error can harm our Cause or a true Christian Scientist.
Good is supreme, it is all, and evil is powerless.
Our arguments cannot be reversed.
Truth is not hindered. It brings forth.

WATCH—Watch and pray against becoming worldly; also for spiritual sense to govern all your motives and acts.

WATCH—Never argue all on one side.
But handle the serpent.
Then claim the real, the Love.

WATCH—A lying argument has no power.
What we reject cannot be forced into our thought.
No involuntary contraction of the muscles of the pupil of the eye nor of the eyelids.
No lessening of the eye.

WATCH—Cannot make you worse when you are better.
When you are better, you are better.
You are not a hypnotist.
You do not send disease from place to place.
You heat it.
One Mind—no other.

WATCH—Watch that M.A.M. does not dull your thought to the clear Word of God. I gave so much to your class—my last class—and *so little* has been done with it! Why? Because sleep overcomes the thought. Students must be watchers against the 'thief that cometh in the night'.

WATCH—Declare daily:
No mesmeric influence can prevent the law of spiritual growth, understanding, development, expression, discernment, humility,

freedom, health, wealth, and healing from having boundless freedom in your consciousness.

No mesmeric influence can separate you from the infinite Mind and its faculty.

WATCH—Take this thought earnestly twice each day:

There is no evil thinking and no evil argument; the lie and liar are a lie, an illusion; there is no such person nor thought. *God is all there is.*

WATCH—You have no faith in evil.

You have no power to do evil, or cause others to sin.

You cannot take away from anyone mind, or any of its faculties.

There is no power in evil.

Good is the only power.

You cannot poison anyone.

There is no poison.

These are God's laws and you cannot escape them.

WATCH—Christian Scientists must work daily to annul the prayers of the unrighteous, those who unrighteously pray that the Christian Science prayers cannot heal the sick.

WATCH—*Better* for her *teaching* and help, etc.

No relapse, etc.

No reversal of Truth, etc.

No pain, no night (fear or doubt). All is joy and peace.

No arsenical or mercurial rheumatism or neuralgia.

No Catholic prayers to harm us, for the wrath of man shall praise Him

WATCH—The claim of hypnotism, mesmerism, electro-magnetism, and animal magnetism, is that they work through nerves.

Now let us cut their wires and know that there are no nerves.

Mind does the talking and Mind is God.

WATCH—There is no animal, vegetable or mineral kingdom; there is no poisonous thought or mind.

There can be no inflammation from fear, hate, lust or poison, through mental malpractice or mental malpractitioners.

There is no mind to transfer or be transferred, telegraphed or transmitted, and no man or woman to operate those claims.

WATCH—Know that M.A.M. has no intelligence to make a law that mercurial or arsenical poison can be mentally administered to produce catarrhal condition of the body. God is the only law-maker. There is no belief in a mentality through which poison can be hypnotically administered.

WATCH—They cannot be swayed by malicious hypnotism.

They are governed and guided by the one Mind, and say and do according to the divine government and guidance.

God governs it.

Justice, truth and love govern it, and nothing else can or does affect it in the least.

WATCH—I cannot harm myself.

I cannot be made to harm myself.

I cannot harm another.

I cannot be made to harm another.

Another cannot harm me.

Another cannot be made to harm me.

Because we are all God's children, we all love each other—Divine Love.

WATCH— Know daily, there are no accidents, no disease, no old age and no death.

WATCH—Every lying argument of hypnotism, theosophy, esoteric magic, etc., is reversed in its effects. Guard this statement of truth by knowing that it cannot be reversed. Their arguments bless us and do us good because the reverse of them does us good. And all things shall work together for good to those that love God.

WATCH—Mortal mind cannot send me a belief that I cannot heal through Mind; cannot make me believe there is any law, or so-called law of mental malpractice that I cannot break and annul. Sin cannot hold a patient. There is no man to treat.

WATCH—I am not hypnotized, not self-mesmerized to believe a lie.

I am governed by God.

I am not glamored.

There is no hypnotism, no mortal mind, no presence, no power in evil.

God is all and my only Mind.

He gives me all my thoughts, words and acts.

He teaches me how to pray aright.

WATCH—There is nobody hurting you.

You or your students cannot help yourselves by taking up others, for nobody is hurting you.

God, Love, governs, and Love is not overcome by hate.

You cannot tight against God.

God, good, is supreme and does govern.

There must be an outpouring of love to meet this hour.

WATCH—Truth cannot be reversed; it bears the fruit of health and holiness.

Life cannot be reversed; it bears the fruit of immortal harmony.

Love cannot be reversed; it destroys all fear and heals the sick and the sinner.

Nobody can suffer or produce any suffering for speaking the truth. Nobody can affect others through a lie.

WATCH—There are no thoughts sent here but the divine Mind.

There is no malicious mesmerism nor hypnotism, no evil thoughts in this house, or that can be sent here.

All is God, divine Love.

Divine Love is infinite and there are no other minds.

One Mind and this Mind is Love, divine, immortal Life, health and holiness right here in this house.

No malicious thought coming here.

All is divine Love and its manifestation, health, holiness, immortality.

WATCH—There is no psychology and no R.C. prayers frightening us in this house.

There is no *sin* and no *fear* of *sin.*

Christian Scientists love the psychologists and the Roman Catholics and they love us.

Good is all *power* and the *only* power.

WATCH—Hold on and persist for good, because there never is a hopeless situation. When error meets with resistance, it begins to be scattered. Where a situation seems unbearable, it is because error is letting go.

Being is one and cannot war with itself; and there is nothing outside of it to strike a blow.

No shadow of mortal mind can touch me; there is nothing to fear. God works in me to will and to do, and I shall perform my work. No cloud can touch me or my patients. All that is within me is the spirit of victory.

WATCH—There is no hypnotism, no theosophy, no electro-magnetism, no animal magnetism.

Awake from this dream!

You are awake to the Truth, you see it, you realize it, and no mortal mind can hinder you from realizing it.

There is one Mind; Truth, Life and Love govern all your thoughts and annihilate all that is unlike them.

WATCH—no fear.

No poison, arsenic, etc.

No suffering caused here by the readers of *Science and Health.*
No evil minds.
No feeling the beliefs of patients.
No relapse, no reversal of Truth.
There is but one *Mind,* God, good. Evil is *not mind,* it has *no power.*
We can help ourselves and help others; *we do.*
We are not self-mesmerized. *God, good, alone controls us.*
We feel no mind but His; there is no other mind to feel.
God gives all the thoughts we have, governs all we do and say and think.

WATCH—Everyone in this house is better every hour, every half-hour, every moment they are gaining health and holiness.

All things work together for good to them that love God, etc.

(Mrs. Eddy says all things are possible to God and it is He that worketh with us both to will and to do His own good pleasure.
(This is the rule for healing.)

WATCH—

1. No fear.
2. No loss of sight.
3. No law of mesmerism that we can't help our Leader or that it hurts us to help her. We do help her. We can help others and do help ourselves, and it benefits us to do good.
4. No sleeplessness and no suffering from sleeplessness.
5. No return of old beliefs of disease or sin.
6. That good that we would do, we do, and are better for doing it.
7. There is but one Mind, the divine Mind is the only Mind. Love is All.
8. We cannot be separated from divine Love and Life, and no mortal affects a person in this house.

WATCH—No form of error can make a C.S. treatment produce an opposite effect, nor can I be made to overlook or forget anything in the treatment that is necessary for its certain accomplishment of good. We must go ahead of error, and keep ahead of error all the way. Error is nothing but erroneous thought, and we must never give in to it, or go down before it. Mental activity must be tranquil—not lazy; it must express force, be exact, and it must know the reality of man's oneness with God, and the utter unreality of evil in all its forms of beliefs.

WATCH—You can heal the sick; you have power to do it, and no one can take it from you, or make you suffer for doing it, or your patients suffer when you are trying to help them. No mortal mind can make a poison for you or your patients. They cannot reach your patients through you, or in any other way. You do not suffer from your head, from any argument of poison. There is no power but God, and with Him all things are possible. You have no fear of mesmerism, for there is none. There is but one cause and there can be no effect from any other cause.

WATCH—Blood is thought and your blood is pure thought, a health-giving, life-giving thought, and nothing impure can enter into that thought; it is perfectly pure.

You are not in body. You are not governed by matter; there is no matter; but you are governed by and govern with divine Mind. You are perfectly well and you know it and are not afraid. You do know the truth and you don't know error, nor see it, nor hear it, nor can you be governed by it. There is no reality to it. You hear divine Mind, the voice of Truth, Life, Love, and there is no other mind to hear. No rheumatism, no sore joints, no inflamed or weak eyes, no old age; but the meridian of being.

You don't need to be told these truths by any person for God has told it to you abundantly, and you hear the divine voice and are strong and perfectly well.

I can know the right thing to do and do it and not have to repeat it. I can know the right place in the roads. I don't forget; there is no sensuality nor effects of it.

WATCH—You, lie, cannot fasten your fault upon me.

You cannot unload your filth at my door.

You cannot argue fear, inability, lack of understanding, paralysis, inaction.

You cannot rob me of my God-given dominion.

You cannot rob me of my property.

You cannot rob me of my good name.

You cannot rob me of my friends.

You cannot take away from me what God has given me, nor deprive me of what God has in store for me.

You cannot cause me to make mistakes, cannot blind me, cannot accuse me.

This *lie* has no origin, is not a creator—there is but one creator, that is God. This *lie* cannot rob me of the fruits of my labors. Cannot rob me of my individuality. It cannot reach me through jealousy, hate or malice. It cannot argue that I am misunderstood. It has no activity, no intelligence, no personality. It is neither person, place nor thing.

WATCH—God's law is justice and Truth, which is strength, and the law of extermination to envy or evil, which is weakness. There is no law of suggestion or evil that can cause me to be unfaithful or disobedient to our Teacher and Leader, or to the Cause of Christian Science. Ignorant or malicious minds cannot make me believe that I can be made an avenue for error to come to me, or go from me, for there are no malicious minds. God is the only Mind; so there can be no other minds affecting me. Lies have no other power, nor has envy, jealousy, hatred or avarice. They cannot be made use of to harm me or mine. Love is omnipotent, all-seeing, all-powerful, All-in-all. Thy kingdom come. Thy will be done on earth as in heaven, and earth is heaven.

WATCH—There is no fear to prevent us from seeing the results of our labor. It is as easy to help ourselves as others, for we have a clearer understanding of God that destroys fear. We have the Mind of God. Because there is no atrophy in the Mind of God, there is none in our Mind; and as God's Mind is All and made all, there is no atrophy.

We are joined by God, divine Science, to Himself, His power and love. And what God hath joined no man can put asunder. Our work does good. We have not the ability or power to do harm. There is no law that can give anyone the power to do harm. God's law is the only law and that does good, not harm, and can give man only the power to do good; not defeat, but victory. We cannot get away from God. If I ascend up into heaven, behold Thou are there. Everybody loves us and everybody reflects love.

WATCH—Nobody that is trying to hurt us can make laws.
The lies they whisper hurt no one but themselves.

Lies, hatred, revenge, have no power but to destroy themselves, every time they try to hurt someone else.

This is God's law and it cannot be broken, and it cannot make anybody suffer because we tell you this.

You cannot help yourself and nobody can help you till you stop trying to hurt others.

You can never prosper while you try to hurt others or make your students believe anybody is harming you, for nobody is doing this.

Then turn to the right side in your own consciousness and know this truth:

God alone reigns and all is Love.

WATCH—Pray that God destroys this effort to harm Christian Scientists; and hypnotism cannot prevent this result. Know that God makes the wrath of man to praise Him and He restrains the remainder thereof. All things work together for good to them that love God. Pray that there shall be no *law-suit* and realize that it is put down now by the right proceeding. Realize that it is stopped now by the divine Mind who alone governs. There is but *one Mind.* Evil is *not* power. It *cannot do anything.* It is *powerless.*

God governs the court. Truth prevails. God governs the lawyers and they cannot make a mistake. Divine Mind governs them and guides them and they say and do according to this divine government and guidance. See that they do not become demoralized, that M.A.M. cannot prevent their thinking, saying and doing the right on the case—that God governs them. Look after the judge that he simply is governed by Truth and that M.A.M. does not touch him.

WATCH—Cruel lie trying to make itself thought, that the children of Christian Scientists will be the offscouring of the earth. This is *not* a thought! It cannot be held or thought—not a law. Same history as any other law of mortal mind—and *no* history.

WATCH—Beware! Beware! Beware!!
Watch and pray.
Study.
Demonstrate Truth!
See *Christian Science Journal,* Vol. V, page 199.

WATCH—Animal magnetism, you cannot produce in me any new beliefs, neither can you bring back any old beliefs, for in divine Mind there are no beliefs. *You* cannot harm me—neither can you make me harm others, nor can you harm those on whom my thought may rest. See I Cor. 14: 33.

WATCH—Animal magnetism, you are a liar.
You know you are a liar.
You know that I know you are a liar.

WATCH—I do not feel the effects of a lie or of hate.
It is the liar that suffers from the lie and not I.
The effect of the Truth I think and utter is not and cannot be reversed.
All is Love and harmony and health and Life and this cannot be taken from me.
They are forever present and there is no reversal of the Truth and Life and Love.

WATCH—No fear.
Love.
No arsenic nor any other poison.
Telling the truth destroys error; it does not make it seem real nor hurt anybody.

We know the truth and it has made us free—everyone in this house.

We can and do help our Leader, and nothing can hinder us. God is her ever-present help.

We are better every day and hour-healthier, higher, holier, better for the approaching dedication.

Good governs this hour and us. Evil is not power nor presence.

There is no evil, no hatred, envy nor revenge. It is all Love, Love, Love, health, harmony, immortality.

WATCH—No fear: God, Love, is all, and ever-present, and the *ever-present help.*

No *metastasis.*

No *pain;* no disease changing forms, and the last worse than the first.

No animal magnetism; all is *Good,* there is no matter, no mortal mind.

We have dominion over the earth, over *the body,* and over all evil.

Good is supreme; evil is unreal; good is all, there is none beside God, *Life,* Love, Truth, holiness. These are right here, and no *other consciousness is here,* no *other* mind, no other power.

Good is all, and *governs* all.

There is no *arsenic, mercury, rhus radicant,* no electric poison, no belief that there is. We know if they take any deadly thing, it shall not hurt them. *God has said it.*

WATCH—

No law of incomplete demonstration.

No law that healing disease brings up a worse one of heredity.

No law of limitation, malnutrition, non-assimilation of food.

No law of rebound of hate from attacking sin or disease in treatment.

No law of continuity of error.

No law of astrology or horoscope.

No law of obstruction.

We cannot be fettered by another's thought.

WATCH (Found in one of the attic rooms at Pleasant View after Mrs. Eddy had moved)—LOST OPPORTUNITIES:

No fear, no arsenic, nor any other poison.

No pain.

No relapse into error.

No reversal of Truth.

No return of old beliefs of disease nor new beliefs of disease coming here.

Then establish in your thought the Allness of God and know there is no hate, revenge nor envy.

All is Love.
No diseased gullet.
No catarrh, no inaction, no diarrhea, no stoppage, no disrelish of food.
We are Christian Scientists and can help ourselves and help others; *we do.*
We are not self-mesmerized.
God, good, alone controls us.
We are not hypnotists, and cannot be.
One God.
One Mind.
Love is All.
No pain.

WATCH—It is my right to exercise dominion; next, I can exercise that right and do exercise it; the right to cast out fear.

WATCH—There is no fear and no thoughts of poison can come. There are no such thoughts.

There is no arsenic and no opiates producing any effect on anyone in this house and no one can be made to believe there is.

Love reigns here.

Truth and Life eternal reign here and nothing else can come here.

There are no evil suggestions, no hypnotism, theosophy, no electromagnetism.

God is All, etc.

WATCH—Every argument to hurt anyone (if reversed) does that one good. All things shall and do work together for good to them that love good, as the Bible teaches.

Sin and sickness are not infectious. We do not catch sickness or sin; good alone is catching.

Divine Love governs. This is the law of Christ and it is fulfilled and it cannot be reversed.

There is one Mind, in all, over all, and governing all.

Remember that malice exultant is no greater than malice defeated; both are false. But to know and understand that malice is nothing is to defeat it.

We can and do trust in our God to deliver us from the persecutions of those who war against Truth and Love.

The holy sense of God as All and Love, and that there is no other Mind, is the best way to meet the malicious arguments of evil.

The law of God says, 'Bear ye one another's burdens, and so fulfil the law of Christ'.

The law of evil whispers, 'You cannot help your Leader, neither can you help yourself'. Now if you let this law of evil govern you and master you, you cannot fulfil the law of Christ; you cannot be a Christian Scientist.

Should the thought come to you that you cannot help yourself, then know that you have your reply in the Scripture, that even as Jesus said, 'I can of mine own self do nothing', but 'the Father that dwelleth in me, he doeth the works'. Since God is omnipotence, there is no power nor person that can hinder His healing work.

WATCH—All is peace and Truth; there is no error, no hatred, no sin, all is *Love,* love for God and man.

There abide, for if you abide in Love and Truth, and Truth and Love abide in you, no evil can come of it, and the result must be, is health, harmony, heaven. The freedom of the children of God comes from this true consciousness.

WATCH—Evil is not power, not mind, and nobody has any power to accomplish evil of any sort (here stop and dwell on this argument till you realize this truth).

Then declare that Love is All and *in all,* in every thought, and all power is in Love. There is no other power. Evil is powerless; there is no evil.

Hypnotism, theosophy, and esoteric magic have no power to do evil, and cannot reverse Truth—but Life, Truth, Love *have reversed,* and they have destroyed all evil.

There are no false suggestions, lying arguments or hatred—these are illusions. They do not exist. I have no fear of them. *I am not controlled by them.* Divine Love is supreme and controls all I think, say, or do.

Pray daily twice at least to divine Love to give you success. Then realize for yourself that Love and Truth and action on your part (for Truth does not work for you unless you work) will give you the victory. Guard reversal. There is no law of hypnotism to reverse God's law. Truth is unchangeable and cannot be reversed.

(All the following Watches are mainly instructional, rather than specific treatments.)

WATCH—Dear one, realize for yourself and *all* each day, clear and strong, that the Christ, Truth, does not merely open 'the windows of heaven' for us, or promise us heaven, but the knowledge of the Christ in Christian Science *is* heaven here and now. This knowledge of Truth as it is taught in Science is heaven's open door for all.

WATCH—Try to realize the omnipotence of Love and Life, the in-breathing of His presence. Arouse yourself to a true sense of God's power, the eternal and ever-conscious Mind that knows only Life. Fear and death are powerless in even a faint perception of the meaning of these declarations of Truth.

WATCH—Make supplication to God daily that you may be delivered from all beliefs of sin or of sickness, and after doing this, then turn to and demand of yourself to realize their unreality, and recognize your power over the temptation to yield to any such illusion.

WATCH— Should you awaken from sleep and find yourself in pain, get up, put on your clothes; take yourself up for alcoholism, poison and -, and don't take them off until you have realized His Allness. Conquer the error.

WATCH—The first thing in the morning, call on God to deliver you from temptation and help you to be *awake.* Then do your chores, not as a dreamy hashish eater, but with a clear sense of what to do and just how to do it.

Then sit down and first get yourself into a consciousness of your power with God, and then take up the outside watch. Sit until this is clear,—if two hours.

WATCH—God is your only Mind. Divine Love is caring for you.

No mortal mind can stop the functions of being. God holds them intact and eternally. You *are awake* to the truth; you see it; you *realize it*; and no mortal mind can hinder you from realizing it. There is but *one Mind.* Truth, Life and Love govern all your thoughts and annihilate all that is unlike them.

WATCH—I want you to take up the Watch every two hours as long as you live or until you can make the right side real to your consciousness.

When I work for the weather, everybody wants fair weather, only they believe there will be bad weather, and I only have to overcome that belief; but when malice comes in and declares there shall be storms, then I have a task to overcome that. Now make real to yourselves: There is no envy, malice, hate nor revenge. God is Love and Love is All. All is health and holiness. There is no opposite.

WATCH—Work every day to know that the belief of impossibility has no power over you. Know that it cannot possibly affect you in any way, and can never for an instant hinder your demonstration, whether you are working for health, peace, joy, or any mental quality, thing or experience. Know that you are conscious of the possibility and realization of all that is good and true.

WATCH—The thief is ready to rob and steal all treasures. But our Master saith, 'Had the good man watched, his house would not have been broken open'. I beg you to watch and pray to this end. You are in danger unless you do. The more useful and prominent you become, the harder the mental robbers will work to rob you of good thoughts, a strong purpose and wise efforts to do God's will.

(Mrs. Eddy sent this to some of the workers in a time of dire strait.)

WATCH— Remember that the power to heal is gained through peace, wisdom, love, dominion over ourselves, and good will toward men. You possess these graces of Spirit, or Christ power, only by loving God, good, supremely. After this cometh the recognition of but one Mind, which enables you to know there is no power or presence that can resist good, or can prevent your prayers being effectual. While you remain in this attitude of mind you are obedient to the Principle of your being, and naught can hinder your healing the sick and the sinner.

WATCH—Every C.S. treatment is accumulative; the work goes on to bless all mankind. Error is non-scientific thinking, and scientific or true thinking is all that is needed to destroy it. A treatment must include the realization that it goes forth with power and truth, and cannot be reversed by any law of nature or of *materia medica.*

When you argue on all subjects that should end well, be a law to your own consciousness that what you say cannot be reversed and inverted, and made to produce the very opposite of what you argue for. This is a late phase of theosophy and M.A.M. that needs to be met.

Be careful not to use human will but speak in the power of divine Love that is a law to human hate and destroys it.

WATCH—Declare daily, 'I am healed, and scientifically healed'. Christian Science is the victor, and vanquishment is unknown to omnipotent Truth. I cannot be grieved or disappointed, since God is All and my life is hid with Christ in God. There is nothing lost. Mental malpractice cannot reverse my declarations, cannot touch my conscious or unconscious thought, for there are not minds many. There is only one Mind, divine Mind.

No aggressive mortal suggestion can cause me to forget my duty to God, to our Leader, or to mankind. Mind is unlimited in its source and supply. Man's substance is in Mind, and cannot be impoverished. There is no poverty, no lack. Fear is no part of consciousness. Consciousness is cognizant only of the things of God, good. There is no reality in discord. God's child cannot suffer and be unhappy, because God is the only power and He never made anything but love and peace.

WATCH—The book of Isaiah is called the 'Gospel of Promise'. We should apply it to our daily needs. Declare daily that no hard, wicked, irreligious or anti-Christian thoughts can touch us from any mortal mind. There is no mortal mind, no evil. There is no decay nor death to the nerves, no destruction to the fluids, nor death to the secretions. Tomorrow you have no business with. We steal if we touch tomorrow. It is God's. Every day has enough in it to keep us occupied without concerning ourselves with the things beyond.

Delay to perform a duty is not obedience. The Scripture declares that 'Now is the acceptable time'. The good that can be done today cannot be done tomorrow; and sufficient unto each day are the demands thereof. The model Sermon of our great Master pleads for our daily bread. We need the bread of heaven each and every day. The Scriptures discard delay; they prohibit the poor protest: 'Tomorrow shall be as this day, and much more abundantly.' A word to the wise is sufficient.

There is nothing within me that corresponds with, or responds to, any form of evil. There is no illusion of poverty. God made all, owns all there is, and it is good. I am joint-heir with Christ, in God, and have my share of everything. I am exempt from want, loss, lack or limitation of any kind. There is no material resistance that can limit me. 'The Lord is my Shepherd, I shall not want.' Abundance cannot lapse into lack, since God is my fountain source of infinite riches and plenty. I can and do demonstrate the wealth which comes from God with no interruption in its flow. I am prosperous and successful, kept so by an inexhaustible supply. There is no mental self-mesmerism. I have fulness of supply and abundance. There are no adverse circumstances, no avarice, no greed, no trust in money, nor love of money. I live in the land of promise.

WATCH—I am glad the mist is melting and hope it will be put under your feet. God demands a more Christian, zealous and persistent effort to resist evil and overcome, or our Cause will again be covered by the rubbish of centuries.... God has said, Do My prophets no harm, and inasmuch as you bless them, I will bless you. But the strange infatuation to forget and not watch, causes the worst of results and leaves the student at the beck of sin.... Oh, may the divine Love keep you from *sleeping* and bless you ever.

WATCH—Watch, pray, labor and have *faith*! *Know* that you can be what God demands you to be and *are now*—His image and likeness—reflecting God, the one and only Healer, reflecting good, Life, Truth, Love.

WATCH—Mental malpractice must be met daily by all the students; met by your mental protest that breaks the so-called law of a lie, or you are liable to be affected by this lie all *unconsciously*. Dear one, *remember this*. Our Master said, 'Had the good man of the house watched, his house would not have been broken open'.

WATCH—Let our finite judgment never settle on *who* is troubling us, and never defend ourselves against a person. Rather ask *what* is troubling us, and then meet the *what*.

WATCH—Never fear a lie. Declare against it with the conviction of its nothingness. Throw your whole weight into the right scale—this is the way to destroy evil. Never weigh against yourselves by admitting a lie.

WATCH—First we must see the error, then repent and then forsake it. You will have to continue with sin until you have overcome it. Then you will have another form of evil to meet—the envy and jealousy of mortal mind. That is where your Leader stands.

WATCH—Take time each day to say: 'What is the most powerful thing in the world? It is God saying "I am" in His own creation.'

WATCH—Any event is every event and 'I am' the law to it.

WATCH—Just go alone and close your eyes, and in the depths of your own consciousness say over and over again, I am, I am, I am, I am. Your whole being will be filled with the sense of the power to overcome, the power to accomplish, the power to do all things.

I am because Thou art (Mind is)—I am.
I am what Thou art (Mind is)—I am.
I am where Thou art (Mind is)—I am.
I am one with Thee (Mind), oh! Thou infinite I AM.
I am good.
I am well.
I am abundantly satisfied.
I am holy.
I am free.
I am because Thou art (Mind is)—I am.

I am, spoken upward towards the good, the true, is sure to outpicture in visible good, in success, in happiness, in abundance.

SAMPLES OF SPECIFIC WATCHES
(Recorded by two Students)

First Series

(2/6/91) Handle the serpent of age. No belief of cyanide or mercurial poisoning. Free use of all faculties. Love is All. No hate, no darkness of malicious mesmerism. One Mind.

(7/16/92) Mother says take up each day, no fear; all is Love. Mind controls all. No malicious mesmerism to hinder his thoughts. Do not name the person or persons by name.

(9/16/92) Christ wore a crown of thorns as easily as a seamless robe. How? By demonstration of his oneness with divine Love.

Handle the serpent that hisses at the heel and the animal magnetism will be silent. No fear. All is harmony.

(4/5/00) Hold the line every day; no fear; God governs all. No M.A.M. to feel or be felt. Mind controls all.

(7/6/00) You are to take up for the Directors daily Mind is All. God is here. There is no darkness, no mental depression, no failure in God's Cause. *Do not name them by name.*

(9/27/00) Are you a Christian Scientist or not? Then take up the work and put an end to these scandalous attacks on your Leader and *Best Earthly Friend.* God is judging us this hour, and we shall be accountable to Him for all. Now take up the work *as you can do* and let us have a peace at Pleasant View.

Your Leader has work important to do, and these attacks must *stop;* see to it.

(3/25/02) Mother asks you: Drop all patients and take for your one unworthy patient The Mother Church of Christian Science which needs healing from its sins this day.

(4/10/02—Work for lecturers) A city that is set upon a hill cannot be hid, and the life of their Leader must be shown as it is. Never did I neglect Jesus in my sermons in the first days of Christian Science; now they must not forget me. The scandalous attacks on the Discoverer and Founder of Christian Science will stop if the *truth* about her be shown to the world.

(10/17/03) Take up at once: Students shall know their duty to their Leader. Grace divine yet lays many burdens on human hearts *unworthy* to bear them. When will blind eyes see their Leader as she is?

(3/18/04) The Mother Church is founded on *Truth* and cannot be removed nor taken down. Mother knows days and nights of anguished prayer that none know aught of, lest the sheepfold be taken down wherein the lambs are sheltered. Weary in days of trial but freshened in His service, she waits till all unworthy ones come neath the shadow of His wing.

(2/2/06) Take up, clear voice, strong, clear, for Christian Science Lecturers. Error tries to hinder Truth being *heard* in public. His

Word must be *shouted* from housetops, not buried in soft voices to tickle ears. The *lambs* of His pasture must be fed and the sheep also.

(11/5/06) Have six of your best students loyal and truthful take up every day with you, work mental to sustain the Cause and do their *duty* to their Leader and Mother.

(Enclosed: Argument for Transgressors—One Mind; Truth controls all. You are set free in the Love of God and you cannot make nor believe a lie. Truth declared is not reversed. It does appear and is manifest. No return of old beliefs. No M.A.M. to work through R.C., hypnotism, mesmerism or theosophy, demonology or old theology to hinder the work of the Cause of Christian Science. Divine Mind governs every hour and evil is powerless.)

Second Series

(2/15/01) Mother sends you this message: Rise up and defeat the evil one in the gates. The hour of deliverance is at hand and all must do their *duty* as Christian Scientists to defeat the evil that tries to find entrance here. Love, Mind, Truth rule this and every hour. *Error* is not met by prayer alone, but by *fasting*.

(4/4/01) Watchfulness is the word of this hour of trial for our Cause. Keep apart from the Sunday students in our midst who trample His divine Word under foot all week and expect forgiveness on the Sabbath. Their reward awaits them.

(6/9/01) Truth declared heals the sick. Prove this and help the Cause at once. Students asleep M.A.M. has already handled. Know that your Leader cannot be deprived of the helpers she needs by the glister of the world. Mind is All. Divine Love rules this hour. *Know this.*

(9/4/01) Healing alone built this Cause and will not be lost if hearts open to His Truth and Love sustain the hands of those appointed to voice God in this age. Form in service means nothing; only healing can build His temple in the wilderness. How Mother longs, prays to hear of more healing in the service of divine Love!

(9/5/02) One Mind controls this and every hour. When the Discoverer of Christian Science in this age must deal with *sinning,* so-called Christian Scientists, those who *know* their Leader as she *is* must be *awake* to the delusions of M.A.M. that would make Jerusalem a waste and desert place. Take up those transgressors in our midst who would undo the work of their Leader. Love is All. One Mind. Dear one, Mother knows your heart is active in His service, Waken to the need of this hour that those who would set aside the Manual of The Mother Church with its *just* By-Laws see the sinfulness of their ways.

(11/17/03) To my Household at Pleasant View: The rules of this house do not permit of evil being spoken, thought or heard. Love rules this and every hour. M.A.M. is without power, powerless. Darkness is nothing. Mind is All, God is All and His voice is heard in all places. God judges and His judgment is sound and righteous. Know this now and every hour. No theosophy, no malicious animal magnetism to lie or hear a lie. God reigns and loveth whom He chasteneth. No work is done until I say it is and no student will forsake his post in any moment. God is Love, Love is All. Truth reigns.

(2/16/05) No fear, no theosophy, no mortal mind, no M.A.M. Love reigns this and every hour. God is All. Life, Truth, Love destroy M.A.M. R.C. cannot lie or produce a lie. Mind controls all. One God, one Life, Truth, Love.

(4/7/05) Mother sensed a little grief in her student's bearing today. Surely he knows that she *loves* him and all those *loyal and true* workers in the Cause of Truth. All poise, power and strength come from Him who runs and is not weary, walks and is not faint in One Mind. Christian history shows that those who have waited never doubting have had their *sure reward* in righteousness. Mother has proved this many times. Now take up again for yourself every day, Love is All. Truth reigns. There is no lie and nothing to make a lie. No M.A.M. to darken thought. Love reigns and rules this and every hour. Truth declared *heals.* No reversal. God is All. 'Commit thy ways unto Him and He shall bring it to pass.'

(5/27/05) One Mind demonstrated *handles* serpents, casts out demons of sense with power of Truth. When will Christian Scientists learn that *blab* never made a single demonstration in building up this Cause? How Mother longs, prays, hopes, for *healing* in Truth and Love!

(7/16/05) Beloved Students at Pleasant View: Handle electricity of mortal mind; no arsenical poison, no belief of nerves. Love governs all. One Mind, one Truth. God is All-in-all. Jesus knew the hour of temptation and *wept,* but he also knew the power of Love supreme over all the errors of sense. No lie *stands* in the presence of Truth. No theosophy, black magic. No destructive electricity. 'He commanded and it stood fast.' God, good, is All.

(Take this up every morning and evening until I tell you to change your prayers.)

(9/22/05) The Cause of Christian Science is founded on Principle, not person. Loyal students of the Scriptures and *Science and Health know* that when the Discoverer and Founder of Christian Science appointed these Books as the *only preachers* in our churches, God was leading this Cause as surely as He led the Children of Israel in the desert.

(2/20/06) The Directors of The First Church of Christ, Scientist, must work in this hour that the dedication of the earthly tabernacle in the wilderness be accomplished sure this year. For this reason Mother places upon all loyal students this word of warning-healing the sick and sinful is the greater part and all must join in this work, who wish not to see this Cause go down.

(8/19/06) Your Mother in Israel calls upon you this day—rejoice with her in sense spiritual—*know* there is One Mind, Truth, Love and all will be met. Behold I make all things new is the promise Christ-like. Do you, dear Lewis, understand this? Then *rise up*—defeat the enemy without our gates that defileth and maketh a lie. No night, no darkness, all is Mind. All is God, good. *Hold to this* until I say change.

(8/06) This Cause depends upon healing, healing and *wisdom*. If these are not added, the salt will lose his savor and this Cause drop down into darkness of oblivion of centuries again.

> [STATEMENT enclosed, with instructions that it be handed to Mr. Armstrong: To the Christian Science Board of Directors: No student of Christian Science shall occupy a position of trust or confidence in this Cause who does not *daily* declare the truth at least three times in his prayers for the well-being of his Leader, the Discoverer and Founder of Christian Science, the Rev. Mary Baker G. Eddy. (Can the above be made a By-law in our Manual?)]

(1/12/07) If your Mother and your best earthly friend directs work to be done in sense and Science spiritual in the Cause of Christ, why can't, won't you and other students before this faithful always in His sight, do it? The calling of Soul is man's highest example, this I know forty years. Dear one, Mother rejoices at your growth in His cause and that is why she seeks always the chastening rod of His Spirit for you, Do you understand this? Kinter and Mann will take the watch this night. Be you at work; if Mother calls you, you win be ready. One Mind; Love over all; Truth *reigns*.

(1/22/07) Hold the ground: Life, Truth, Love reign this and every hour. No fear, no night dream, no day dream. M.A.M. is not power.

Only reality; God, and His will *is done* on this earth *and at Pleasant View.* Keep the line; hold your aim, thought externalized is the guide.

Please receive from Mr. Carpenter the texts for thinking and I will name the hour in the morning beginning 5 A.M. The above named watch is uniform.

I do not ask you to treat anyone. I only show you what is in belief and man's daily duty to God.

WATCH PRAYERS AND OTHER ITEMS OF INTEREST

WATCH PRAYER—Pray all the time. Pray this way: Love, just take me in. Give me one Mind, one consciousness, and make me love my neighbor as myself. All is Love, peace, harmony. Heaven is right here. Love reigns. There is no strife. Peace, be still. Truth has destroyed the error. Love has destroyed all hate. All is Love, peace and joy. After praying, be willing to be fitted to receive the blessing you ask for.

> (Mrs. Eddy said: These 'watch prayers' are righteous prayers which are for the purpose of antidoting unrighteous prayers, and are in accord with the statements of Jesus, Mark 13: 37 and Luke 12: 39. The Lord's Prayer is a 'watch prayer'.)

WATCH PRAYER FOR THE WHOLE HOUSEHOLD—All is Love, peace and harmony. Heaven is right here. Truth reigns. There is no strife. Peace, be still. Truth has destroyed the error. Love has destroyed all hate. All is peace. Love and joy. Run and not be weary. The need of the hour is simplicity, meekness and obedience.

THE PRAYER OF THE WATCHERS—The effect of this prayer *is not reversed.*

God, good, reigns; there is *no other mind.*

Love reigns; there is no envy, no revenge.

All things are working together for good to those that love good.

We do love good, God, and He gives us all our thoughts, and governs all our acts.

The divine Love preserves our life and health, and they cannot be taken from Christian Scientists, and Christian Scientists cannot be made sinful.

We love God and God loves us and is guiding us every moment.

This prayer cannot be reversed.

This prayer bears fruit after its own kind, it does good, and blesses us and all others.

(Charge them not to change, add to, or diminish this prayer. Something is out of tune. This will be a chord.)[1]

TO THE WATCHERS—'Hear, O Israel, for the Lord, our God, is *one* God.'

You are not to come in your own name to pray.

You are not to control any mind.

You are to come only in the divine strength, and know that God will rule and does, and that hypnotism and evil minds cannot and do not control men or governments.

All power is God, good.

This is my only formula to Christian Scientists for prayer, and God will give you faith that will remove mountains.

IN YOUR WATCH INCLUDE THIS ALWAYS: When a good point in health or progress is reached, it cannot be lost and the case made worse, but it *does remain* and *no relapse can occur.*

INSTRUCTIONS REGARDING WATCHERS—(5/19/06) C.S. Board of Directors

My beloved Students: Consider this, my proposition: that you require some of the best Christian Scientists in Boston and vicinity to pray once each day that no thought of earthquake, tornado or destructive lightning enter thought to harm it, but that He who reign's in the heavens and watches over the earth saves from all harm. Again let me say, pray not on *hire* but the demand of love to God and man.

Mary Baker Eddy.

[1]Historical Note: Membership in The Mother Church was largely recruited from the ranks of the sick who had been healed in Christian Science—some of them of so-called incurable diseases. This life-saving quality of Christian Science with its membership in the Church of Christ, Scientist, was met with the suggestion or argument of reversal and death. So Mrs. Eddy, detecting the effort of malicious mind, formulated the *Prayer of the Watchers* as given above, and had it passed to a number of Christian Scientists who might profitably be alerted on the subject. Then the claim came up of reversal of the prayer itself, and she stopped its use. Later she saw that it might be used again to good advantage and so ordered it, writing as follows to William B. Johnson, Clerk to The Mother Church at that time: 'Have the "Watchers" use that prayer so long as it works well. I find that the law of mesmerism that relies on *reversing* the effect of Truth, is sometimes forgotten and in this case the prayer does not work well. Perhaps it was this that caused my order to discontinue it. Another cause existed at that time: Mr.— managed to some extent the "Watchers". This must not be so. Let no one but yourself consult with them on this work and be sure that you give it sufficient attention to know as to its results, and, if good, continue the Watch an the same terms it had in the beginning. Please have the dear "Watchers" resume the prayer you sent to me at once and charge them to let no one know it but yourself.'

(6/26/08) *Confidential* Beloved (C.S. Board of Directors): Have several Christian Scientists who are best adapted to it, take up the weather and know that 'God sendeth the rain upon the just and the unjust.' Hence the latter, *it is raining*. Continue this prayer till the result follows it. Let none know, that will tell it, what is being done.

(Adelaide Still, Mrs. Eddy's personal maid, reported that at this time a student whose duty it was to work on the weather opened the Bible at random to Gen. 2: 5 in her work and then showed it to Mrs. Eddy. At once the latter took the work out of her hands and wrote the above letter.)

ALERTNESS To Duty—It shall be the duty of every member of this Church to daily purge himself of all aggressive mental suggestion, and not be made to forget, nor to neglect his duty to God, to his Leader, and to mankind.

(Changes made in Mrs. Eddy's handwriting in the 34th edition of the Church Manual, 1903)

TO THE WATCHERS WHO ARE MISTAKEN—(12/21/01) Beloved students: Disband your meeting *today* and never meet again to do what is not carried out *scientifically*. Each one do the work of daily duty. Each one realize the allness of God, good, and that there is no opposite evil. Do not meet together to discuss or to direct the prayers of Scientists unless I call you together. Each one pray daily and not ask amiss. I have known of the discord before of prayer that is amiss. You all can know that newspaper men will not publish aught against Christian Science. Please *know this*—and also know that you can do this separately as well as together.

With love,
Mother,
M. B. Eddy.

WATCH—We must strive—I had to do it—so must you. This human is the very element of error and must be overcome in all points.

Someone said to her. 'It isn't difficult to destroy mesmerism when we see it hasn't any power.' She answered, 'If God is All, there is nothing to destroy. There is nothing but God and what God creates. I have to go back to the book and so must you.'

(A student's conclusion: So we must struggle with mesmerism. To keep watch—is to watch, our thought perfectly poised. Words without desire is not prayer. Prayer must have no *selfishness in* it. You must not let the mesmerism of mortal mind make you think you can't keep your watch.)

One day Mrs. Eddy said to a student, 'Are you working?' He began to tell of his hours of study and work. She said, 'When you see old age, do you declare that Life is eternal activity, beauty and joy? When you see the leaves falling and hear the wind blow, do you declare that there is no change, decay or cold? When you see deformity and disease, do you declare that man is made in the image and likeness of God?

The student answered, 'Mrs. Eddy, I am not working'.

When the plenipotentiaries of the Russian and Japanese governments were in America (1905) on invitation of the President, negotiating peace between their countries, Baron Komura was taken ill. A student reports that Mrs. Eddy assigned him to handle the lie of disease and to know that medical thought could not hurt the Baron. She further told him to get another student to handle mesmeric influence so that it would be seen that only one Mind operates. In addition he reports that he was assigned to tell the Christian Science Board of Directors that they would be held personally and individually responsible for the Japanese delegate's restoration to health.

This was accomplished; and after peace had been signed, the students concerned were congratulated on the ability they had shown to see the matter brought to a peaceful solution.

CHAPTER THREE

PRAYERS

Given by Mary Baker Eddy to Students

Here I am, dear God, free from the body, Thy humble servant. Mind's idea. Uphold me with Thy right hand. Uphold my voice, Send me where Thou would'st have me go and teach me what to say.

Beloved Father-Mother, God, give me wisdom to meet the problems I may have to meet today; give me understanding to deny error and to proclaim the truth. Give me grace to keep silent when speech is unnecessary. There is no strife, for Truth, risen Truth will destroy error of every sort. And heaven is right here. God gives abundance of intelligence and opportunity. I cannot be impoverished mentally, physically, spiritually, or financially. God is substance and I reflect that substance.

Realize to yourself daily more than once that the fields are white and ready for the harvest, that divine Love always has met every human need, the need for work as well as any other; that Mind is ever active and you reflect divine activity; that the source of supply supplies every need; that there is plenty of work for all, and yours belongs to you and no one else can do it. *It comes to you direct* and the supply is abundant, and know all the time *that this is so.* Never let a lack of anything stay a moment with you. It is rank error and brings all sorts of disease and difficulty.

Love is all powerful.
Love is all seeing.
Love is ever present.
Thy kingdom has come.
Thy will is done here on earth as it is in heaven, and earth is heaven.

(Mrs. Eddy told her students to put this prayer in their pocket book, and, if they did, they would never want.)

O God, show me Thy way and keep me in that way.

(This is what Mrs. Eddy gave, when one asked her to give the shortest prayer.)

Father, teach me how to still the clamoring of sense, and fill my place as listener, that I may hear Thy voice and grow to understand Thy Word, and so become Thy messenger. Then teach me how to banish pride and stubborn will that I may be Thy representative with no false sense of human zeal, that every word may bless and heal, when I Thy message give.

Be like a little child. Turn your thoughts to Love and say, O Love, just take me in; give me one Mind, one consciousness and make me love my neighbor as myself. Let your heart cry out to divine Love. A child cries out to its mother for more light, more truth, more love. Ask Love for what you need and for what Love has to give; then take it and demand of yourself to rise up and live it.

God will direct you in all your ways, if you *trust* Him; faith must take hold before sight or fruition, and this faith will, when instructed in divine Science, become understanding and you will have no doubts, but every proof of His promise, 'Lo! I am with you alway'.

Trust Him, dear; read daily the Bible and *Science and Health*, and pray the prayer of our Lord's in your own words; ask for His kingdom to come, for Love, Truth and Life to govern all your desires, aims and motives, to feed you with faith and a clear knowledge of good, to make you patient, forgiving, long-suffering and merciful, compassionate, even as the dear God is thus to you, and you desire Him to be, and thus reflect this God, good, in all His qualities, etc. My desire is that this year shall be crowned with mercies for you and all.

Oh, keep me ever seeing Thee and seeing as Thou seest, my Life, my joy, my All.

Oh, that an influx of divine light and glory may enter each, and every one of our hearts, and that you be endued *anew* with power from on high.

God, forgive me for having any doubt, fear or lack of faith that all things are not possible with Thee.

We should pray for that Mind to be in us that was in Christ Jesus, not the man that was mortal, but the idea or Christ which was immortal. Never pray to have my mind as a person, for God is my Mind and yours and there is but one Mind. Christ expressed the Mind that is God, for Christ was the spiritual idea for that age and all ages, for this idea never changes; it is the same forever; it expresses Science. The female thought is its last fleshly embodiment because this thought expresses the Mother-God, the mate the Father. But remember these are concepts which we entertain; they are neither male nor female in the spiritual universe of God, and we shall gain this true sense of ourselves as God's ideas, spiritual personalities, when the sense of life, substance and mind is gone forever from matter and Spirit to us is All-in-all.

Study the Bible constantly, daily, and, dear one, pray. Ask the divine Love every day to give you all that the Lord's Prayer inculcates. Go alone by yourself one half hour every morning and ask God, good, 'Thy kingdom come—ask to establish the reign of honesty, peace and purity in your consciousness and to overthrow and cast out all that is unlike the Christ, Love. Ask to forgive those that wrong you even as God forgives you, and see how this must be for you to reflect God. Ask for deliverance from temptation, ask for patience, meekness, peace, and so may the grace of God be with you.

May the divine light of Christian Science which lighteth every enlightened thought, illumine my faith and understanding, exclude all darkness and doubt, signal the perfect faith wherein to walk, the perfect Principle whereby to demonstrate the perfect man and perfect law of God.

(8/10/97) Pray God to take away my testimony of the lying senses, and increase my faith and spiritual sense.

Students do not pray enough, They should go by themselves at least three times a day to pray. Their prayers should consist of much giving thanks, more realization of the perfect, as well as the denial of error. There is too much denial of error and too little realization of the perfect. Lord, make me upright.

The need of divine wisdom and Love—Christ's assurance of prayer answered-and the absolute Science of God's Allness, moves the Christian Scientist to pray for the peace, prosperity, and brotherhood of all nations and peoples. No will-power is used in the Scientist's prayer, since human will must be lost in the Divine, for prayer to be efficacious. In the words of Zechariah, 'Not by might, nor by power, but by my Spirit, saith the Lord of hosts.'

I would ask that all Christians unite in prayer for the cessation of sin,—the oppression of the weak,—the accession of power at the sacrifice of individual rights; and especially that divine Love shield the innocent from the wrath of the guilty, and cause it to praise Love.

Thou infinite Life, Thou infinite strength, Thou art here. You are strong in the Lord and in the power of His might. You are strengthened with might by His spirit in the inner man. Flow through me, spirit of divine Love, to do this healing. Divine Love flows everywhere and is reflected through you as well as through the most advanced Scientist. Look up and feel its beams of warmth and live in it.

PRAYER FOR YOURSELF—I am the child of God. His care and love surround me. Animal magnetism cannot reach me to make me *fear* or *be afraid.*

PRAYER FOR ONESELF—I thank Thee, Father-Mother God, that neither ignorant, fraudulent, nor malicious mortal mind can reach me, or affect me mentally, physically, financially, or otherwise; and I *know* it, for God is the only power; that I am not the victim of aggressive mental suggestion, nor the target of M.A.M. claiming to operate through any channel whatever, but I am the blessed legal child of God, spiritual, immortal, all-harmonious, perfect, happy, healthy, pure, sinless, free, and fearless and diseaseless, and deathless, expressing the substance of all good.

Hold yourself constantly and consciously under God's eternal law of blessing, of happiness, harmony, health, peace, joy, power, progress, protection, abundance; there is no other law,—only a contrary mortal mind lie which you are awake and alert to, and not under.

INCLUDE THIS IN ALL YOUR PRAYERS—All the individuals in this house can and do help themselves by prayer,

God helps them.

His promise is fulfilled: Seek and ye shall find. 'Because he has put his trust in Me, therefore have I delivered him.'

THE CHRISTIAN SCIENTIST'S PRAYER—There is no matter and no mortal mind. God is All-in-all. All is harmony, health, holiness. This is the prayer 'unceasing' to be used on all occasions and at all times. It lays the axe at the root of unreality, materiality (that forbidden tree) and cuts it down. Preserve a sacred silence on this subject of prayer.

(Signed, Author of S. & H.)

MORNING PRAYER IN MRS. EDDY'S HOUSEHOLD—This is God's spiritual household. Nothing can enter to annoy or destroy. Nothing can enter to manifest sin, sickness or discouragement, for God, good, keeps this household in perfect peace. There is no will-power, obstinacy, or animal magnetism that can darken the atmosphere of my home, for God does in very deed dwell on earth with men and governs every event. There is no evil condition of thought that can argue or suggest or make any law to dominate or control me, intimidate me, or crush me, bring any evil to pass upon me, or shut out of my consciousness any good. There is no law of failure, want, poverty, lack or limitation. There is no law but the divine law which is plenty, abundance, harmony and dominion. No mortal mind or minds or mediumship, can touch me, or anyone within the radius of my thought this day, for God, good, governs every member of this household in perfect peace and love.

DAILY PRAYER—Let your prayer be daily: Reveal to me, O God, my secret faults, every error, every sin. Earnestly desire to know thyself, to have thy heart searched, to let thyself be humbled, and the man of God stand revealed. Never for one instant say, 'Thank God, I am not as other men'. There is no I. If you are a personality, you are as other men; but if you are the *idea* of God, there is but one I, God.

DAILY PRAYER—Thy kingdom come; let the reign of divine Truth, Life and Love be established in me, and rule out of me all sin; may Thy Word enrich the affections and govern mankind. Save me from hurting any one or harming myself.

(Changes made in Mrs. Eddy's handwriting in the 45th edition of the Church Manual.)

DAILY MENTAL INVOCATION—Divine Love: Give me grace, meekness, understanding and wisdom for each hour of this day.

EVENING PRAYER—Before you are ready to close your eyes in sleep, be sure you are not holding anything unlovely in your consciousness, anything unlike God; laying aside every fear, put yourself entirely in His charge. Quiet yourself with the thought that He who has all power will protect you, give you health, and all you need in abundance, and know that whether sleeping or waking, you are safe because your life is hid with Christ in God. To declare that you are well is the exact truth; you are not flesh, but rather the ray of divine light that, shining upon flesh, makes it appear alive. This *you* is spiritual and cannot be sick. Remember that power is exerted by merely stating a truth. All truth is the word of God. Assert it constantly, even though your so-called human mind screams falsehood. It is to acknowledge Him, to have your mind stayed on Him, to be directly benefited by the activity of good.

CHAPTER FOUR

ARGUMENTS

Given by Mary Baker Eddy to Students

You have no faith in evil.
You have no power to do evil, or to cause others to sin.
You cannot take away from me my mind or any one of its functions. There is no power in evil. God is the only power.

God governs all, is All-in-all. God is our constant Guide and Guardian. No mortal thought, known or unknown, seen or unseen, can interfere with the manifestation of Love's presence with us. The weather manifests God's government, and no evildoers can change this fact. The devils of human thought—all the powers of many minds—are powerless in Love's presence. God is All. God is Mind.

Divine Love maintains man forever at the point of *completeness, preserves* his *every faculty* and his individuality; guides each separate idea in continuous unfoldment of the infinite grandeur of spiritual creation.

We are the channels, transparencies for the reflection of His goodness in proportion to the demonstration we have made over self, and the understanding gained of the Truth of being, the love for the brotherhood.

The deadliest poison is a secretion engendered by the working of hatred. Handle arsenical and mercurial poison to prevent rheumatism. Strive to work from God instead of up to God.

We, as God's ideas, are free from, and cannot be touched by the errors of unfavorable comment, disapproval, criticism, fault-finding, censure, blame, condemnation, hate, murder.

Man has no constitutional liability to disease, no inherited weakness; is not subject to abnormal growths, decay, decomposition, A.M. or vital poison; is not subject to or liable to death, sin, sensuality, vice or consequence.

Mind is infinite, supreme, serene, complete, perfect and forever at peace; all substance, being, action, faculty, influence, power; is already complete and in evidence, and there is no other influence and no other evidence. Law is a ceaseless, harmonious restful activity of the infinite, and there is no other law. This law is the law of this day and every day, and all its activities and duties. The law of Mind to this day sets aside the belief of fear and doubt, and obliterates the possibility of disease, accident, mistakes, fear, sin and death. The law of God, of Mind, is ceaseless action, presence and infinite protection. This day is merely a step in infinite progress. It is unfoldment, not time.. It brings no belief of delay in success, no disappointment. It adds no fear, no age, no deterioration, no decay, no sin, no materiality, no belief in matter. It only adds wisdom, power, dominion, law, and the presence of well-done. My treatment now establishes the law of this day, and obliterates the supposition or belief in any other law. Principle governs me and mine this day. This day is unfoldment in which every detail and incident is but an illustration of divine presence, power and wisdom.

God knows the things I have need of: the quality and the fact that seem to be lacking; therefore, I, as His child, must also know it. You have no faith in evil. You have no power to do evil, or to cause others to sin. You cannot take away from anyone, Mind, or one of its faculties. God is the only power. You cannot poison. These are God's laws; they control you, and you cannot escape them. No mortal mind can harm Christian Science. The clergy and press will not; they cannot and they do not want to harm Christian Science or its Leader. They love Christian Science and they love the Leader thereof.

You are face to face with both Truth and error, and this must come before the power of Truth is understood, and the powerlessness, yea, the nothingness of error is proven. Wait patiently on the Lord. Why? Because He has said it, and because the escape from sense is slow and if we are patient, it is accelerated.

Overcoming age is not resuming our youth; it is thought going into new paths which history has never recorded.

The laws of health cannot be broken. There is no law of transmission, contagion, heredity, no poison, microbe, or germs. With God there are no limitations, no sense of limitation. No sense of limitation can be manifested by God's image and likeness. The law of God maintains my health from a spiritual standpoint. The divine Mind supplies all the wisdom, all the power, all the opportunity for every man, and prompts every man to the right action at the right moment, so there is no conflict of interests; no possibility of failure; no discord of any sort. There is no material substance to lack, and no cause for the lack; therefore no lack. There is no hypnotism or mesmerism for R.C. to operate through, no activity, energy, will, law, mind or minds to give operation to hypnotism or mesmerism. Every idea of Truth acts according to its own law. Try to realize the allness and presence of God. You are His image and likeness. There is no lack of resuscitation. God's law is the law of resuscitation. There is no inaction in Mind, no lethargy, no insanity, no stagnation, no hypnotism, no evil; nor can any of its claims subtly take possession of the so-called mortal mind, for Mind is God, ever conscious, ever acting, all motion. There is no electricity to poison the nerve centers. There is no deterioration, no disintegration; no form of woman to waste away; no destruction, no cohesion.

Be Christlike, tender, merciful, temperate, humble, pure. Wait for the test of our sincerity. Long to be good, and seek daily prayer for divine teaching. Nothing can enter into God's kingdom that worketh or maketh a lie, a discord, or a disease. The action, the force, the power of the Truth is self-evident, self-acting, self-sustaining. Declare the truth for *all mankind.* You will be made to know what to handle, and you cannot be apathetic or forgetful, for God is our Guide and Instructor.

There are no impure or improper secretions or organisms, or substance that can give forth impurities, and no such thing as impeded circulation or imperfect action. Mind is All, is God, is Spirit. I know that my treatments, and my affairs can never be reversed or interfered with. No family relations or human associates can dispossess me of the Truth or interfere with my success. I believe that my work is satisfactory. I know that my treatments are good, and fear cannot come and abide with me. A treatment is never afraid that it will not work, for the declaration of Truth brings with it a consciousness of its sure and immediate effect. I do have faith in God and know that spiritual facts are the only facts. Fear is nothing. It cannot rob a treatment of its effects or of its purpose. The Word of God cannot return unto us void.

Our home is in Mind, in spiritual consciousness, the eternal harmony of Soul. The builder and maker of this home is Mind. It is built and established in the eternal. Nothing can destroy the harmony of our home. Mind fills it with the glories of the kingdom of God. No fear of sin, sickness, or death can enter this home; no sense of poverty or want. No lack of supply has any presence or place here. These are illusions, nothing but M.A.M.—sin, a belief in a power apart from God. They cannot find us, for we dwell in the secret place of the Most High, God, and we are eternally conscious of the infinite riches and abundance of Love. God is our supply, is inexhaustible. The lie that argues poverty does not know us. We do not know it, cannot see, fear, hear, or manifest it, for we are living in God. God governs our home. Truth fills our household, is recognized, received and sought. There is no resistance, no rejection, no indifference. Love destroys *all* unlike itself—removes *all* that is offensive. Mind plans every detail of our affairs. Nothing can obstruct the path of Truth—the only path in our consciousness.

I am not A.M. I am not mesmerized with the fear of beliefs, or the beliefs of fear. Cast it out. Mortal mind is a criminal malpractitioner. Divine Mind is the only true practitioner there is or ever was. It creates, rules, governs; hence we are free, healthy, happy, harmonious, peaceful, mentally and spiritually free.

Order M.A.M. to get out; deny M.A.M. Affirm: Truth is keeping us in a strictly scientific way.

You have your place and work in God's kingdom; I *have mine.* We are in the place prepared for us. Nothing can hide this place, or remove us from it, or withhold from us our spiritual blessing. Overcome self and care for others.

God is good, and omnipotent, and goodness is your safeguard. The physical question is overcome the same as the moral. Your strength is omnipotent; your unerring wisdom is the same, and both are in proportion to your grace to meet the temptation that God, good, is not all in origin and end, in Principle and phenomenon. Now gird up your strength in Christian Science, and know what you believe, and understand omnipotence just a little, and you will be impervious.

There is no hypodermis, no softened brain, no worn-out brain cells. Why? Because there is no brain, no mind in matter. If your mortal mind aches, you have only to change your mind on this subject, and the pain is gone. Mental work helps your head (or, rather, your belief of head) the same as use is said to strengthen muscles. I know this is true.

You cannot suffer when you have one Mind, God. Watch—and acknowledge no other.

Enter into the joy of Love, heaven within you. It is His kingdom come. His will be done. You are in health, in peace, and have all help in God.

You are not over-tasked. It is a lie of M.A.M. Be strong, and hold the fort. If the diabolism of M.A.M. does not incite sanguine natures to mental conditions deplorable, it turns them to stone; or other lymphatic temperaments to make sullen and morbid. I pray that He will keep you unspotted from M.A.M.; also the world, the flesh and—the devil.

I rise in the strength of Spirit to resist all that is unlike God. I am spiritual; I feel, I know that I am one with Christ in God who hath all dominion.

There is no sin or error, to mesmerize me into seeing or feeling a body.

There is no malignant animal magnetism to prevent me from reflecting light.

There is no self-mesmerism to hide me from Truth, or Truth from me.

There is no hypnotism or mental malpractice to harm me, to affright me, touch me, for divine Love surrounds me. Intelligence, power, substance are the source of my being. Life enfolds me.

There is no motive power but God, no universe but Life, Truth and Love. There is no channel, nor channels, personal or impersonal, through or by which animal magnetism, either malicious, wilful, or ignorant, or sympathetic, conscious or unconscious, can approach Christian Science, its Discoverer, its adherents, or their patients.

Do not think of personality when protecting yourself or patients as a rule. Think only of the all-absorbing Love that destroys all hate. Realize the allness of Truth and good and the absence of error or evil. Realize the right side, and only side.

Take four hours each day for your reading, prayer and meditation alone with God.

Remember this fixed fact: You have no material heart. Your heart God gave you, and He governs all its functions. It cannot cease to act so long as God acts, for it is His reflection of Love. Let alone all sense of anatomy, and hold this true consciousness of yourself, *Pain is not pain, and you know it.*

Joy! Joy! Joy! Praise the Lord!
I am whole. The darkness disappears.
The bright light shineth.
Joy! Joy! Joy! God is my Life.
My soul doth stand revealed.
And I know, know, know, I am whole.

Life is eternal and unchangeable, and can never grow old, for time is not, and youth is immortal—you have always existed, and always will exist, a perfect, complete and finished work, a spiritual being created of and by Spirit and subject only to spiritual laws. You do now and ever must manifest the God—life that is shining in you. It is working always in every part of your being to will and to do. There can never be any loss of your faculties—for they are of Soul, and not of sense. The Life and strength of which you are the constant recipient, are indestructible and infinite, and nothing can prevent their inflow. You are governed and sustained by perfect Love in which there is no fear of helplessness or death. Your faith and trust in the omnipotent power of Truth are perfect and unclouded, and you know that God is your sufficiency. Never was one of God's children palsied or helpless, for all His works are good and eternal. There is no mortal mind to say you are old or feeble. There is but one infinite Mind, which is the understanding of the truth of your being, and holds you in perfect harmony and health.

Do not fear your sense of fear. It is nothing. We are as safe as omnipotent God. God's idea absolutely cannot fear; he knows there is just one Mind. Is he going to use that Mind to fear with? Is he living in God and still afraid? Is there anything outside of or beyond God? Is there anything inside of God to fear? God made all and proclaimed it good.

Fear is godless, mindless, powerless, not included in consciousness. Fear cannot act on mortal mind, body, understanding, does not manifest self either as subjective or objective; not mine or anybody's, and if I seem to fear, it is not my fear or anxiety and doesn't make any difference. God isn't afraid. My treatment isn't afraid. A Christian Science treatment dissipates all the supposititious presence, power, law of fear. Fear is a fake belief within a fake belief, without cause, effect or continuity.

There is no personality. There is no mortal mind to embody itself and call that embodiment by my name, and hold over it laws of limitation. God is Mind. I have the senses of that Mind. I have no mortal mind to look for pain or pleasure, health or sickness, strength or weakness, life or death.

Mortal mind cannot mesmerize me into a belief that I can have any disease so-called, for I am an idea of God, perfect, harmonious, and eternal, and cannot be mesmerized. It cannot say to me, 'It is yourself that has a disease, etc.', for I am perfect, and it cannot make me think that I am it.

Divine Love fills every avenue, flows through every channel, and removes every obstruction. There is one infinite Mind and that Mind is my Mind and governs me. All my thoughts come to me from this

Mind and return to their source. In this Mind there is no material sense, no other mind, no mortal mind to tempt, to harm or control. Know this, realize it, and you are master of the occasion, of yourself and others. Hold on through all this animal magnetism and fear, and though fear make you suffer even unto death's door, God will—He will deliver you.

The kingdom of heaven is God's government of His ideas, His wise and compelling enforcement of law, His unerring jurisdiction. I am a citizen of His dominion, governed by His laws and protected by these laws; my affairs are administered justly and harmoniously by these laws. The laws of divine Principle operate because infinite power and intelligence are back of them, not because we invoke them—and they no more stop working than the laws of this country.

You are the child of the loving God, surrounded and protected by infinite Love. There is no hatred or evil to frighten you. You have no disease, you have nothing to fear, you are not in danger, you are entirely well, and continually held in the presence of God.

I am the unresisting channel through which Love shines with its full healing force. In the reality of being is all I can ever want, need, desire or long for. In fact, I have perfect satisfaction. It includes more than 1 can possibly now discern or desire in the measure of happiness and the completion of every wish or prayer that is wholesome or right for me to have. All other longings are destroyed in this realization. I must work to know that the definition of man in *Science and Health* applies to me. I am God's image and likeness, reflecting a full, perfect image of Life, Mind, action, and so forth. I am not under any material law of limitation.

There is no material plane. We live, move, and have our being in God, and we cannot pass out of that.

You must know that malicious animal magnetism cannot gain or assert power or act through any mortal or mortals—if you know it, it cannot touch you or make you afraid. The word you will need is, 'It is I. be not afraid.' 'Because he hath set his love upon me, therefore will I deliver him.'

Occultism cannot know to hinder the work of God, good. Occultism cannot embody itself mentally or physically. It cannot rob, steal, persecute, annoy, or destroy me or mine, for there is no *occultism.*

There is no arsenic, mercury, morphine, rustox, or ether that can cause any inflammation of the pneumogastric nerve, thereby affecting the sympathetic nerves, causing any inflammation of the head, stomach, or bowels. There is no pneumogastric nerve, materially or in belief.

Ever-present Love is the very nearest thing to me at all times. It is the nature of God to bless and care for me. I never reach out for Him in vain. He is always available. He never delays. God will remove our sins from us as far as the east is from the west as soon as we are ready to give them up.

Mental malpractice and malicious animal magnetism are utterly without power, and cannot voice error to me in the nature of arsenical, mercurial, electric, opium or any other poison or overwhelming soporific influence, mentally, physically, morally, or in any other way, for I am panoplied in divine Love where human hatred cannot reach me. Love, not hate; Truth, not error, govern man.

My life is a manifestation of divine Life from which I derive all moral and physical health. Therefore my life should be beyond the reach of accidents as the divine Life is.

The birth out of matter into Spirit is not gained by *argument,* nor by force. It is *growth, hourly;* it is forever getting nearer Love that is *Love;* universal, divine *presence* and power, alias *might* and dominion; first over the body; then its reflection is dominion over all the earth.

Neither I, nor my source of supply, nor my demonstration of Christian Science, is subject to any malicious mortal thought or limitation. There never was a moment when evil was real. There are no mortals who can reflect evil on the earth, and I must disargue (disarm?) the claim of personality to make room for the dear Love which destroys malpractice. There is no mortal (me) that can be touched by malicious minds. If God is All, I need not be afraid. Anything of which I seem to be afraid is unreal (ANOTHER VERSION adds: and the fear both senseless and useless).

Abide in the 91st Psalm. Inasmuch as I am God's child, spiritual and not material, I must be perfect. I am whole; I am free; I have all that I need; I live in Spirit and not in matter. I am without care and without anxiety. No one can hurt me nor take from me anything that is good. I know no such thing as sin, suffering, want or disease, for I am the perfect reflection of Life, Truth, and Love. I am never disappointed. The harmony of my being cannot be disturbed, because I live in the infinite.

The law of divine Life, Truth and Love is a law of instant and complete expulsion and elimination of all poisons and impurities from the system. Why? Because the floodtides of divine Life, Truth and Love are pouring and surging through consciousness, uplifting, purifying, nourishing, healing, elevating, sustaining and energizing mankind.

Take this thought earnestly twice each day: There is no evil thinking and no evil argument; the lie and liar are a lie, an illusion; there is no such person nor thought. God is all there is.

It is a shield to mentally remind yourself daily that *God* is the only Law-maker for man, morally, spiritually and physically.

Treat yourself three times each day on the basis I name, and let a student treat you once, and make the basic point this: that you can help yourself and need not the help of man. God, good, Truth, Love is all the help you can have, for they are all power.

Every day—every hour—your work increases in effectiveness and power.

This is my support, that the male and female natures are equally expressed, coexistent in me. This is the way that I exist and is the reason I never lack. It is because I am of the nature of infinite completeness; there is never anything in my experience in which the male and female qualities are not infinitely at one, supporting each other. It is because my spiritual inspiration is perfectly balanced with scientific understanding; because my joy is perfectly balanced with courage, and because my love is perfectly balanced with strength. My tender emotional nature is perfectly balanced with thought, reason and understanding; therefore I am a state of perfect protection, perfect substance, and I am supported by my own infinity. I am the presence of substance, because there is no unsupported idea in me.

My manhood takes care of my womanhood, defends, protects, and supports her. My joy is defended and protected by my courage. My love is protected and defended by my understanding, by the strength of my scientific understanding which is omnipotence. I am never undefended and my womanhood cherishes my manhood. My tender affection cherishes my scientific understanding and unfolds love to it, takes care of it, watches over it with love, and gives it every opportunity to unfold and demonstrate itself in perfect harmony, unity, equality, and unfoldment. So my nature is complete.

There is no evil mind to make a law to prevent us from bearing others' burdens, and so fulfilling the law of Christ, nor to produce an opposite effect nor to prevent us from accomplishing that which we desire.

There is a continuous demand for all I have to offer. Neither malicious animal magnetism nor any erroneous mortal thought can hinder me from meeting those who desire to get what I have to give. No erroneous mortal thought, opinion or judgment can hide, hold or take from me those persons who can help, elevate or benefit me.

Neither mesmerism, hypnotism, theosophy, esoteric magic nor wicked mental or audible arguments can affect me. God governs me. Justice, Truth, Love, govern us, and nothing else can or does affect us in the least.

(Thrice each day from one half to one hour.)

Then have faith in God. Know that faith as a grain of mustard seed can remove mountains, and have no faith in evil. Know that it cannot do anything, that it is nothing. Know that God is all. The wrath of man shall praise Thee and the remainder of wrath shalt Thou restrain. All things work together for good to them that love God. See I Thess. 5.

I am awake. I cannot be glamored.

There is no hypnotism. I can see the need and meet it, for it is God that worketh with me.

God has a plan for all His children, and it is a gracious plan. I have my place in His plan. I have my work in His plan, and malicious mental malpractice can neither hinder nor prevent me from seeing a full, complete and perfect manifestation of what God's plan is for me here and now.

Hurrying cannot affect the heart. It cannot beat like a trip-hammer. nor perform its functions with difficulty. Hurrying cannot produce heart trouble. There are no unsound hearts. There is no slow nor hurried motion to the heart, no shortness of breath ascending stairs.

With the sword of the Spirit, God cuts from me the lies of animal magnetism, mesmerism, clairvoyance, esoteric magic, *materia medica,* religious anarchy, theosophy, atheism, aggressive mental suggestion, mental malpractice, thought transference, telepathy, Darwinism, false science, and all other pretentious forms of error. None of these counterfeits can harm me, mentally, morally, spiritually, financially, or socially—through employees, business associates, publishers, creditors, debtors, friendly or unfriendly, competitors, rivals, friends or foes, Scientists or non-Scientists. Neither can they harm me in any way, in any manner, in any degree or to any extent whatever, through my correspondence, telegrams, telephone messages, advertisements, leases, contracts, business successes or failures. They cannot plant the *lie* of *limitation* on me, my agents or my company. God reigns over all, through all, in all, above all.

This omnipotent goodness is a living, palpitating presence, before which the error of mortal mind, personal sense and human belief must fall into nothingness—dust.

Catholicism is brotherly love, while Roman Catholicism is the Pope's intention. Roman Catholicism is a false conception of Catholicism. a false conception of true theology. No cloister, circles, Jesuitism, priesthood, Papal power or school of cardinals or bishops can be a channel through which mortal mind can work or rule upon my consciousness or the consciousness of any individual to bind or hold you, or him, through ignorance, fear or superstition.

No Roman Catholic prayer or prophecy or anathema nor curse can dim, deaden, darken or confuse your consciousness, nor blur the Christ image in your thought. There is no God in any prayer of condemnation—no Christ in it—no Truth in it, and, therefore, there is no *power* in it and *you cannot fear it.* There is no power or rule or government or control apart from God. There is no power or belief of power that can hinder you from any right achievement. Remember your efficiency and capacity are unlimited, and no effort of evil to reverse the words and works of Christian Science can hinder your success. All ability, all achievement, all accomplishment are possible to men because they are man's. It is the law of man's being from which he cannot escape, even if he would, to know all that God, Mind, includes and is.

I do not lack anything.
I do not lack wisdom or love.
I do not lack judgment or intelligence.
I do not lack energy or industry.
I do not lack and cannot lack anything, or the means by which to acquire anything. I am not outside infinity.

(When Mrs. Eddy gave the above to Margaret Worthington, she said, 'I give thee this'. Some days later she gave it to her again, saying, 'I give thee this because it is a fact'. Finally she gave it to her the third time, saying, 'I give thee this; now go and *prove* it to be a fact.')

If thy liver offend thee, cast it from thee. There is no liver, for there is no matter. There is no stomach, no sour stomach, no pneumogastric nerve, no connection between brain and liver. and there is healthy digestion. There is no pain; matter is not pained, and Mind is Love, and Love is *not pained.*

There is no paralysis of rectum, nor abdominal muscles, nor of the colon, nor in mind, for there is no mortal mind. Action belongs to God; it cannot cease. There is no evil, no hate, no sin; mortal mind is not affecting you. God is the only Mind, and you *reflect* God, and there is no other *you*. Wake, wake to *know this*. You control mortal mind, it does not control you. There is no body; Mind is all; you reflect God, and God governs all, and mortal mind does not exist,

As malicious animal magnetism is only a false claim and really nothing, it cannot separate me nor anyone else from the best and greatest good, nor limit my supply in any way. It cannot touch me with a claim of poverty in any way in myself, nor in anyone, for Spirit is my unlimited source of supply.

I am not dependent on any personality for my needs. Malicious animal magnetism cannot hide my work nor blind my judgment, nor make me feel failure, nor lack, nor incapacity.

God gives to each and every one of His children abundantly all they need, and that supply is not—cannot be—hidden at any time by any mortal mind law or claim, for all laws and claims of mortal mind are false laws, and of the no-mind, which has no real existence. It is destroyed by Truth *now.*

There is no unconscious or subconscious mind to be affected. There is only one Mind, the consciousness of good, This divine Mind cannot receive suggestions. It cannot be impregnated. It is invulnerable and infinite. There is no subconscious mind to hold to latent fears and beliefs. The divine Mind being all, it obliterates and destroys such latent causes and effects.

There is no mortal mind, or man, or personality, that can think through me, or read my thoughts, or change, influence, beguile, bewilder, or darken my consciousness.

It is impossible for darkness to destroy light. Nothing that divine Mind created can be perverted, reversed, relapsed, or changed.

The infinite light forever protects its idea in the substance of Soul. Evil minds have no power to reject, deny, oppose or defy God; no power to stop the work of Christian Science.

There is a spiritual reversal for every argument of evil and to declare it agrees with your adversary 'quickly'.

God will reverse every argument of evil before it reaches us, through the Word, which is the two-edged sword, which liveth and abideth forever.

We must handle the claim of trickery, slander, meddlesomeness of the human mind.

Animal magnetism does not deceive me. It is not my consciousness. I do not hear it argue, neither can it argue. It is neither mind, life nor intelligence, neither person, place nor thing.

Animal magnetism, ignorant or malicious, you cannot separate me from God, good. You cannot dim my spiritual perception. You cannot make a law that I cannot heal myself or others. God is my refuge, the only intelligence, the only power, the only Mind. Animal magnetism is not intelligence, is not Mind nor any of its attributes.

Animal magnetism, you are a non-entity, nowhere, nothing. Animal magnetism cannot think or feel. It has no existence nor creation. It never has been nor ever will be. It cannot maintain itself in my consciousness as life governed by a sympathetic system of nerves, neither as an organism sending forth impure secretions; neither as impurities, deformities, or abnormalities. For God is All-in-all, the only *creator* of the *only universe* and *man.* We are His children and we do realize the all-fulness of the omnipotence of God.

Animal magnetism cannot sever the modes of good; cannot impel my mind into error of thought or action, cannot make me dormant or stupid or drunken with its subtle, evil influences.

There is no error of any name or nature in my consciousness that can resist, hide, or escape the Truth. The light of Truth and Life and Love shines straight through my belief of evil and banishes it, chasing it into its native nothingness.

My desire is to know and obey God's law, to be filled with all the fullness of Spirit, knowing only the consciousness of God, good.

My health, strength, life, intelligence, action, etc., are subject to the governing and controlling power of the divine Mind, and to nothing else, for there is no other power.

There is no insufficiency of any kind in Truth, in infinite Love.

Good is ever-present, and is the only reality of existence; this renders evil obsolete.

There is nothing present or has power apart from God that has any reality.

Error cannot strangle, smother or choke the Truth or its manifestation and the Truth cannot be reversed.

There is no belief of evil in the bodily senses that has any reality, and that is the Truth and cannot be reversed.

Impersonal error is obsolete, absolutely obsolete, in the presence of Truth, of God, of the Christ, or the spiritual idea, of Life, Love, Spirit, Mind, Soul.

The law of my so-called mortal mind concerning my body or any part of it, is *unreal, nothing,* rendered *null* and *void* by God's law.

No mesmeric law of my conscious or unconscious thought can formulate any inharmonious condition in my body that has any reality in the presence of God, LOVE.

M.A.M. cannot work through *materia medica* to hinder my work in Christian Science.

The mesmerism of the patient's own thought regarding *materia medica* has no reality.

No law of evil of any name or nature can separate my thought from the function of my real being in the Truth.

My mental concept of brain cannot hide, resist, or escape the Truth.

The law of divine Life, Truth and Love does supersede the so-called law of my mental concept of brain, my belief of brain.

There is nothing present nor has power apart from divine Life, Truth and Love as infinite Mind, that can possibly control or confuse my thought, obscure my spiritual perception or hinder my progress in Christian Science, spiritually, mentally, morally, physically, financially, or any other way.

God's will is all good always, is harmony, perfection. The will of God is health, gladness, all good, Life. His will is the consciousness of divine ever-presence, of Life eternal. It is to know what it is to act in conformity with the divine purpose and to be wholly governed by God.

There is no physical law that has any reality to operate through my personality to harm me, to separate me from my true spiritual being in the Truth, to separate me from the love of God in Jesus Christ, to separate me from harmony.

I have no belief that matter, brain, can control, derange, or confuse my thought, or can suffer or cause suffering in the Truth, in Life, in Love.

Look away from body to Spirit. My being is spiritual, my life, my intelligence are spiritual; my senses are spiritual; my life is hid with Christ in God, and there is no other existence.

The Christ, or Truth, the manifestation of God, does supersede my belief that my true being, that real life and intelligence, are in matter. We have immortality *now, not* shall have.

There is no life in fire.

There is no fear, *conscious* or *unconscious,* that can restrain the power of divine Love to heal.

I was born free, not in bondage to anything nor to anyone, for Principle leads me ever. Infinity includes only the man who is well, and all he needs. There is no mind to put forth a law of reversal. Love governs all, and there is only one governor. Mortal mind cannot make a law to reverse God's law, for God's law is not reversible.

Every sexual emotion is a conspiracy against Science.

There is nothing about me that attracts, corresponds with, or responds to, any form of error or evil. In proportion to your realization of this are you *immune* to the mesmeric and hypnotic influences of A.M.

May the allness of God, Love, and the nothingness of aught else serve to cover the question of your protection, and the allness of good, and the powerlessness and non-existence of evil be the reality of your thought.

The unseen silent forces of God are standing sentinel over me and mine and all, silencing, destroying, and annihilating the unseen, silent arguments of the serpent, material sense.

Malicious mentality has no power to make me sin or to separate us; yourself alone can separate us, *they cannot.* Therefore be of good cheer, *love the brethren,* love God, and go to Him, not me, for guidance. This *alone* can save you, and *this will.*

You know you cannot be swayed by malicious hypnotism, You are governed by the one Mind to see and do according to divine government and guidance.

Hypnotism cannot nauseate, irritate, cannot keep up nervous symptoms; cannot control organs or functions of the body. Deny claim of old age.

No sexual poison, no sexual disease to cause arsenical poison to act on the stomach, joints, muscles and nerve centers, as a specific curse. No curse able to cause diseased bones or disintegration of tissues.

There are no electro-magnetic currents to convey poison to nerve centers or to send dispatches over the body physical or mental.

Evil arguments and mental suggestions cannot frighten, interfere with, or keep me from doing the work that is mine to do today.

All is Mind and Mind is God, omnipresent, omnipotent, omniscient good. God is my Mind. Divine Mind expresses every function of my body. No morbid nor torpid secretions can lodge in any part of my body. Nothing can obstruct the channels of Truth. No mortal or human opinions or theories can produce fear in my consciousness. The bowels of mercy are free and cooperate action daily, because good is the cause of all action, the same yesterday, today and forever. No illusion of fear can produce any abnormal manifestation on or of your functional action, since God governs all that He has made and there is nothing made that He did not make. Truth is an alterative to that entire system. Love is the only laxative and frees us from all bondage. No self-righteousness, no self-will, no self-fear—no fear of self. I live in God, good, the eternal consciousness of good every day, every moment.

Children, you are a perfect thought of God, made in His image and likeness, surrounded by His love as by a strong fortress through which no evil can reach you. God is your Mind, your Life, your strength, and you are governed by Truth and Love. You have no material conception or birth, no father and mother in the flesh. You were not born of the flesh (mortal mind) and you are not the reflection of beliefs.

Belief is not reflection. You are not weak or easily led astray. You cannot desire to rule and lead others. You are not rebellious or obstinate. You have no human will. God's will is all and you are its reflection. Therefore you will only do right, for you reflect and inherit divine wisdom and understanding. You are spiritual and Spirit knows all things.

Sensuality has no power over you, for you are not conscious of the lusts of the flesh, but you are the pure conception of divine Truth and Love and co-eternal with your Father-Mother God. Your every thought and action are love, goodness, tenderness, gentleness, beauty, holiness, joy and peace; that peace which passeth all human understanding. In God we live, move, and have being; therefore we are in Life, health, strength, forever. To be conscious of this is to be in the presence of God—with the Father who is Life, Truth and Love. Amen.

We are the children of the King; why should we mourn?

My work is in Mind—it comes from God—it cannot be intercepted nor diverted into other paths, being governed by divine Principle. It is progressive, prosperous, satisfactory, joyous, continuous. It reaches from pole to pole, from ocean to ocean, perfect, infinite, going on all the time, for the glory of God. Perfect idea is already located, with absolute satisfaction in Mind. In this perfect place in Mind, I am able to support myself, have all the recreation and companionship needed. In the perfect place of Mind is complete satisfaction. I live in the affluence of Spirit and am one with the inexhaustible, unobstructed, omnipresent source of income, and infinite as is the source, so infinite is the supply. It is the Spirit that profiteth. I am the ceaseless intake of God's eternal giving.

You, false claim of malicious mind, whatever or wherever you are, you cannot mesmerize me, or hypnotize me to think I haven't understanding to meet any claim that comes to me.

My identity is not lost. I am God's child and His child can never be deprived of her birthright or any other good necessary to her happiness and well being.

We do not suffer from mortal thoughts or arguments, for if true, they help us, and if false, they cannot hurt us. They cannot reach us. They cannot be heard.

No evil communications here, no old age, no diminished power to resist error, but increased power to receive and demonstrate Truth and bring it out in our lives.

There is no educated mortal mind through hatred of the Truth, or through jealousy, that can hypnotize me into believing that there is any reality outside of God, Love.

The activities of Life, divine Mind, are a continuous going forth of the elements of perfection, which cannot be reversed, polluted or forced into wrong channels.

Your constitution is not predisposed to the reception of any unseen mental influence nor any specific poison. There is no evil influence operating injuriously in your system, for Mind is the only system and there isn't any evil.

There are no hindrances, interruptions, personalities, conditions or circumstances that can make inactive or suspend the law of Spirit. I cannot be mesmerized to doubt the power of Truth over this and every other error. I know that I have confidence in all my treatments. I know how to handle all error and handle it instantly. All that I need to know in handling error is revealed to me, for it is God who handles the case and it is God who gives all right ideas.

Know that your treatment, the word of Truth, is with *power*; it is more powerful after it is spoken. There is no lapse in its continuance. It goes on unbroken forever. There is no reversal in Truth. No relapse.

(To meet the claim that after treatment is given, error can work.)

I am a Christian Scientist. I cannot be self-mesmerized. I cannot be self-hypnotized. I can help myself. I can help others. In the fiery furnace it was the individualized spiritual consciousness that the King saw. When we work together as one, it will be seen as the Son of God.

Malicious hypnotism cannot operate in my thought when I am asleep and manifest itself the next day as sin, disease and death.

Life is God. This treatment is the power and activity of divine Mind. It cannot be found, it cannot be reversed or return void. It does accomplish that for which it is sent.

SENSE AND SOUL'S LAW—There is no law of sense making me forget what I should do or do it wrongly. There is but one law and this law is God's, making me remember what I should do and do it rightly.

TRUTH'S ARGUMENT—Right cannot be reversed.

I cannot be made to think wrong or do wrong.

I cannot go opposite to what Mrs. Eddy needs in any way nor in anything I do.

I do not believe that she is unjust or unmerciful and I will never find her so.

I am not mistaken in her and I know I am not.

And when I know this, then I will progress and never till then.

I can help her, I can.

I cannot and I will not afflict her in anything I do.

I can help, doing what you say and just as you say, and I can do what she tells me.

(Written at Mrs. Eddy's dictation by Calvin Frye and passed around to the members of the household.)

POINTS To ESTABLISH—It helps you when you help others.

You cannot be made to hurt another and nobody can hurt you, and you cannot harm yourself, for there is no sin, disease nor death.

When you help others, it helps yourself.

When you heal or help one belief of disease, it helps and heals all the others.

You are not hypnotists but you are Scientists.

No relapse, no reversal.

God, good, divine Love is the *only Mind,* etc.

No loss of hearing or of sight.

No sleeplessness.

Sundry Brief Arguments Preserved by Students

I have time for every manifestation of love and tenderness in the abundant present.

There is no mindlessness. Mind is God.

I have perfect understanding to know all that I need to know in this case.

There is and there can be no such thing as abnormal secretion of phlegm in your throat.

There is no matter. There is but one Mind to govern man and there is no evil to interfere with man.

No subtlety of evil can blind or paralyze my human capacity to apprehend and love God.

Malicious mental malpractice cannot reach me through the nerve centers to produce hallucinations.

Mortal mind cannot outline my experience.

I cannot be made to carry out the works of evil nor be prevented from working in the interests of Truth and the Cause.

No suspension or depression nor loss of power to resist error, but increased power to stand and demonstrate Truth.

Love cannot be shut out of my life.

Mind has no sad memories. Mind, God, knows only the good, true, beautiful and perfect.

Error cannot outline, formulate, personalize nor embody itself to my consciousness.

Error cannot voice itself to me, through me or about me.

I do not see evil as evil, but I cannot be blinded to it nor governed by it.

God's law of reversal is the only law of reversal from which there is no escape.

There can be no law decreeing a crippled condition, mental, physical or financial.

SUNDRY SPECIFIC ARGUMENTS

For the Weather

The weather is in reality the atmosphere of the Mind that is God. It is His idea. God and man are not two, but *one,* in the sense that Principle and idea are one, inseparable.

That is why we can handle the weather of mortal belief just the same as we would meet a case of rheumatism.

Don't argue there is no rain, or drought will set in. Watch the clouds and if a bad looking cloud is gathering, scatter it and allow the rain; but no cyclone or tornado or dangerous lightning does God send; hence you can know it does not come.

For Transgressors

There is no fear or effects from fear—no reversal. Malpractice with its supposed malpractitioners cannot send any thoughts here. There is but one *Mind* and that is good. No evil spirits, no poison, no theosophy can come, no evil suggestions, no suffering coming here or sent here because of the (law) court. Affirm without limitation the truth that *perfect health is here,* etc.

Ps. 91. No reversal. You cannot make laws. Divine Love governs all. You are governed by divine Love, you feel no envy, no revenge, no hatred. All you feel is *Love, peace,* and Love fills your thoughts and makes you happy and satisfied.

One Mind, Truth controls all. You are set free in the love of God, and you cannot make nor believe a lie. Truth declared is not reversed. It does appear and is manifest. No return of old beliefs. No M.A.M. to work through R.C., hypnotism, mesmerism, or theosophy, demonology, or old theology to hinder the work of the Cause of Christian Science. Divine Mind governs every hour and evil is powerless.

Malpractitioners cannot make laws. The lies they whisper hurt no one but themselves. Lies, hatred, revenge have no power but to destroy themselves every time they try to hurt anybody else. This is God's law, it cannot be broken and it cannot make anybody suffer because we tell you this. You cannot help yourself and nobody can help you till you stop trying to hurt others. You can never prosper while you try to hurt others or make your students believe anybody is harming you, for nobody is doing this. Now you do see this and love God and man. Then turn to the right side in your consciousness and know this truth:

God alone reigns and all is Love.

A sinning thought should not be comforted but aroused, just as with anyone who is suffering for sin.... Now retrace your mental practice, if it were a soothing treatment, and mentally rouse the patient.

For Poison

There is no one to administer arsenical poison. It cannot be administered behind an unsuspected lie of cold-taking, sewer gas, or any other lie to hide it. Arsenic cannot be concealed. Arsenic cannot kill. The law of divinity—declaration is demonstration—overcomes and destroys the law of arsenical poisoning and its effects. There can be no fear of it. Arsenical poison cannot cause mental apathy.

Handle hypnotically administered poison.

Sundry Treatments

Protection from mortal mind

I am not separated from God and divine Science.

There is no intelligence in hate, envy, cruelty and revenge.

No law for the students of divine Science-no law of old beliefs. No law of relapse or poison.

There is no substance in poison, mercury or morphine.

No law that I cannot help myself. No law that I cannot heal my patients. No law that I take my patients' beliefs.

There are no beliefs.

No law that I cannot understand Christian Science. No law of discouragement or failure.

I cannot hear a malicious argument.

No law of an accident or a disaster. No law of discord, electricity, polarity.

All things work together to them that work good, to them that love God.

No law of discord or enmity for our class. No law that we may not seek each other's good and forget ourselves. No law that we may not enter the straight and narrow path that leads to life.

I am under no law but the divine Love that uncovers all error, and brings to light all truth.

Omnipotent Truth uncovers all error.

Overcoming hypnotic attraction

You do see that this is sin, and you are afraid to sin; you can and do see that this is hypnotism and M.A.M. trying to make a fool of you to ruin you, and you can resist and overcome it. You are strong. God has given you power and strength and understanding to resist it and rise above it. You do care what they say; you do not want them to talk evil of you; you do love purity, chastity, virtue.

God made man in His own image, after His own character, and as God's reflection you do reflect goodness, righteousness, the beauty of holiness, honesty, truthfulness. There is no happiness or joy outside of good.

Now arouse yourself, open your eyes and see what I say to you is the truth; error cannot reverse it. Hypnotism and M.A.M. is a lie. Love is All.

Spiritual Friendship:

God is with you and God is Truth. So you have it, Truth, right with you every hour, and never can be without Truth, and Truth is telling you just what to say and what to do, and how to do all that is good.

May the Love that guards its own and owns all ... make you happy without any other companion.

Samples of Adverse Arguments that Ask for Acceptance

TO DISCOURAGE CHRISTIAN SCIENTISTS—Christian Scientists shall not believe that they can heal the sick, or that Christian Science can heal.

They shall not believe that they can handle mesmerism; they shall not recognize mesmerism.

All the work of Christian Scientists shall be and is reversed, and is a law of reversal—an enactment.

Christian Scientists do not want to handle malicious animal magnetism, aggressive mental suggestion, mental assassination.

USED BY ERROR TO PREVENT CHRISTIAN HEALING—All your old beliefs are back, and worse than ever.

You cannot help yourself.

You *do not understand the Science.*

You cannot heal the sick.

Mrs. Eddy is a deceiver; she is not what she appears. You hate her.

You must not join the Association of Christian Scientists.

You don't want to read the book. You *must not* circulate it.

You cannot fix your thoughts. You cannot argue.

You are frightened.

You are in despair.

Nobody can help you, and you cannot help yourself.

It is not me that is doing this. It is your old beliefs.

Take medicine, or if you were ever a spiritualist, call on the spirit or an orthodox.

Go back to the church and you will be happier.

It is Mrs. Eddy—take it up so, and you will be better.

ADVERSE ARGUMENTS—You cannot help yourself.

You feel everybody's disease and state of mind.

You are poisoned to death and cannot demonstrate Christian Science upon yourself.

You cannot have any faith in God.

You cannot get help through Him.

You cannot write, teach, lecture, or travel.

You have got to die.

You take everybody's disease, and cannot get rid of it.

You are perfectly helpless; you cannot help yourself, and no one can help you,

You suffer for telling the truth about M.A.M.

ARGUED THROUGH A MALPRACTTTIONER—I never leave a Scientist after I have separated them from Mrs. Eddy until I have taken all the damned Christianity out of them.

I make them believe that Mrs. Eddy is making them sick, and suffer, while I am the one that is doing it; and when I succeed in making them believe this, and hate her, then I can take all the Christian Science out of them. This way I calculate I can stop the Cause.

LIES' LAWS—If you do anything right once, the next time you will do it wrong.

If you improve in health or in spiritual understanding, it will cease and you will lose it and *forget* and grow worse.

All the wrong beliefs are real to you, and you cannot make them seem unreal.

Laws of *Good* believed and adhered to will obliviate the lies. *Realize* this.

ITEMS OF AN INSTRUCTIONAL NATURE

When you lie down to sleep, know that you have self-control, and that the everlasting arms are about you, and nothing can intrude into your quiet sanctuary—your peace and rest. You say you cannot sleep—why not rather say you rest in God who does not sleep? You need no sleep. Realize this, and the fear that you will not sleep will disappear and you will sleep. It is the assurance of knowing that makes us master of the situation.

How many Christian Scientists give treatments as though they knew that Mind really heals the sick? The real thing is the presence of Mind and the realization that there is no other presence. Do not be afraid to take this stand and demonstrate it. Make *God All*, for God *is* All, and there is nothing else. It is just as though Mind were saying: 'I am here, and there is nothing else here. I am the practitioner and I am the patient and there is nothing else and neither can be, other than I Am.'

It is this Infinity, this infinite Presence that makes disease impossible. Don't squabble with yourself mentally and wear yourself out with arguments, either audibly or silently—but be firm, and know that God is the source of your intelligence. 'Be still and know. Quiet the material senses one after another, and withdraw to the secret place of the Most High', and after you have shut out the material clamoring, you can hear the still, small voice. The Bible tells you, 'The battle is not yours, but the Lord's'. Meet every problem that comes up as its master, knowing that 'that which hath been is now, and that which is to be hath already been, and God requireth that which is past.' This implies that nothing which is not good can remain permanently in consciousness.

Christian Scientists shall daily accentuate God's law in knowing that it is supreme and that obedience thereto brings immediate and permanent health, happiness and success.

If we go at an error with a determination to conquer with Truth we should know that an error is a coward; it will retreat.

Try not to see mental work as treatment, but as a watch to keep out the enemy. Jesus said, 'Watch and pray lest ye enter into temptation.' We have 'to work out our own salvation', and this is one of the ways to do it. We have got all things. Dominion is our right. It is necessary to realize this by arguing down the evil which says we have not.

The enemy will try to make us do wrong, or make us sick or try to kill us to the end, so we must stand guard, and the way to do it is to declare that evil cannot do these things. Mortal mind will try in every conceivable way to prevent this thought from being declared. Why? Because it means death to error.

I trust you are strong and know that there is but one Mind, and that this Mind governs you, permeates your body and brains with Truth; hence there is no room for error to steal in, and matter is not you. You are spirit, the idea of God and the Mind that was in Jesus must be in you, for God is *All*, the outside and inside of Truth and its ideas. *Watch* that no *secret* influence changes you and your children from the affections that you had when first you joined my class and learned you were free in Christ, Truth.

You have nothing to fear from 10,000 mind-curers. Why do you feel shocked at things *unreal?* There is no power in evil, A million of ciphers makes no number. Evil is a naught. Why do you call it a unit and units? You must not forget my teachings. Rise from this *nightmare* of mesmerism. Quimby left this stain on your mortal belief; now wash it off *in Science,* Christian Science that rests in calm strength on the sure foundation that *God is all,* and whatever else seems to be *contradict* and *know it is not*. The woman was not hurt reading *Truth*—if error says she was, it lies and you know it, and you must *establish* the Truth in your own and your patient's mind. You know there is but *one Mind* and there is no other to be deranged. There is no deranged mind—*know this* and make it appear.

Your experience at this time is most *promising*. Every one that stands by me and is governed by God, the divine Principle of his work, will experience from the influence of Satan *trying* him just what you do. It is only the influence of malicious mesmerism, the influence of a *lie*. Now remember, dear, your cardinal points in Science, viz., a *lie is never true,* that Truth and Love are your only Life, substance and intelligence, or *Mind,* and you cannot lose your true mind any more than God can. You cannot suffer for defending me which is acceptable in God's sight. 'Inasmuch as ye do it unto one of these little ones, you have done it to Me', are His words. You cannot love me too much, for the love of good fulfils the law of Truth, and you cannot love the evil only sensually, and you do not love me sensually.

Now awaken from this spell of animal magnetism!... God, good, has all the power on earth or in heaven, and 'He doeth His own will and *none can stay His hand'*. Waken from this dream! Look and behold the *Truth* of what I say. It is all a *lie* that you have written me. This is the hour of the lie, yea, for the *snake* and Red Dragon to do their best. But you are privileged to have this battle with the *lie early* in your labors, and why? Because God knows you are equal to meeting it and putting it *down.* If you were not, you would not be called to meet this temptation. And blessed is he that can endure temptation, said our Master. He even was tempted and you are enduring temptation, that is all, and are *growing* under it. You will come out of this ten thousand times as strong in Truth as you went into it.

Just know there is *no power,* no spell in animal magnetism, no electricity, no brains, no nerves, and no intelligence or power in mortal mind, alias evil,—and that Truth, good, is omnipotent, has *all power* and it *governs you,* and all error, evil, is under your feet. *See this, know it,* and after your forty days and nights experience, like the blessed Master, you will have angels minister to you,—white winged higher and holier views of divine Science, and thank God for what you have learned.

Declare without thought of material organs and knowing that all is Spirit and spiritual, my stomach is already perfect in God; and so on with other things. There is nothing the matter; a belief of fear is all that frightens and disturbs you. The false belief will flee before the right idea. Thought will govern; therefore declare the right idea.

Know that electricity has no power to send any poison through the pneumogastric nerve. Deny all kinds of mental poison. Mental poison is the mental atmosphere of conflicting human opinions and beliefs. We must handle the serpent and know its arguments are false and powerless, since Mind alone is real.

In beginning with a patient one must see the spirituality of his being, and then be fortified to deny the beliefs with understanding. If you were in a house that had caved in, you would keep on working until every timber was removed which kept you from freedom; so you must see all that holds the patient as removed, and has no power to hold. Man is free, and freedom is the God-given birthright.

Do not admit that error is, or can be, in your consciousness.

We must not deny our understanding, for thereby we are denying Christ, for Christ and understanding are one. We must not admit that we are mortal, for all there is is God, or Love and its manifestation.

Knowing is being. We heal when we know that God heals.

Students must avoid mesmerism. They are not Christian Scientists if they do not throw down mesmerism. Self-immolation is essential; fear to offend God is a wholesome idea. Money for God's work comes through us as His stewards. It is God, not man, who furnishes the means. When the receiver of Christian Science funds is right, money will flow in.

If I burn my hand, or have a pain, is that mesmerism or an effect? It is mesmerism itself. It is never *your* fear, never *your* pain, never *your* mesmerism. Mesmerism is a lie about God and man. Malpractice is the activity of animal magnetism; its law is that we cannot detect it, and that we do not want to handle it.

Theology, spiritualism, theosophy, psychology, occultism, false philosophy, false science, mesmerism, hypnotism, oriental witchcraft, black art, black magic, astrology, palmistry, demonology, diabolism, thought transference, are things to be handled occasionally; they are arguments which tend to perpetuate evil and death in the name of good.

Exceedingly important for children and heredity: Handle the belief of a latent, unconscious, subconscious, or human mind or instinct, as a possible channel for animal magnetism; also prenatal mesmerism, hereditary contamination.

Put away all selfishness out of your thought, such as thinking you have been wronged, or *any* sense of injustice or any ingratitude from others. Bury it out of sight forever, and let Love pour in where that seemed to be. Forgive as you expect to be forgiven. God knows that I *live*. I am not in the body and the body cannot talk to me.

(Mrs. Eddy told Laura Sargent that this was the way to escape from the belief of pain and flesh.)

Take courage from every experience and power will be yours. Go on, dear one, and prove that you are the child of Him who cares for His own. Be faithful to Principle in all that you say and do, and success will be yours. Be happy at all times and in all places; for remember it is your right and a duty you owe to yourself and to God to retain this right no matter how loudly the senses scream. Depression belongs not to the child of God, neither is it real, nor can it affect one when his motives are right.

I am rejoiced to hear of your progress and more than thankful to know that God will bless you in all that tends to benefit yourself and others. But you must watch that you are not led into temptation. To think of me mentally for the purpose of preparing yourself to treat the sick, is a great mistake! It is a mild form of *mesmerism* and will tend to destroy your power to heal in Science. My great desire to prevent this result causes me to name it to you. May God prosper and bless you in all your good work.

If you go to a case with a sense of poverty, squalor or uncleanness, how can you bring it out? For poverty means an unclean God. The only poverty is unclean love. If you have a poverty of compassion, there will be a lack of action.

Do not be discouraged when you see a man apparently acting much worse than ever before, but know that he is growing better, for the very error that besets him will drive him *out* of the false sense and destroy the error.

Affirm that neither malicious influences to harm the innocent, nor physical causation, can produce any result, for there is but *one Mind,* even *Love,* and this Mind and none other *governs all;* is *All.*

Relapse—it is a belief of theosophy, astral or planetary influences, earth currents acting through nerve centers, mortal mind. And God gave us dominion over all the earth. That when our work did well once and the next time failed, we must know that error could not make a law that we were not Christian Scientists and could not heal, and that our work was hypnotism, mesmerism. We must know that God is the Healer and have faith as a little child, and must *love.*

I will show you how, having done all, to stand. Isn't Love the master of hate? Isn't Truth the master of error? Isn't omnipotence the master of death? Yes! Well, you have Life, Truth, and Love right here. Then *realize* it; when you do, your work is done.

Give no intelligence to sin, disease and death. Is God All-in-all? Do you believe this? Then is it not a sin to give intelligence and power to anything else? Then know there is no hypnotism to make you forget or me suffer. Give it no power; destroy it utterly.

We are not to say, there is no stomach, no organization, etc., but to say there is no diseased stomach, no diseased organs, for if we have not grown spiritually where we can maintain our position when we declare there is no stomach, the mesmerist can use that declaration against us for harm in belief. Error may argue, you have said that matter has no intelligence or law, and I (error) say, if there is none, then heart, nerves, muscles, bowels or stomach and kidneys do not act, and you cannot live in the suffering this inaction produces. Christian Science replies, 'All is Mind, Spirit, God, and this divine Mind gives me life, for God is Life. Life is action and this action is harmonious; it is mental Life. It is Life in Mind outside of body.'

When you leave a thing with a negative, you have left it nowhere. You have established no point in your own mind. Take the positive side; know the right side. You can negative error without individualizing it so much. God is All. Never leave the negative without the affirmation in which our thought must rest.

When tempted to personalize evil, let us pray to God for grace to grasp the divine understanding, the tender touch of pardoning Love.

The camp of a defeated enemy is always completely destroyed. We must destroy in our daily consciousness the motives and desires which feed mortal mind.

Psalm 1: 1. Do not listen to the voice of error as you go along, for if you do, it will get you to stand or believe in it a little more, and finally you will sit down and be entertained by it.

We do not have to make money. God is our Father and He has all things, houses and lands, everything needful. If this is true, then man has them just as surely. He does not have to get them, he has them now, just as much as God has them.

(Mrs. Eddy illustrated this by saying, 'If I stand before a mirror and pick up a book, my reflection does the same thing. It does not wait until I have held the book for some time, but picks it up at exactly the same time as I do and, therefore, has the book just as soon as I do.')

Beware not to harden the heart when often reproved, for that shuts out the light and leaves you in darkness. Cultivate tender-heartedness and sympathy with the good.

Hold steadfastly to the truths of the Scripture and divine Science and know that others' hearsay cannot affect you and that Truth cannot derange the proper functions of Mind for God is Mind and Truth is the Way and the Life.

There is no mental sexuality or syphilis engendered from that belief. No spiritual wickedness in high places, and know there is no infection or contagion of mental or material *sin*, and no effects of it.

Destroy penalty, condemnation, eternal damnation, Roman Cathol-icism in your thought of man. Christian Science practice is knowing that there is no sinful man, no diseased man, and knowing the Christ is getting into heaven. Every treatment is an instant in infinity, the unfoldment of Christ. Jesus proved that what he knew was the Christ, was the presence and power of God. Love is wisdom, and without wisdom there is no love.

The character of God, *alias* the essence of good, its nature and tendency, is all that should be worshipped or loved in man or God. By this true worship, we approximate, appropriate and assimilate the qualities of good in ourselves.

Matter is self-will, grief, disappointment and depression and will cause heart failure. Paralysis—handle specifically that no force or action or strength can be lost.

When we overcome self-wrong, self-vindication, hatred in ourselves, we are masters of all error, and then we can help others.

Love is the Way. Love worketh with us. It does not work with hate, hence we *must* love. Love 'worketh with us to will and to *do*', that is, to accomplish. 'Love never faileth'; hence we cannot fail in our demonstration.

His ways are not made known until He tries our obedience, and then He will *reward it.* Be of good cheer. It is Love, unquenchable Love, that loves you better than you can love yourself; Love that cares for every moment and will not leave you comfortless; Love that saith. 'none shall be able to pluck them out of my hands'.

Don't say, God help me to do so and so, but say, God, open my eyes to see that I can do so and so, overcome evil with good.

We must not argue too long against sickness; the wheat and the tares must grow side by side, but they must not be seen as being the same. Do not mix them. Do not confound good and evil and call them one. All is good; there is no evil and it is false.

Belief of duality and unity in duality is the claim of the Red Dragon, swollen with lust and hate. Hermaphrodite mentality, both sexes. Appendicitis is a belief of evolution. We must demonstrate, but not evolve. No Darwinism and no remnant of tail.

Poisonous influences from people's thoughts are nothing when you prove them to be nothing. Go right on and keep your thought on the real. Never for one moment look back at the past. It was a lie; it never was, because God was not in it.

What is the root of mortal mind? Selfishness. Lay the axe of Science—Love, Principle that He revealed—at the root, working out the harmony of Life and Love.

God's plans are going on as best for you and me, whether we know it or not; but *in the knowing* and in *the glad supposition of that fact,* there is rest and peace. Reliance on God's plan unfolds faculties, capabilities, and opportunities heretofore unknown; it overcomes obstacles and removes obstructions.

Do not try to build up matter or make it comfortable and prosperous, but destroy matter with Spirit. Then all these things shall be added, and in the right way. The latter is Science.

Do not let anything interfere with the healing; the instantaneous healing must be brought out. Jesus proved his faith in this way. It is not only to dispel aches and pains, but to heal the sin—mental suggestions that would try to turn your thought from the truth of being; make you think you cannot heal; are afraid to try; that your work can be reversed, can relapse; that Christian Science is mesmerism, etc. To believe a lie is sin. You know those suggestions are all lies. Then it is a sin to believe them. Heal the sin. You cannot be made to yield to such a belief. You *know* better. You are in Mind alone, and the so-called claims of matter cannot touch you, cannot make you an avenue through which to reach any one in belief. You are a child of God, *reflecting* Him. Nothing can force you to believe differently. It is *now* that Truth is—not going to be. Destroy the sense of time.

We must see the nothingness of mortal belief of health, and see true health —wholeness, which is always the same. You and all reflect it. Keep your lamps trimmed and burning, ready to give light at any call.

Sensualism, living in the material sense, eating, drinking, etc., is an open door through which mesmerism comes in to affect us. As we cease to live in the material sense, we do shut the door upon it.

The Scientists should make error unreal to themselves that they may make it unreal to others; and sometimes can do more for others by going by themselves and meditating on spiritual realities.

Have no will opposed to God. Meekness is not weakness. It is 'not my will but Thine be done', throwing ourselves into God's power.

Spiritualism claims obsession, says the dead can and do control the living. It is mental poison. The so-called laws of spiritualism are, first, a person has died, and the one he longs for on this plane, he is continually beckoning to or calling. Second, people who have died can control those who are here.

Do not let the material things hinder our progress in Science. It is a trick of the devil to keep us chasing after matter. You cannot serve God and mammon.

When do we need to look at disease? When our faith in God is not sufficient to destroy it instantly with the command of Truth. We only need the argument against disease to strengthen ourselves. When we can heal by knowing All is Mind, we do not need to know anything about disease.

Know that you—your God-reflected self—has God-health, God-peace, God-happiness, etc., and that the evil one or devil cannot take this from you.

For one look at error, take ten looks at the ideal Christ, and stop explaining error, or we will never get rid of it; it clings to one as long as they excuse it or explain it.

To G. C. C. [Gilbert Congdon Carpenter]

Include this in all your prayers. Eddy. All the individuals in this house can and do help themselves by prayer. God helps them. His promise is fulfilled: 'Seek and ye shall find.' 'Because he has put his trust in Me, therefore have I delivered him.'

Good is infinite. If we limit good and concede power to evil, how can we expect to escape that which we believe has power to hold us in bondage? The First Commandment forbids us to believe in a power apart from God.

To J. F. K. [Julia Field King]

Trust in God and leave evil to do its own work of self-destruction. Always overcome evil with good. Never descend to the warfare between evil and human will trying to do God's will. But forgive all offences and love every enemy you may think you have.

Watch and pray against becoming worldly; also for spiritual sense to govern all your motives and acts.

To L.H. [Louise Hovnanian?]

There is no fear and no thoughts of poison can come. There are no such thoughts. There is no arsenic and no opiates producing any effect on anyone in this house and no one can be made to believe there is. Love reigns here. Truth and Life eternal reigns here and nothing else can come here. There are no evil suggestions, no hypnotism, theosophy, no electro-magnetism. *God is All,* etc. M.B.E.

(This message was left in the student's room and on reading it she found herself free from a cold and sore throat from which she had suffered all day and which she was trying to keep from Mrs. Eddy.)

To C. C. H. [Calvin C. Hill]

We never can know who is in reality a Christian Scientist until he is tested under fire; then what is left are dregs unfit for use till purged and purified, or they are qualities that evil cannot destroy and are held by the power of God.

To L. E. S. [Laura E. Sargent]

My work is mine—it comes from God. It cannot be intercepted nor diverted into other paths, being governed by divine Principle. It is progressive, prosperous, joyous, continuous. It reaches from shore to shore, from ocean to ocean, perfect, infinite, going on all the time, for the glory of God. Perfect idea is already located, with absolute satisfaction in Mind.- In this perfect place in Mind, I am able to support myself, have all the recreation and companionship needed. In the perfect place of Mind is complete satisfaction. I live in the affluence of Spirit, and am one with the inexhaustible, unobstructed, omnipresent source of income, and infinite as is the source, so infinite is the supply. It is the Spirit that profiteth. I am the ceaseless intake of God's eternal giving. You, false claim of malicious mind, whatever or wherever you are, you cannot mesmerize me, or hypnotize me to think I haven't understanding to meet any claim that comes to me.

(The following is not a written statement by Mrs. Eddy, but an approved record of some remarks she made. She told Laura Sargent to go and write them down and on being shown the result, wrote across the page: Well done—Mother.)

(4/24/94) Mother said, write it on tablets, begin with the law: 'Thou shalt have no other gods before me.' This revelation seems like the transfiguration where Moses, the law, prophecy (Elias), (Christ) Science, were revealed. Mother said in the old way mortal belief had one devil; now it had many, but we must not call it *they*, but evil. She said when we take up our watch, we do not help *her* with *our* thoughts, we simply clear our own thought of the belief of evil, and this is getting rid of *our* thought and getting out of God's way, so the light can shine through, and this blessed light helps *us* and *all* in its shining. This is the blessed, blessed way from sense to Soul.

Signed Statements

In answer to on-coming questions, will say: I calculate that about one half century more will bring to the front the man that God has equipped to lift aloft His standard of Christian Science.

(11/28/10—Dictated to Laura Sargent five days before she left us) "It took a combination of sinners that was fast to harm me."

To the Directors

(6/14/08) Faith without works is the most subtle lie apparent. It satisfies the students with a lie, it gives them peace in error, and they never can be Christian Scientists without that faith which is known and proved by works. Words are often impositions, and faith without works is dead and plucked up by the roots. It is not faith, but a deceiving lie lulling the conscience, and preventing demonstration. A satisfied sinner is the most hardened sinner.

To the Field (through W. B. J.) [William B. Johnson]

Is poverty crying aloud in the land? Then we should know the purpose of God is rich in blessing to the poor—in Spirit, The fullness of the earth belongs to the healthful circulation of honesty, virtue and progress in the footsteps of Truth.

To the Mother Church (through W. B. J.) [William B. Johnson]

(1/15/95) Make broader your bounds for blessing the people. Have Friday evening meetings to benefit the people. Learn to forget what you should not remember, *viz.* self, and live for the good you do. Conduct your meetings by repeating and demonstrating practical Christian Science—tell what this Science does for yourself, and will do for others. Speak from experience of its Founder- noting her self-sacrifice as the way in Christian Science. Be meek; let your mottoes for these meetings be, Who shall be least, and servant; and 'little children, love one another.' (See *Journal,* Vol. XIII, p. 41.)

Statement in Print in Lyman Powell's *Mary Baker Eddy,* First Edition, p. 232

You must get rid of the 'old man', the old woman; you cannot make them better and keep them. You are not getting rid of the old man if you try to make him better. If you should succeed in making him better, he would stay with you. If you patch up the old and say it is good enough, you do not put it off, but keep it. If you try to make the old satisfactory, you are preparing to keep it, not to put it off. We have but one Mind; and to abide in this perfect freedom of individuality is the resurrection, is to have risen above material or lower demands. The resurrective sense is positive; it is 'yea, yea and nay, nay'. The resurrective sense does not listen compromisingly to error. It is *always* about its 'Father's business',—reflecting Principle. Jesus' whole life was resurrective; that is, his life was a constant conscious rising spiritually above sin, sickness, death; and his resurrection from the grave was to sense a type of divine Love's final triumph over the human belief that matter is substance, or has power to impose limitations to Mind or man.

Sundry Brief Instructional Items

Psychology is the study of foolishness.

Don't think pain and handle suggestion, animal magnetism, but think animal magnetism and handle it.

Know every day that the world is ready for Christian Science.

Just when the mortal mind says, I can't, you must know you can, for *I can* is the son of 'I am'.

Do not say, 'This is my error or my pain'. Say, 'This is an attack against my Christ'.

Handle fear in case of sickness, belief of hate to heal sin, and keep at it over and over.

You do not have to keep saying all the time, God is *All*; just know it.

When throbbing of body or sleeplessness is spoken of, take up fear.

Babylon is the world in the church.

While you know the truth, defend yourself against the subtleties of error's claims.

You will never get any crops to grow by thinking of the growth.

The call for help is to the divine energy of Love, which always answers, and is without fear.

Malpractice commenced first by making sick; then by calling back old beliefs; and third by the belief in poison.

(7/19/07) Life understood spiritually is heaven here.

MEMORANDA—
1. Pray God to help you awake to the claims of error, and awake to the truth that destroys them.

2. Whenever error would try to make sin, sickness, disease or death seem real, Good overrules it, and it makes them more unreal to us.

3. Good reverses every evil argument and effort and brings out the opposite good.

CHRISTIAN SCIENCE RULES—Subdue all imperiousness, self exacting, and resentment of wrongs. Bear afflictions as you ought. The Scripture saith this is the proof that we are sons and not bastards. Matt. 5: 11, 12 is our rule for consciousness under afflictions.

ANIMAL MAGNETISM—This delusion must be met in all its subtleties—in all its so-called pleasures and pains of sense, (1) passion, (2) appetite, (3) lust, (4) pride, (5) hatred, (6) envy, (7) malice.

MOTHER'S LESSON—Take this lesson to yourself, and whenever anything happens to you of an unfortunate nature, do not admit anything on the wrong side, but instantly declare that the experience does you good. Even if you should fall down and break your leg, get up and say, 'I am the better for this experience'. This is the truth as God would declare it, for every attempt of evil, when surmounted and destroyed, helps the one who is attacked, and your quick and right declaration to the effect that instead of harming you, it has done you good, breaks the claim of evil, and you become a law to yourself that evil cannot harm you.

WONDERFUL LESSON 6/3/94 (in the handwriting of Laura Sargent)—Mother explained what Jesus meant when he said, 'Thou shalt love the Lord thy God with all thy heart, and thy neighbor as thyself; on this hangs all the law.' In order to love God we must honor and love the Way. How can we love God unless we love His idea which shows us the way and which is the Way, and in order to honor and love the Way we must have a true sense of the individual through whom the Way has been manifested to us, else we are not keeping the law to love our neighbor as ourself, or doing by our neighbor as we would be done by. Mother explained Matthew 15: 4 and showed us that the Truth which gives us spiritual birth is our Father and Mother and is what we are to love and honor. Then she explained the difference between a human sense of love and the spiritual sense. Our whole salvation rests upon the manner in which we treat her, since the Way comes to us through her and God demands that we love our neighbor by having the *spiritual sense* of our neighbor, and the *spiritual sense* of our Teacher and Mother as God's *idea* that we must love and honor. Now when we try to kiss her, and caress her, this is not loving and honoring the *Way;* it is *dishonoring* the Way or idea, and thus dishonoring God, and this material sense is what God is rebuking in us; and then when the rebuke comes, we look through the material sense to the *person,*—which in the *spiritual sense* is not our Teacher and Mother or the Way at all—and think she is unjust and (does not) love us and blame her for the discord, when all the time it is God rebuking us through the *Way,* through the idea of God that is expressing God's condemnation of this *false material sense* that would forever shut us out of His presence. Our *material sense* of Mrs. Eddy is person or a personal sense, which is a dishonor to her and God, for God's idea of her is the *spiritual sense* of *man;* namely, the *Way,* the *Truth,* the *Life, Christ,* the *spiritual sense* of Love, of good, which is the divine Science of God and man. Now, when I kiss and embrace the person, I dishonor God and His idea, and this material sense of love which is false, opens the way for another false sense i.e. hate to come in; then we blame the one that rebukes us and hate them, when the spiritual idea or real individual is showing us how much she loves us by showing us the Way, voicing God's idea, which would give us dominion if we only followed obediently.

Mother explained this Scripture, 'Ye ask and receive not, because ye ask amiss to consume it on your lusts.' We ask from a selfish motive and she illustrated it in this way: If we have a pain, we ask to have it destroyed. Why? Because it makes us suffer. Is this the way? No! We should ask to have it removed because it dishonors the *Way* that God has

"I am, the Truth, the Life and the Way"—Christ... the firm knowing that God is all in all & All." That is 'the Way'.

revealed, and this dishonors God. We ask to have the pleasures of sense destroyed. Why? Because they make us miserable.' Is this the way? *No!* We should ask to have them destroyed because they dishonor the *Way* and thus dishonor God. Then our prayer *will be* answered because we ask from an *unselfish motive* and with an honest purpose to honor and love the Way that is God's idea. This is the great lesson that He has given to us, that if we would 'love Him with all our heart and our neighbor as ourself'—thus keeping the whole law—we must have the spiritual *sense* of the Way and love and honor His Way or idea—*the real individual that voices good*—with the spiritual sense of *this individual and not* a material one, and do this by *prayerful watching* to see that in forsaking the material sense we love *more* instead of less and are ever reflecting this spiritual sense of Love, which is all tenderness and compassion and loving kindness and which is the *Way*, the *divine idea* of *Love.*

Mother explained the difference between a material sense of love and a spiritual sense. A material sense of love dishonors the one it professes to love through lust, as in marriage the man dishonors the woman he claims to love by taking away her virginity, thereby exposing the falsity of such a sense by showing it is not love, but lust, i.e. hate.

Mother said this is the 'Lamb slain from the foundation of the world', that is the spiritual sense of Love that is slain from the foundation of a material sense of sexuality.

HOUSEHOLD LESSON—Rom. 2: 22. S. & H. 476: 32. Hold to the correct view of man that heals. We adulterate the Truth when we have a false sense *of* God and man. We have idols when we hold in thought the beliefs of sin, sickness and death, and believe them to be real. We break the law when we believe that evil is as real as good, for this is a false sense which sees only the inverted image and not the true idea of God; hence it prevents us from reflecting the healing Truth, having but one God and loving our neighbor as ourself.

TEACHING—Mrs. Eddy said 'no mortal mind can affect you'. Then she said in substance that we could not be prevented from helping others any more than the rays of light could be prevented from reflecting the sun, for it was not we at all that did the work, but God. and to have faith in God and to know the Truth that makes free,

Again she said (that) error tried to make a law that we could not help ourselves and we could find a remedy by knowing that not we ourselves, but God did the work.

Mrs. Eddy said to a member of her household, 'You have a belief that you suffer for doing good. Now it is not you that does the good; God does it and it shines through you. Now don't you get the benefit of the shining before another feels it? Then it is proved that we do not suffer from the good that shines through us.'

INSTRUCTION 10/22/90—Overcome the love of personality and the fear of it. God is Person, but He is incorporeal. God is infinite Mind, and there is but one Mind, one God. He is the only Person, the Ego, the only I. We are not Person but the reflections of the one Person; members of that one Body which is Christ. That Body is not corporeal. It is infinite Mind, Spirit, substance. It is Love. Person is not finite, it is infinite. Person is not human, it is divine. I have contended against the personality of God because lexicographers define person finitely. Now as Christian Science defines Person, God is infinite Person and there is but one infinite. Let us not humanize or finitize personality.

(2/27/92) The law of mortal mind that says our work, whatever it may be, will not amount to anything, must be broken.

Know first that no such law can interfere with Truth.

Second, that there is no such law. All law is divine and this law of mortal mind is only the inverted image of the law of God. Reverse it and you will find the divine law that all thoughts of Truth *must* have an effect. Is. 55: 10, 11.

(6/27/92) Ever keep the fact of the Allness of God and the nothingness of error before us; then begin at home and root up every sin or belief of A.M. Destroy them with the Truth of being. Let them learn first to show piety at home. Then we are fitted to heal or apply the Truth to error which disappears as Truth appears. Harmony of belief (the body) will appear before the understanding of Truth comes to the individual whom we are healing, one of the signs of Truth.

'Error is a *coward* before Truth.'

(8/1/92) See all false claims as conditions of (mortal) mind entirely distinct from the person.

Handle each one as it appears to your thought.

Watch your own thought that you be not tripped and used as a channel to prevent the good work you are trying to do.

This is most important, as the subtlety of evil is to prevent Truth from appearing.

Another subtlety is the claim that to 'handle the serpent' will not do any good. *Look well to this.* II Cor. 10: 5. Heb. 4:12.

(9/92) Mortal thought awakened is startled at its own shadow. While it slumbered the shadow was unperceived. It must needs learn the nothingness of itself and its shadow, then the fear which in its ignorance was unconscious, and became conscious at the awakening, will pass away, for mortal mind will see that it need not be afraid of itself. II Thess. 2: 8.

(1/22/93) The condition that sees another condition as one that is 'bound of Satan', and bows before it, or fears it, and thereby gives it power, is the more dangerous of the two and needs more to be looked after and rebuked. All conditions have their individuality (or claim to) and stand distinctively apart from every other condition, and yet there are links connecting them with each other.

INTERPRETATION—Romans 8: 16. Love beareth witness with our love, and true love is abiding affection for good, impersonal, pure, loving not the body but the ideal wherever seen.

QUESTION: How much Christian Science do you know? The approved answer: Only what I can demonstrate.

DEFINITION—What is demonstration? It is not declaring the Truth till the result is brought out, but absolute demonstration is being in that spiritual condition of thought where the *work is done* without taking thought of it.

DEFINITION—Animal magnetism is starting a belief and getting others to fear it, until evil is done to those that hold the belief and a law is made, and the error goes on gaining ground until the serpent becomes a dragon.

Sundry Other Recollections by Students

Mother said, 'Science says just the opposite of sense and sense just the opposite of Science', and we are separated from her and God through the false sense that clings to personality, that wants to grasp it and caress it and thus make something of *nothing*. Thus we fail to meet with her on the stairs of spirituality through a corporeal sense, which is either the 'fear of personality, or the love of it'. In order to overcome evil, we must master both the fear and love of personality.

When the work did not go well, Mother said we needed to rise to the consciousness of love, and when we did, it brought the demonstration.

Mrs. Eddy said in substance that the higher we rise in Science, error, by reversal, makes us believe that that which is in our conscious ness, comes from outside and is in another; while that which is without our consciousness, comes from within and is in our own thought.

When a suit in law was pending, a student said to Mrs. Eddy, 'I know the case is all right and we will win it'. She replied, 'If you feel that way about it, you had better stop handling it, It is already all right, but it is the demonstration of the fact which will win it.'

Student: I am ready to obey when I understand.
Mrs. Eddy: Be ready to obey before you understand.

Mrs. Eddy said, if we use arguments, they must be correct. For instance, we could not say, 'Roman Catholics cannot use malpractice', because malpractice was a corruption of her teachings, where Roman Catholicism was a corruption of Jesus' teaching. So we must say, 'Malpractice cannot use Roman Catholics'.

(4/11/96) Mrs. Eddy said this morning there are just two things to guard against in our life work, apathy or stupidity, and making a reality of evil, sickness or sin.

CHAPTER FIVE

LETTERS FROM MRS. EDDY

To E. N. B. [Erastus Newton Bates]

(Jan. 28, 1892) God did not make the infant Jesus. Mary's spiritual concept of progeny exceeded the average human belief, therefore she believed that He did. If her conception had been wholly from God, it would have been the concept of a man instead of a babe, and could not have been born *materially* of Mary. Here is a supposed partnership between God and Mary which is not Science but a human concept in *part*. God is the only Creator. He needs no help. He can have no help, hence Jesus was a material man between the human thought of Mary that was half right and the Christ or idea of God that was wholly right because it was never a *babe* and never a *material* phenomenon. Now I charge you drop this subject from your thought. Think no more of it; let this seed that I have now sown lie still in your thought until you are ready for the harvest. Obey me once more and you will find the good effects resulting from it. The way your mind has been stirred since I saw you is not profitable. Now if you rest, are not stiffed on this question, God will clearly show you what I mean in *due* time.... (Part lost.)

N.B. You said you must be with me in your teachings. This is impossible at present. You know not what you ask. 'Are you (now) able to drink my cup? No! You could not take my place and hold your phenomenon of human life. Now give up that thought or it will become a mad ambition that will be a weight in the wrong scale, weighing downward.

To Mrs. C.

(Dec. 29, 1890) The old year is stepping out in storm and shine The New Year will have come before you see my face in a locket mailed with this letter.

Darling, what a joy it will be when we meet face to face in a bodiless bliss, where the face of the Father is reflected in us, and we are all of one family, loving and beloved.

I was sorry for our dear Annie, but when father or mother forsake, God is nearer, for the joys of sense only becloud the joy of Soul.

I should startle you by a rehearsal of what I experienced in this line, without a fellow mortal to solace me, when I began in the field of Christian Science to sow and water,

But all these trials enrich the heart and quiet the forbidden pleasures or longings for the things of time and sense. It is good to be afflicted. In the world those who are growing away from it, must have tribulation; but knowing that Christ—Truth—hath overcome the world, our dear Master said, 'Be ye not afraid!'

He who understood Love could 'wait patiently on the Lord', well knowing that all our 'light afflictions' work out for us a mighty joy, a joy imperishable.

With a bounty of love for our child-hero, sweet Annie, tell her all this and much more. God is Love. He careth for her, for you and for me,—what more need we? Yes, the years of my pilgrimage have taught me deep, deep lessons-and high, O, who can attain unto them except it be through experience!

To E. S. D.

(March 24, 1896) My precious child: Yes you are that. As I read your letter the mother heart yearned for you and said, 'How long, O Lord, how long?' I thank you deeply for the oranges received from you. They are excellent and I think of you as I eat them. Dear indeed are your words of wisdom on the subject of theatres. I disapprove of them and all other alluring amusements, but more especially the sensual theatre. You have contributed shining lights to our church communion. I shall write to dear Mrs. Eastaman to receive gladly the names of all applications that you endorse. When to prop weakness or foster conceit, the taunt comes, 'You are not Mrs. Eddy's student'—I give you liberty to repeat my words. Yes, you are my student more emphatically than are those who have more of the letter than the spirit of Christian Science. I would endorse you for a teacher of this Science as soon as I would some of my normal class students. I have not had time to read your MSS but will read it when I can get the moments requisite. Now dear one, rejoice and be glad for great is the reward of a pioneer of Christian Science in the far West, such as you have been. Your name is very dear to me as a staunch spirit-filled Scientist. I love the thought that sometime I may have you in a class of my own.

[original letter was signed "Lovingly, Your Mother in Israel"—see Sargent reminiscences.]

To D. A. E. [D. A. Easton]

I feel it my duty to state to you the spiritual need of my old church in that city. It is in short a revival, an outpouring of love, of the

Spirit that beareth witness. I found it essential when the pastor of this church to lead them by my own state of love and spirituality. By fervor in speaking the Word, by tenderness in searching into their needs and especially by *feeling myself* and uttering the *spirit* of Christian Science—together with the letter.

O, may the God of all grace and peace and joy and love give you wisdom to feed this dear flock and He will if you trust Him and obey Him. These are His only conditions.

One more candid hint I will throw out on things less sacred, but very requisite. Give the mesmerists no points to your disadvantage. The wicked horde of this class in Boston exceed any other place. Never name (and caution your family also) any belief of sickness in the past or present; no private experiences of any sort unless they are good and true.

Have your sermons not at all commonplace, but well chosen, eloquent and adapted to the Boston high culture. To this end you will need much study and contemplation.

Unless we have *better healers,* and more of this work than any other is done, our Cause will not stand and having done all stand. *Demonstration* is the whole of Christian Science, nothing else proves it, nothing else will save it and continue it with us. God has said this and Christ Jesus has proved it,

Preaching and teaching are of no use without the proof. I find that the teachers and preachers are the poorest practitioners.

(March 26, 1889) Allow me my dear student to say—if you will make a study of S. & H. for one month and go through the book as you would any textbook in college, it will be of great advantage to you.

(Oct. 18, 1893) The edition of S. & H. revised is now finished. May the light God has set upon its pages illumine my students and all mankind.

God is giving each of us the experience best adapted to lead us to Him.

(In reply to his query whether he should perform wedding ceremonies of Scientists) I hope you will not have to perform such a ceremony. The marriage problem presents before the world a question, the most critical belonging to Christian Scientists. I dread the ordeal through which it must pass, and we with it.

To A. G. E. [Asa Gilbert Eddy]

I know the crucifixion of the one who presents truth in its highest aspect will be this time through a bigger error, through mortal mind instead of its lower stratum, or matter, showing that the idea given of God this time is higher, clearer and more permanent than before. My dear companion and fellow-laborer in the Lord is grappling stronger than did Peter with the enemy—he would cut off their hands and cars. You, dear student, are doubtless praying for me—and so the modern Law-giver is upheld for a time.

To J. F. K. [Julia Field-King]

(1893) Now dear, let not sorrow be the master of joy for it *is not.* The burden is light, the yoke is easy, and if I can say that, any mortal can; for never mortal before drank my cup. Yet I bless God for every dreg. Be of good cheer; *Love is supreme.*

(Jan. 25, 1897) Be *guarded,* and fear not sexuality; it has no power over you. A Christian Scientist is as exempt from that temptation as an angel....

You are master of the bad tendencies of Socialism and not at all at their cruel mercies.

(July 12, 1897) You need not discontinue giving those private written directions to any and all your students who need them. I do foresee that the handling of serpents wisely and harmlessly is the pending need of the period. I have taught mine privately how to do this as I could not publicly, inasmuch as the symptoms or seeming effects demand different arguments and according to the hour. The 1st Commandment is the full remedy. Possess yourself of good and dispossess yourself of any other mind and all the mystery of iniquity beateth in vain against your house.

(Nov. 26, 1897) God bless you dear one for the good you are doing. But be wise, calm, slow to judge, patient, *pure, loving.* These are the graces of Christian Science. The Chicago dedication has stirred the waters. I am informed that millions will read my simple address. Mr. Kimball writes as if inspired, Mrs. Ewing also. My few words on that occasion healed the sick! This is all I ask since my faith without works is nothing but a tinkling sound. People seem to understand C.S. in the exact ratio that they know me and *vice versa.* It sometimes astonishes me to see the invariableness of this rule. May the Father-Mother Love keep you in peace and joy, prosper your labors, unite you to Spirit, separate you from matter and receive you hourly into the Heaven that *is Love.* (See *Journal,* Vol. XV, pp. 526-33.)

The virginity of Jesus' mother is a cardinal point of Christian Science.

To C. M. F [Caroline Foss?]

(Aug. 12, 1906) It comes to me in my prayer to tell you that disobedience and self-justification are the cause of your not mastering m.a.m. I have begged of you to quit telling me why you did a thing wrongly, but you have not obeyed me. I have told you it is like the sick excusing sickness—tell *why they are* sick, and you do know that this would tend to make it real and to *justify sickness.*

To C. W. F. [Caroline W. Frame]

The first experience of mine in entering upon the discovery of Christian Science was the entire stoppage of the periods that are believed to be concurrent with the moon. Hence that saying of the Revelator of the spiritual idea, 'The moon was under her feet'. Often it seems to be *discouraging* to hear my female students talk of this period as if it was part of their life, normal and scientific.

To J. F. G. [James Franklin Gilman]

(Jan. 25, 1894) When you protect yourself from mental malpractice you will rise and continue to grow, and never till you see this need and meet it can I trust even your word. Much less your delineation of Christian Science.

To S. J. H. [Septimus J. Hanna]

I can do you most good by pointing the path, showing the scenes behind the curtain. The united plans of the evildoers is to cause the beginners either in lecturing or teaching or in our periodicals to keep Mrs. Eddy as she *is* (what God knows of her and revealed to Christ Jesus) out of sight; and to keep her as she is *not* (just another white-haired old lady) constantly before the public. This kills two birds with one stone. It darkens the spiritual sense of students and misguides the public. Why? Because it misstates the idea of divine Principle that you are trying to demonstrate and hides it from the sense of the people.

Keeping the truth of her character before the public will help the students, and do more than all else for the Cause. Christianity in its purity was lost by defaming and killing its defenders. Do not let this period repeat this mistake. The truth in regard to your Leader heals the sick and saves the sinner. The lie has just the opposite effect, and the evil one that leads all evil in this matter knows this more clearly than do the Christian Scientists in general.

(Aug. 26, 1902) Whoever opens most the eyes of the children of men to see aright and to understand aright that IDEA ON EARTH that has best and clearest reflected by word or deed the divine Principle of man and the universe, will accomplish most for himself and mankind in the direction of all that is good and true.

6/8/07

(In reply to a query whether a Christian Scientist should go into politics) There is more present good done by being in the midst of error and neutralizing the old with the new. The old bottle of dishonesty in politicians needs *emptying* and it needs your purpose poured into it, the purpose to accomplish the most good for the largest number. If you are now sufficiently rooted and grounded in Christ, Truth, and all its sweet savors of patience, wisdom, grace to bear the strain, you can do more good by occasionally working among politicians than by taking yourself away from them. It will be a great strain upon your *Christliness,* but if you take it up as a *cross,* and bear it meekly, God will direct and *sustain* all such endeavors, and you will grow in the stature of Christ by all the things that await you.

To C. H. [Camilla Hanna]

Your allusion to your mother gone before us is easily answered. As you have been, and are, my dear faithful student, I will answer it. Would not a student in mathematics that could not work out the sum given him be relieved by seeing the solution? She at least learned that what she thought must kill her, did not, and was relieved of this belief, but she has yet to learn how to master death. She must meet death again, but with how much more courage she will meet it!

To C. C. H. [Calvin C. Hill]

I am glad that you have left all, left but nothing for something, and this something is all, God bless your brave, honest intent with its fullest fruition. There are the sick, the halt, the blind to be healed. Is not this enough to be able to accomplish? Were I to name that which is most needed to be done of all else on earth, I should say, heal the sick, cleanse the spotted despoiled mortal; and then you are being made whole and happy, and this is thine, 'Well done, good and faithful', enter thou into all worldly worth and the joy of thy Lord, the recompense of rightness.

(Aug. 2, 1906) Your dear letter strengthens me. I am having much of the experience that you name but on an opposite basis utterly. 'When first I learned my Lord' I was so sure of Truth, my faith so strong in Christian Science as I then discovered it I had no struggle to meet; but stood on the height of its glory a crowned monarch triumphant over sin and death. But behold me now washing that spiritual understanding with my tears; learning little by little the *allness* of omnipotent Mind; and the nothingness of matter, yea the absolute nothingness of *nothing* and the infinite somethingness of *All*. O bear with me, loved one, till I accomplish the height, the depth, the Horeb light of divine Life,—divine Love, divine health, holiness and immortality. The way seems not only long but very straight and narrow.

To E. A. K. [Edward Ancel Kimball]

No need of leaving home. God, Truth is *there* and everywhere, Awake right out of your dream; nobody is hurting you and you know and I know there is but *one Mind,* and none other to harm you. There is nothing to relapse, since God is all and does not relapse. You are not hypnotized, since Truth and Love are not hypnotizers, and there is no other mind or power on earth, or in heaven, but Love, Truth, Life. You cannot die if you tried to; you cannot be poisoned unless you consent to be and so kill yourself, as the Oxford boys by (making a man think he was) bleeding to death. *Pshaw*—you, a man glorious in every respect, yielding to such illusion! I cannot credit it. Now, know you are not, and cannot be, poisoned by a lying argument, for a *lie* is *nothing,* not even an argument, and not one word of what you believe is *real,* and you do not believe it is.

The belief that scares you is your own hand uplifted against yourself. Put it down. The Truth that is good is your life, and doing good you sustain it, but fearing evil you lose it. Body and mortal mind are one. I know this and take no thought for the body. Look out that your thought is right and your stomach will be forgotten, for you have none in Truth. Stick to this Truth and all is well. If thy right hand offend, cast it from thee. Cast out your liver! God is your life and you are the liver and there is no other liver. This is casting out evils and these signs shall follow them that believe.

There is *no liver,* no pneumogastric nerve and no nerves, no solar plexus. Then *stand,* having done all, *stand* on *this Rock.* There is no matter, no *substance* but *Spirit.* Stand there, know it, draw all other physical conclusions from this one *all Truth.* Stay in Boston and vicinity always if you please. I know you can master it, the lie, there as well as elsewhere. To run before a lie is to accept its terms. This works like running before the enemy in battle. You will be followed, pursued, till you face about, *trust* in *God* and stand on *Spirit* denying and facing and fighting all claims of matter and mortal mind both one, and you have grown to be honored by God with entrance into this department of learning.

(1893) For the world to understand me in my true light, and life, would do more for our Cause than aught else could. This I learn from the fact that the enemy tries harder to hide these two things from the world than to win any other points. Also Jesus' life and character in their first appearing were treated in like manner, And I regret to see that loyal students are not more awake to this great demand in their measures to meet the enemies' tactics.

(1893) 1 have learned from bitter experience that the head instructed before the heart is ready, costs me and our Cause dangerous difficulties and sore defeats.

To G. H. K. [George H. Kinter]

(Dec. 2, 1901) Trust your God, our God, in divine Science. There is no other way than for us to *trust always*. This I have proven consistently for forty years. Can you, will you, do the same, my beloved student? Remember this, and live continually in the thought and attitude of trust, confident expectation of good. Nothing else can do for you what this can.

(July 7, 1903) Yes, come at once. Mr. Frye has written you for me as to what to bring with you. God is leading you into a blessed privilege, a wonderful opportunity. May He in His infinite mercy grant that you be kept right, sound in mind and body, free from the a.m., 'The sin that doth so easily beset us'. Notify me immediately upon your arrival in Concord.

(Jan. 26, 1907) Yes, dear, you are right. We must go to the Scriptures always and often for in them we go to God. Mother only wished you to understand the letter of the Science in its larger sense. I know of Mrs. L. God will mete out and measure to her for, 'With what measure ye mete it shall be measured to you again', says the Scripture. Beloved, do not let this effort of the evil one enter your thought to disturb you, for nothing shall enter there that worketh abomination or maketh a lie.

(Jan. 12, 1908) Life is the law of health, and you are the manifestation, the embodiment of this law. Know this, *feel it*. The ways of God are often hard to determine, but Love is preparing us all for a great work.

(Oct. 14, 1908) My word to you at this time is that of the Scripture, 'Rejoice and be exceeding glad for great is your reward in heaven'. Gladness and rejoicing are divine in essence and their reward is manifold in its effect.

To F. S. K. [Flavia Stickney Knapp]

The case named of rupture is considered very difficult, but God says all things are possible to Him. You have only to rouse yourself from a stagnant sense of God's power and presence.... Never yield for a moment to doubt or dismay, . . . God is perhaps trying you as He has tried all His own, and if you stand the test, all at once you will come into the kingdom of our Lord, a clear and abiding sense of your power to heal. Only be faithful over a few things and He will make you ruler over many, and then you will enter into the joy of your work. Rupture is only a thought of matter, but there is *no matter* and man's entire substance is Spirit. *Rouse* yourself from the dream of matter, and pluck the beam out of your own eye; help others and you are helping yourself; help yourself and you will help others. You know what I taught you is true. Now do not let the *enemy sow tares* while you *sleep*—be awake and watch. Deny with all boldness that you cannot heal, for to admit it is dishonoring God, since He it is who heals, worketh through us, and we must see that we reflect Him,—reflect the divine power. I know, my dear students, the way is the way of our Master, full of crosses and crowns. I have more to meet than my students, so much more, you cannot conceive of my cup. But still I drink it, thankful that I am found worthy to suffer for Christ.

Work right on, dear Mrs. K., take pay for your labor, for the laborer in this cause is worthy of his hire, and God has employed you and He will *pay* you sure.

Yes, take the class you name.... Be careful to separate the old from the new, and empty the vessel you fill. No greater mistake can be made than to disobey or delay to obey a single message of mine. *God* does speak through me to this age. This I discern more clearly each year of my sojourn with you.... My books have produced such results in the community, that now it may be safe to teach clergymen. But it was not, eight years ago.

To I. O. K. [Ira Oscar Knapp]

Answer to question physical. The cause is *personality.* You must have no pleasure coming from personality and no suffering coming from personality. You must hold no intelligence in finite forms. Your love or your dislike of another personality or your fear or your love of your own personality puts your weight of thought in the scale of error and this weighs against yourself.

Oh, do not sleep again, do not let the word go forth 'sleep on and take thy rest', 'mine hour hath come'. You will always think you are fully *aroused* to the present need when the glamor is deepest. You are always most safe when you realize you are in need of more conscious truth relative to the be, and its action, and feel sure it is nothing, and His strength abounding in you, and see the path of the serpent and handle the error without fear....

The birth out of matter into Spirit is not gained by argument, nor by force. It is *growth, hourly;* it is forever getting nearer Love that *is Love:* universal, divine *presence* and power, alias *might* and dominion; first over the body; then its reflection is dominion over all the earth.

To Miss L. [Miss Land?]

Now beware of what our Master warned his students against, *viz. 'The doctrines of men'.* Waldo Emerson was a man fitting a niche in history well, and we all in Mass. love him; but he was as far from accepting Christian Science as a man can be who is a strict moralist. Bronson Alcott is far in advance of him. I saw Emerson some months before his demise; went for the purpose of *healing* him. Let no one but my husband, Dr. Eddy, who went with me, know it. As soon as I got into the deep recesses of his thoughts I saw his case was hopeless. I can work only by God's graces and by His rules. So when I said, in reply to his remark, 'I am old and my brains are wearing out from hard labor'—and then chattered like a babe—'But you believe in the powers of God above all causation, do you not? he answered 'Yes', and this followed in substance: but it would be profane for me to believe a man does not wear out. I don't believe God can or wants to prevent this result of old age. Now Miss L., what would this be for an item of history—that Normal Class Students from the only College or School in our land teaching the supremacy of Mind over all error should relapse into studying the ethics of one who died in that belief? Can you find in any work higher ethics than in *Science and Health?* Can you find in any work as good a system of hygiene? Do you understand all that work? If you do not, then it is your bounden duty to do it; and, if you wish to graduate at my College, under the seal of the State of Mass., you must know this great textbook sufficiently to be examined in it throughout, before you can receive a diploma and graduate at the only chartered mind-healing College *on earth.*

To H. A. L. [Hannah A. Larmine]

(1887) Words are inadequate to express the love that flows from the human hearts touched by the Divine.

That *sweet,* dear offering of thine, reached me as a *prayer,* that unites us in Christian fellowship.

Now, darling, I hear of your success as a healer, I knew it would be so. The Christ heals, the Spirit and not the letter is the potency of Christian Science.

One thing let me ask of thee. Do as David did when his heart was wrung at the severance of earthly ties. Lay off the sackcloth, exchange the bitter tear for the oil of gladness. This is Science, to 'rejoice alway', as Paul admonishes.

Now, darling, death is as *unreal* as sickness; your dear one never died, No, he never died! Lift up your eyes and lift up your heart to behold Life *eternal.* Let this comfort you that you only sorrow in *belief,* or can sorrow except over a belief. Now rise superior to this belief in death, or sorrow, for Science divine, reveals the great truth that Life is the master of death, and joy thus abides in Him, the master of all grief.

Christ hath overcome the grave. Truth and Love, God, our Father, as taught by Jesus, hath taken away death; for He hath shown us that *all* the evidence or testimony of the senses is *untrue, unreal*! Now let us rejoice this Christmas morn that Christ hath so arisen to our understanding that all sense material is hushed; and the great facts spiritual of Life and Love are more apparent. All else, which belongs only to human, mortal belief, is false.

(1887) 1 was sad on reading your letter, but it all arose from sympathy with your loss, not that of the dear departed; it is his gain.

Let this console you, for woman's love is so unselfish it can sacrifice for others. Let the good you *can do* and the stimulation of action keep your mind from dwelling on the past, for the present demands your care, and you must go forth to meet the future calm and strong.

God is your refuge and a strong deliverer. He will hide you under His wings till the storms are past and the sunlight of His presence cheers and invigorates you with new strength and exaltation.

When will we all be anything but poor and naked and hungry? I thirst, I hunger daily for the living God, for such an active power of Love as will touch every child of His with love, joy, peace, longsuffering, faith, meekness, temperance. God bless you all, my little children; I long to see you. Be strong in Love, the bond of perfectness; forgive everyone his trespasses. 'Be kindly affectioned one to another, in brotherly love preferring one another', are Paul's words. Do not doubt the talents God has given you, but use them in meekness.

(Jan. 4, 1891) Your present to me is such a sweet reminder of yourself, your head and your heart—that I just love to look at your offering to my useless feet, useless I mean in the sense of material toil, and faster I hope than ever and more beautiful upon the mountains of Holiness and in the dwelling place of the Most High.

Dear one, I felt a little cloud no bigger than a man's hand pass before my eyes, and the raindrop of a tear, as I read your letter. My heart goes out to you with a prayer 'comfort ye my people', give her an abundance of love this year and love so divine that a human sense of love would only mar it, and spoil its joy. Oh! Father, make her home here sweet, a resting place from the world, and where no memory of mortal joy or sorrow can come to cloud the immortal peace, for there is no peace, no pleasure, no bliss in mortal things.

However dear they may be to sense, to Soul they are not permitted. Now my loved one, which do you choose, for both you cannot have? I would rather drink the cup of pain and anguish than sip the chalice of sensual pleasures in even their mildest and *best* forms. Why? Because they are God's high tides that hourly waft us nearer and nearer the shore of eternal bliss.

'Where no arrow wounds the dove.
Where no partings are for love.'

Even though the waves are dark and tumultuous in this heavenward course as we are reaching the sweet haven home, they will grow calm, and then Oh! then, it is *home at last* and there is no night there and no more sea.

This cause must be carried morally by silent argument just the same as you carry it physically. This is the great duty for Christians that they must do or be accountable to God for leaving it undone.

To J. L. [John Lathrop?]

When you are in perplexity or doubt about some important question that must be decided, keep your mind still; cease thinking and wait, that the still, small voice may speak. No words may come to you; nevertheless you will have asked your question. Wait—when the moment arrives, the decision you will have.

Cultivate the habit of trust by daily repeating, 'I am led by the spirit of infinite wisdom. I consecrate my will, my judgment, my desire, and all my faculty to the direction of the all-wise One. I shall hear. I shall know. I shall do right.'

When you have an earnest desire of the heart and there seems no way of having it fulfilled, cease thinking of the obstacles, of the impossibilities and declare with an earnest and definite faith: 'In my Father's sight there are no closed doors, no obstacles, there are no impossibilities. There is no malignant animal magnetism to prevent me from reflecting light. There is no self-mesmerism to hide me from the truth, or to hide the truth from me. There is no hypnotism, no mental malpractice to harm me, for divine Love surrounds me. Truth enfolds me. Intelligence, power, substance are the sources of my being. The only native power is God. The only universe is Life, Truth, Love. There is no channel, personal or impersonal, by or through which animal magnetism either malicious, wilful, sympathetic, or ignorant, conscious or unconscious, can approach Christian Science, its Discoverer or their patients.'

(Jan. 3, 1891) My work for the world this last year will go on through all time. I feel that you all have in my book, *Science and Health,* the anchor of your being that will prove sure and steadfast in storm and shine. O! how thankful I am that God has enabled me to give to you, my dear children in Christ, a rich inheritance!

To L. L. [Laura Lathrop]
(Mar. 15, 1905) The body and you are not one. You are not in the body, talking to it, and it cannot talk of itself. You are spiritual, not material; you are my good, faithful, follower of Christ—the image of God. Indeed, you are this idea and have no strife with the flesh. You reflect God, and His image is like unto Spirit, not matter. The flesh has no connection with you. Realize this, and you are master of the situation.

To W. D. McC. [William D. McCracken]
The thief is ready to rob and to steal all treasures. But our Master saith, 'Had the good man watched, his house would not have been broken open'. I beg you to watch and pray to this end. You are in danger unless you do. The more useful and prominent you become, the harder the mental robbers will work to rob you of good thoughts, a strong purpose and wise efforts to do God's will.

To Mrs. William P. McKinley (wife of President McKinley)
(Mar. 30, 1898) In this hour of our nation's suspense let me rejoice with thee that its revered Chief Magistrate is in every respect equal to the hour, and fervently hope that Congress be found equal to coinciding with his wisdom, The present prosperity of our country, when compared with its condition under a previous administration, seems almost anomalous.

No greater glory could crown any nation than to rebuke and pardon so foul a crime as the destruction of the *Maine* and the loss of her brave men. And this while the nation was feeding the starving foemen. The question is grave—does God require the best government on earth to disturb its peace by war to give Cuba her independence when other nations offer no help? Foreign nations are allied, but the United States stands alone in her glory.

This suggests to me the situation in our country of the rising sect of Christian Scientists. While Catholic and Protestant churches are leagued together, our churches stand alone among religious sects and have yet to gain their independence —the rights of conscience according to the laws of our constitution. It is a strange thing to say that under a free government a bill is brought against them for healing the sick, and again that they are prosecuted for not healing the sick! Although our courts find no fault with the M.D. who loses his patients or claims to help them.

Pardon my straying into this allusion. But my purpose is to say

Notwithstanding this I admonish Christian Scientists never to take the sword, but always endeavor to overcome evil with good. And obeying this rule the prosperity of Christian Science is unexceptional, for the Principle which governs it is mighty in demolishing wrong and sustaining right. This little leaven of rightness will finally leaven the whole lump of nations till navies and armies are not requisite, and the brotherhood of man is established on the Principle of one God,

Accept my heartfelt hope that you are in health and the enjoyment of a peace that the world cannot disturb.

To A. McL. (Editor of periodicals) [Archibald McLellan]

(1903) 1 deeply sympathize with you in all you wrote. I would quickly, joyfully give you a rule for each need wherewith to supply it. But God alone can do this, and He will do it. Ask for wisdom of Him, the divine Love, and you will receive it, and as ye pray *believe,* and it shall be done unto you, are the words of our Master. Our periodicals stand for a system to be established and a Science to be demonstrated. They are not to amuse or to entertain so much as to instruct the public. They should contain only what tends to this result. The dabblers in literature are not the ones to fill this demand. We need cultured writers to make the abstract interesting; and sound subjects to make our readers satisfied. *Wisdom* and the keen perception of what to write and how and when to write it are requisite in the editor, and a fearless stand as to maintaining the rights and rules of periodicals in self-defence and the dignity due to our paper and its purpose. Wit and wise repartee are sometimes auxiliaries to this end; and sarcasm blent with love may gain a strong point in human thought. Unlettered novices in Christian Science are not the writers that we need.

I recommend that you get *exchanges* with the leading religious or secular magazines and newspapers if possible. This is advantageous in many respects.

(Aug. 11, 1906) Allow me to say it is your right to omit what is wrong in an article contributed to your paper and I advise you to do this and so retain whatever else is useful in said article.

(Aug. 23, 1906) Have no Park nor parks for Christian Scientists. But have more spirituality and power to resist evil. Resist the Devil and he will flee from you: draw nigh unto God and He will be nigh unto thee, St. Paul. I may not have quoted verbatim.[1]

(Aug. 28, 1906) The article[2] ... should not have been published in our periodicals. It contained that which is irritating and unwise relative to priestcraft.

Be very careful not to let appear in our periodicals anything that can offend the Roman Catholics or other religious denominations unnecessarily. And weigh well the results of whatever is published. Let all you send out tend to make friends not foes to our Cause. Let it be a repetition of the angelic announcement at the birth of the Christ idea, Jesus, 'Glory to God in the highest, and on earth peace, good will toward men'.

To M. B. L. [Mary Beecher Longyear]

(Jan. 15, 1905—Full text of letter appearing in part in *Sentinel* of Oct. 7, 1916) My Mary and my disciple: God is moving on the face of the waters of your thoughts and His creations will appear.

I propose that the institution you found be called Sanatorium, also that it be for teaching surgery, training nurses, teaching cooking, and healing the sick. Also that it be a resort for invalids without homes or relatives available in time of need; where they can go and recruit, etc. You who are so capable of financial operations can arrange all without my suggestion.

Our cause demands a wider circle of means for the ends of philanthropy and charity, and better qualifications for practical purposes. This latter lack in students of Christian Science is a great hindrance to our cause and it must be met and mastered. The students need to be qualified so that under the fire of mortal mind they can stand, and 'having done all to stand' (St. Paul).

Special Notice of the Present

[1] 'An Error Corrected', denying plans for an Assembly Park, appeared in *Sentinel* of Sept. 1st, and used phrases from this letter.

[2] 'Little Things' in *Sentinel* of Aug. 18, 1906.

Let none but yourself into this movement or *know of it* now. Do not rely on me at all for I have not a half hour to spare, or a moment some days, and God with you is your majority. Keep your thoughts away from me lest they bring too much of this world with them and, dear one, this would surely not help you. I want this work done wholly apart from me

To H. A. N. [Helen Andrews Nixon]

(July 16, 1890) This is what history will call my *birthday.* But it is sweet to know that I was never born of the flesh but of *Spirit.*

My joy at your new birth is *very great.* I thank God that none which He hath given me can be lost. Now permit me a few words of counsel. The next temptation after a victory such as yours is to either darken your evidence of the newly found Truth, or to cause one to over act in the inspiration of zeal to bear testimony to it, and thereby to help others.

It is always right to obey the scripture and when converted to strengthen the brethren. But there is great wisdom to be used in knowing just how much to say, and when to say it. I recommend that the *C. S. Jour.* preserve a wise reticence on this subject until the world is more enlightened on the awful error of mental malpractice, or Malicious An. Mag. There will be a time when it can be, must be, met and laid bare before the people. But my dear Students show themselves not quite equal yet to meeting this question silently or audibly just as it can be met and thus destroyed to each one's own consciousness. This is done not by a sense that there is no such evil in claim, but only that there is no such evil in *reality*; just as sin or sickness is to be considered. *Love* is the victor over all.

(1891?) Your confiding letter was sweet, delicate and lovely. May the God of all grace lead you *gently* into the gate that shuts out all that belongs to the flesh in origin or manifestation.

Until then, and as you journey thither, may the 'Love that never faileth' strengthen your clear sense that you are in the true way, if indeed you follow afar off. It just pierced my heart to hear you say or rather to read of your saying that you were not a Christian Scientist! Oh how can you indulge the thought that Christ has not shown you this diviner way in Science. I scarcely believe that you do believe what you wrote when you said, 'I know that I am not a Christian Scientist'. I do pray you never to repeat this saying *unqualifiedly*, again. It is indeed a great achievement, but many are regarded as Christian Scientists because they have started in this direction, and this is proper. If it were otherwise we should have to drop the dear name and this will not do. Let us work on, and pray on, in His, Christ's, *dear name,* until we have more and more of His spirit and arrive at the fullness of His stature.

(Oct. 11, 1892) It was comforting to read the divine record of your communion with God. He has shown you the Truth on every topic you wrote.

I bless His holy Love, and pray for grace to keep me in the paths of His testimony always. Yes, this is the class that subjects you to no human opinions. Oh! that I may never have to teach another of my own.

About procreation, I seldom ever speak between husband and wife. I do this freely to those who are not married, but dread to touch the conjugal relations already existing. My Books are explicit on this question.

I reconveyed my gift not because it was not safe to build, as you said, with the first title; but because the Trustees refused to, and I was made willing for the sake of peace, 'when they ask you to go with them one mile to go with them twain'.

Again you see in results that God's purpose was to establish a Church with a new form of means less material whereby to worship Him. Is it not wonderful and glorious to watch the signs of the times! ...

Be as *ever* the same loving tender wife, and God will in His own good way open the eyes of Mr. N.

(May 19, 1893) From what I hear, I fear you are drifting away from Christian Science, especially on your sense of obligation growing out of the marriage covenant. Now dear one, any student misunderstands my books and teaching who believes that she or he is not morally and Christianly bound by the marriage vow to fulfil the claims it includes. I would not hesitate to trust your honesty and sincerity in fulfilling an agreement made with me, and it is of much more importance that you fulfil so sacred an obligation as: the bridal vow.

Your recent notion that it is not your duty to love your husband and parents more than any other fellow-beings is preposterous. While I feel sure that your motives are sincere and your morals sound, yet I am sure that it is wicked for you to entertain such beliefs, and contrary to my teaching of the present wisdom or practicality of such ultra means in Christian Science.

In my work *Science and Health* I say 'The nuptial vow should never be annulled so long as its moral obligations are kept intact'. How can you mistake my meaning? This vow you well know is understood to include all the claims that our laws legalize by this contract and which you have acknowledged and promised to fulfil, therefore this solemn pledge cannot be conscientiously broken except by mutual consent. I commend only this unity of consent.

Now dear one, take up your cross and bear it with woman's patience, hope and prayer, and God will give you wisdom and peace. Do this for the sake of your precious children, husband and parents, and for Christ's sake who taught us to obey the laws of the land in which we sojourn. It is your Christian duty to act on the basis that our dear Master taught—'Suffer these things to be so now, for thus it becometh us to fulfil all righteousness'. What he observed on these grounds he knew were material and not spiritual rites and he saw the wisdom of this condescension. Cannot you then trust our Heavenly Father's promise 'that all things shall work together for good to them that love God'?

Let us hope that sometime your husband will think as you do on the subject that troubles you. Have more faith and 'wait patiently on the Lord'. The advice of loving your loving parents who have more experience than their children, is of great importance; remember this. All remember the commandment 'Honor thy father and thy mother', etc. Not for the world would I have you break one of the Commands in the Hebrew Decalogue, it would unfit you for Christian Science, it would darken your mind so that you could not comply with the requirements of Christ in healing the sick and casting out error. We must take the beam out of our own eye before we can see clearly to cast the mote out of another's.

Now dear student, rouse yourself from your present unnatural and unscientific belief on this subject, herein named, and pray that God (to) leave you not in this temptation but deliver you from evil.

Never notice the sentiments of those hot-headed students of Christian Science who talk foolishly on the subject of marriage. You have never seemed to quite understand all my teaching. Nothing should ever deter us from acting conscientiously for that is our individual right. But conscience tells us we must not be false to ourselves or to others. Cannot you see this ? I seldom talk on these unpleasant questions, as you well know.

If you need help of a Christian Scientist Mrs. Munroe is a good woman and I hear does good healing. I cannot myself conduct your case—you know I have not taken patients for many years and am out of practice. This letter will do all that I can do for you

To W. G. N. [William G. Nixon]

(Jan. 13, 1892) I congratulate you on the success at your home. But I also pray that you be left not to temptation, and understand that God has created all and man is *not, cannot* be, a creator, however much the senses declare against this great truth of Christian Science. To the senses you have gotten a child, but not in Science have you a mind in matter, any more than you have sickness, disease and death. Hence what you believe is a mortal child, is *mortal,* and *subject* to the above, and if you believe you have an immortal child, formed of matter, you believe a lie for this is *impossible.* I felt so strangely[3] it was my duty to say this to you, that I have written it.

Please bring wife and children to Concord and visit me when Mrs. N. is ready for this and all will be loving and Christian in our interview.

Relative to the oft-repeated question, Shall the Spiritual Interpretation of the Lord's Prayer be printed in Hymnal or any other form, I reply always, No. This is properly repeated by the Pastor and not from the pews. The 91st Psalm is suitable for the Hymnal.

To M. P. [Mary Plunkett]

(Sept. 24, 1885) The spiritual darkness that malicious mesmerism leaves on your mind is all that you are really in danger from. I see this darkness in everyone that writes me on this question from Chicago. Now knowing the physical symptoms of disease is no aid spiritually, and you can only heal them by *spiritual,* not by material power. Arouse yourself from this spiritual blindness that seeking other gods occasions, and find *Truth* and *Love* the only powers, for they are and you ought to know this. I want to instruct Mr. W. If you 'take the sword you will perish with it'. That was what killed my husband—he would fight mesmerism on a material basis, with a human instead of a divine sense, and I could not be allowed to do this work for him. To make him *see this* was the effect on him of malicious mesmerism, was the point. His last moments opened his eyes and he said I was right.

(Sept. 22, 1886) Now watch and pray; every wrong unscientific thought, every *fear,* put down; every symptom moral or physical, that is not Science and does not reflect Life, Truth and Love, meet and master, then you are out of the reach of malicious mesmerism and they are only, by trying to hurt you, helping you to difficult problems and you are solving them, and this is your only way to *heaven*—the harmony, peace and immortality of being. Now be *strong* in the Lord, put on the *whole* armor of Truth, and not go to laying it off in the battle and call on other gods—to go to matter for help!

[3]Strongly?

(1890) The delicate conjugal question you asked in one of your letters is to be handled *wisely*. You and everyone has the rights of conscience, but you must be careful to manifest more affection for your husband, and in the proportion that you withhold the conjugal claim. By this justice, many a wife has in *Science* held the affections of her husband and he has come peacefully into her truer sense of total abstinence which is the only true position in Science.

To Miss P. [Sarah T. Prime? or Carrie Potter?]

We understand as Christian Scientists that our varied experiences *are things of the past;* not so the marvelous sense of God's presence resulting therefrom! God has placed us all in our orbit, and like the stars we are held there by His power. *One* does not interfere with another and we cannot fall out. Also, God is abundance. God giveth the only abundance. Mental malpractice or error cannot rob us of that abundance, either mentally, morally, physically, or intellectually. This demonstrated proves the power of Life, Truth and Love for every human need.

To N. R. [Nemi Robertson]

(Jan. 1897) My ideal is Christian Science *demonstrated.* God gives you fresh opportunities every hour for work in His vineyard. Will you take this yoke upon you? I have borne it forty years.

Attacks on the Discoverer and Founder of Christian Science are attacks on *the Cause itself.* When will you see *this,* and stop these efforts of animal magnetism to destroy us? The students *alone* will be responsible if these demon schemes are not ended. Yet who will bear this cross? See Matt. 10: 33.

To F. S. (Mrs. Eddy's lawyer) [Frank Streeter]

(July 2, 1900) You said to me, 'I believe that one of my eyes is shorter than the other' I have often felt I ought to have said to you what I now write, namely, you acknowledged metaphysical healing in that testimony and it should have proved and settled the case in your favor. If you believe that one eye is as long as the other it will be so. All that makes it seem otherwise is your belief, The Scriptures saith, 'As a man thinketh in his heart, so is he'. Now I appeal to you as a lawyer not to testify against your own case. Your physicians have testified for the case against you and you believe their testimony. Your false sense of sight has testified against you and you believe its testimony. But the Science of your being gives you the verdict of Mind, not matter, and it decides the case against atrophy and declares that matter cannot bear witness and that one eye is as long as the other. Believe Science and you are saved.

To V. S. [Victoria Sargent]

'Let God do it.' Do not allow that thought of the person who has tried to injure you enter your thought! Destroy in your thought all envy, jealousy, and hate, and other errors, and the light will shine in your thought and heal you and very likely the other person also.

To C. S. [Clara Shannon]

(Sept. 1, 1893) Be like a little child. Turn your thoughts to Love and say, O Love, take me in; give me one Mind, one consciousness and make me to love my neighbor as myself. Let your heart cry out to divine Love. A child cries out to its mother for more light, more truth, more love. Ask Love for what you need and for what Love has to give; then take it and demand of yourself to rise up and live. Trust Him, dear, read daily your Bible and *Science and Health,* and pray the Prayer of our Lord's in your own words. Ask for His kingdom to come, for Life, Truth and Love to govern all your desires, aims and motives; to feed you with faith and a clear knowledge of good; to make you patient, forgiving, long-suffering, merciful, and compassionate, even as the dear God is thus to you and you desire Him to be. And then reflect this God in all His qualities. My desire is that this year shall be crowned with mercies for you and all. Dear God, I ask for divine Love to leave me not to be tempted, nor to yield to temptation in any direction. I ask for wisdom and grace to know and to do just what God would have me do. (See also p. 61.)

To E. P. S. [Elizabeth Pinckney Skinner]

(Dec. 26, 1891) The Scriptural narrative,[4] that you queried has both a spiritual and a literal significance.

Jesus no doubt supplied the literal loaf and fish to their sense so as to impress upon them at that period, the Christian era, with the fact of his twofold power, as the way shower, or mediator between the things of the flesh and those of Spirit. His mission on earth was this declaratively and demonstrably from the beginning to the end.

Not so is the Christ's appearing at this age. Rather is it now to show through Science and not the senses the power of Spirit and of Good, and to spiritualize all the meaning of the Christ, to name Christ the idea and not the person of God, and to impress, at this period, the Science of Spirit on the mind, through Truth, and the

[4] See Mark 6: 35-44.

phenomena of Mind, and not matter. To voice God less in parable, and more in the facts of Being. This must be the true interpretation of the Parable of the loaves and fishes, because Jesus could in no other way have made the way for the second appearing of Christ in Science.

Darling

I give you permission to read this hastily written explanation to your next Bible class.

Please give my love to all the dear members of this class.

To A. E. S. [Augusta E. Stetson]

I hope the cloud from Boston has not reached you: God reigns, He is showing me through it. His face is so sweet in the gloom, His love so true! I always go up in the cloud, and when it passes away, then the dear Love tells me the why and wherefore, but this is marvelous to even me; that God always takes the one we love most in the flesh wherewith to rebuke our pride and chasten our lives in the flesh, till we are above the flesh and all human designs, and safe in the place of His abiding.

To E. A. T. [Emma A. Thompson]

(Aug. 23, 1887) 1 trust you are strong and *know* that there is but one Mind, and that this Mind governs you, permeates your body and brains with Truth, hence there is no room for error to steal in, and *matter is* not you. You are spirit, the idea of God, and the Mind that was in Jesus must be in you, for God is ALL, the outside and inside of Truth and—its ideas.

To I. C. T. [Irving C. Tomlinson]

(1897) Our Cause is immortal; it rests on nothing temporal; it is the cause and effect of all that really exists. What more is left us to desire than its acknowledgment and the unfolding of God, infinite Life, Love! I rejoice that the young folks, yea, the children, are its supporters, embrace it, love it, and will learn to live it,

To M. W. [Martha Wilcox]

(Dec. 31, 1905) You have been a long time at work without a vacation and now you can have one and get well and rested. True, *you do not* need this for God, divine Mind, rests you and heals you; matter cannot do this, and the Scripture bids us to come to Christ, Truth, and find rest in these words of Christ, 'Come unto me, all ye that are weary and heavy laden, and I will give you rest. For my yoke is easy, and my burden is light.' Working for the good of others is not hard work, it is a burden that is light. You have worked for me to help me many years and it has not hurt you for it cannot. Doing good helps us all; it has carried my life on forty years and it will sustain yours. Do not feel you must come back to work till you *believe you are rested* and able to do so.

Do not *think* of *me;* keep your mind fixed on God. Take no thought about my food. It only wastes thought to dwell on matter.

To Mrs. W.

(Sent on receipt of copies of *Science and Health* and *Unity of Good* bound with the Bible) What sweeter unity can there be for our model than Christianity and Science. I regard the type sacredly and trust that our acquaintance will be built upon this Rock. Hearts unite on some basis, and if the foundation of friendship is spiritual, it cannot cease; it must be perpetual.

May the light that breaks upon the dawn of eternal day illumine your path, cheer, comfort, support you. This divine ray is never obscure in Science; only the shadow of sense can cause temporary eclipse, as we stand in our own light.

To F. W. G. [Frank Walter Gale]

(1891) You are *growing.* The Father has sealed you, and the opening *of* these seals must not surprise you. The character of Christ is wrought out in our lives by just such processes. The tares and wheat appear to grow together until the harvest; then the tares are *first* gathered, that is, you have seasons of seeing your errors—and afterwards by reason of this very seeing, the tares are burned, the error is destroyed. Then you see Truth plainly and the wheat is, 'gathered into barns', it becomes permanent in the understanding.

The healing will grow more easy and be more immediate as you realize that God, good, *is all,* and good is Love. You must gain Love, and lose the false sense called love. You must feel the Love that *never* faileth,—that perfect sense of divine power that makes healing no longer power but *grace.* Then you will have the Love that casts out fear and when fear is gone doubt is gone and your work is done. Why? Because it never was *undone.*

I was pleased to hear from you. Had felt that our Father was giving you line upon line and you had the best Teacher and most loving in all His ways. This abated any care of mine for you.

In reading my revised edition[5] that is, by the way, published this week there is no special direction requisite. The general rule is to commence with the first chapter, read slowly and pause as you read to apply certain portions which meet your present need,—to thought that will carry them out in action. The book is complete in itself, it is a teacher and heater. Has 50 pages more than the old edition just past. The labor I have bestowed on it you cannot reckon, there are more signs of it than you can *see,* but not more than will be *felt.*

To J. J. E., artist of a picture of The Mother Church called *Dawn* that Mrs. Eddy had in her library.

Your picture of The Mother Church of Christ, Scientist, distinguishes the artist, points a history, and illuminates it.

(This was her reply to the artist's letter of July 27, 1907, in which he said: 'I represent the Christian Science Church rising unharmed out of the smoke of contending factions, the struggle of creeds and all sorts of "isms" for supremacy.' See *Sentinel,* Vol. X, p. 732.)

To R. F. [Rose Festner]

You have not to fight, not to struggle, but only to *know,* (See *Sentinel,* Vol. X, p. 792.)

To the Christian Science Board of Directors

(11/23/02) Be strong and clear in your convictions that God, not M.A.M., is influencing your actions. In order to be this, you surely must pray daily that God, good, divine Love—your only Mind—be followed, be loved, be lived by you.

(12/27/03) My beloved Students: May this dear Christmas season be to you a Christ risen, a morn, the break of day. There is nothing jubilant attached to the birth of a mortal—that suffers and pays the penalty of his parents' misconception of man and of God's creation. But there is a joy unutterable in knowing that Christ had no birth, no death, and that we may find in Christ, in the true sense of being, life apart from birth, sorrow, sin and death. O may your eyes not be holden, but may you discern spiritually what is our Redeemer.

I thank you, dear ones, for your kind remembrance of me—the most lone and perhaps the most loved and hated of earth! May you watch and pray that you keep the Commandments, and live the Sermon in the Mount this coming year. Watch, too, that you keep

[5] No doubt the Fiftieth Edition of *Science and Health,* which appeared in 1891. See *Sentinel,* Vol. XLVI, p. 1159.

the *commandments* that experience has compelled to be written for your guidance and the safety of Christian Science, in our Church Manual.

(4/5/09) My beloved Board: You know that God, divine Love, reigns, and the Catholic prayers this week (holy week) or any week, to harm your Leader, are powerless. Will you as my Church realize this Truth that destroys error. Do not take me up personally but know mentally and prayerfully that the Catholic prayers to harm anyone are utterly powerless. Evil and sin are nothing. Good and divine Love are infinite, and there is no other power. They are all and govern all.

(12/14/09—regarding the mooted placing in The Mother Church of a statue of a woman kneeling) No picture of a female in attitude of prayer or in any other attitude shall be made or put into our Church, or any of our buildings, with my consent. This is now my request and demand: Do nothing in statuary, in writing, or in action, to perpetuate or immortalize the thought of personal being; but do and illustrate, teach and practice, all that will impersonalize God and His idea man and woman. Whatever I have said in the past relative to impersonation of thought or in figure I have fully recalled, and my Church cannot contradict me in this statement.

To Editors of 'Sentinel' *and* 'Journal' *and C. S. Directors*

(July 14, 1903) Are you asleep on so important a subject as to make the laying of our Church Corner Stone in Concord a desecration—instead of a quiet, solemn, brief ceremony? You who profess to know there is *no matter* to elevate the usual material ceremony above all precedent.

Not over fifty persons shall be present on that occasion with my consent.

With love and all the patience God would give me for such *sin,* such *folly,* such a waste of time and money only to obey M.A.M. and make sport for our enemies.

N.B. I had not seen your notice in our publications till today.

(The notice, in *Sentinel,* Vol. V, p. 717, was as follows:

Corner-Stone Laying at Concord, N.H.

First Church of Christ, Scientist, of Concord, N.H., announces the laying of the corner-stone of the new church, the gift of our beloved Leader, the Rev. Mary Baker G. Eddy, for Thursday, July 16, at two o'clock. A cordial invitation is extended to all.)

To the Editors, 'Journal'

(Jan. 30, 1897—when forwarding an encouraging letter from First Church, Buffalo, N.Y.) Love, overflowing, makes angels, is entitled to God's care, governs fate, kindles all hearts with delight, and, as in Israel's dream, it rises above earth to Heaven. (See *Journal,* Vol. XIV, p. 573.)

To a Western Church, which sought Mrs. Eddy's adjudication on a minor point—

(About 1888) Be loyal to the spirit of my teachings, then do your own work in your own way. (See *Journal,* Vol. VII, p. 213.)

To First Church, Kansas City, Mo. (telegram)

(Dec. 1898) My heart greets you with Christmas joy. Continue, fellow-worshippers, vigilant in that whereto God calleth thee. Unity imparts the spirit of the trinity. Opinions of men are not substitutes for Science. Be patient with misjudgment. Christ, Truth, overcometh error. Today is tomorrow understood. Love maketh right prosperous. Pure hearts and clean hands upbuild the cause and Church of Christ, Scientist. Have one God; live in conformity therewith, obedient thereto, governed thereby. (See *Journal,* Vol. XXX, p. 227.)

To First Church, Eau Claire, Wis.

(July 15, 1899) Your brief, brave, tender lines of loyalty are reassuring to the woman in the wilderness. Like song of birds at evening, they reach my ear and heart. God bless you, dear ones, and accept my thanks and prayer for your prosperity to be continued. (See *Journal,* Vol. XXXII, p. 348.)

To Third Church, New York, N. Y.

(1899) 1 note what you say about Third Church. 'Three' is a sacred number in our calendar. (See *Journal,* Vol. XXXV, p. 333.)

To First Church, Brooklyn, N. Y.

(April 26,1905) Unity is oneness with God and man. It is the bond of peace; it keeps the first commandment and obeys the golden rule. It rejoices with those that rejoice and ministers to such as mourn. It is the bond of perfectness. (See *Journal,* Vol. XXXII, p. 656.)

To the Readers in First Church, Troy, N. Y.

(December 3, 1897) Your excellent letters were duly received, and each day thereafter I tried to find moments in which to answer them. Today is my very first opportunity. I rejoice to read a notice of the dedication of your chapel pending the erection of a church.

Your quiet, efficient labors specially commended themselves to me. I hope the Church shows are now over. I saw the advantage of giving emphasis to the Chicago Dedication; beyond this, I recommend to all Churches to give no publicity and particularly no public pictures of their Churches. It is too commercial, too cheap looking, too little like things that come in course and to stay, and too like a surprise that one can have a Church edifice. These have always been my views on this subject. I feel so even in regard to The Mother Church although that is an exception to all others.

In His light you have all models, all example, and this light is for the illumination of all taste, culture, scholarship, morals, physics, and metaphysics. A Christian Scientist is as much perfected in the above whole, or in any part of those. My desire and prayer is, 'Father, make them perfect even as Thou art perfect'. Give my love to your dear church, lead thou its members into light.

To all First Readers

I request that you pray once *every* day for the principal editors of the principal periodicals in your city and for the clergymen in your pulpits. The lying influences sent forth to deceive our clergymen and our pressmen, would, 'if possible, deceive the very elect'.

This must be met with a counteracting influence through prayer. Let Truth be heard above error, and God will bless your efforts. Jesus saith, 'All things are possible to him who believeth'. Ask other members of your church to do likewise, each day to pray as above and pour in the truth that destroys the error.

To a Committee on Publication

(1/12/05) Beloved Student: I hasten to ask: Have you—been elected for the Publication Committee of New York State? If so, then I am prompted by our God to write to you solemnly, earnestly and lovingly on this special subject, namely, That you act lovingly and wisely towards Mrs. Stetson and her church. The enemy will tempt you to do otherwise, but if you have the desire to do rightly, and watch and pray daily for guidance, then no one can misguide you in this or in any other respect, and no one can harm you and you cannot be made to hurt any one and will 'do thyself no harm'; and God wilt bless you abundantly.

To Students with Cases

(July 2, 1884) Your very interesting letter has just arrived and I hasten to reply.

The tone of your letter is right; it indicates the working of the 'little leaven' of Christian Science, which if the spirit be not quenched will 'leaven the whole lump'.

You ask why do you linger longer on this case of belief where the genital organs are the fears, and gout the manifestation? The Apostle says 'know ye not that we are the servants of that to which we yield ourselves servants to obey'.

Mortal man rests contentedly on the foundation error that man is conceived through the so-called material senses; hence if pleasure of sense is real, is not the pain of sense as real also? Here the material thought weakens under its own argument, and all you gain over sexual disease is absolute Science that rebukes both the so-called pains or pleasures of sense. The gout is another manifestation animal, as a general thing, and requires a shock oftentimes to start its foundation to tumble into nothingness. Attack the appetites, if it be a case of conscious origin, and startle the dream into loathing itself and craving a higher sense of what supports happiness and is Life.

Treat the genital disease according to the sex; if a woman married, it is often inflammation caused by compulsory indulgence, in which case, realize yourself the myth of mortal thought, that all its sense of action is but a dream. When nothing is done in the right direction, there has nothing been done, and no fears can cause inflammation, and inflammation cannot cause weakness, stricture, pain, prolapsus, because matter cannot be inflamed and Mind is God, and there is but *one* Mind and this Mind creates and acts independent of sexual organs.

There are no sexual organs, only in belief, for all is created, and man or woman are not creators. Destroy the belief of sexuality or its results, take thought into its upper departments and you heal the disease.

I shall be pleased to hear from you. Did you get the Mag. I sent—in sending it my hope was to give you sweet comfort in reading the sentence I marked.

I have a great interest in your success and know that with 'clean hands and a pure heart', you will succeed and finally all cases will be treated. At first you must wait and work yourself up higher, for God worketh with you.

(Postscript) I open my letter to say on reading yours I find some questions unanswered.

Your revery when treating the sick is a belief that comes of a vivid imagination and I would handle it with the intellect, confine myself to sober, sound reason illumined by understanding, instead of imagination, and practise from a calm fixed sense of the nothingness of all error and the conscious harmony of Spirit, wherein are no outlines of *mortal beliefs.*

The length of time in which to treat the sick depends solely on the periods of their waking from the dream of material sense. You can heal them with one treatment if that one wakens them, breaks the dream, and you must treat them until it is broken and then stop.

(Jan. 2, 1885) Your interesting letter should have been answered sooner but this is my very first chance to reply. Yes dear, a case of deafness from fracture of the drum is as readily cured on the Principle of Mental Science as the simple earache. All that hinders your finding it so is the reality you make of matter. The false teaching of so-called mental healing is fastening the belief in matter, and this fastens the belief in disease, and the only way it can be cured after that is through belief, will-power, which *leaves the* so-called cure worse than the disease. Why? Because a stronger belief had to master the weaker.... The basis of Metaphysical Healing is Mental Science and this Science has nothing to do with matter, only to say and to establish in the back of mind that there is *no matter. See this* and you heal all cases of belief since all are founded on matter.

To a Student about to Travel

Remember that unless you travel mentally, that if you don't traverse new lands spiritually, if you don't cross metaphysical waters, that is, and reach shores hitherto unvisited in Soul, you have wasted your time, money, and effort, and you will get nothing out of it. Don't do less Science but more. May God enfold you in the paths of righteousness for His name's sake, where no evil, no accident, no allurements, no blame lies, claiming some world more dazzlingly beautiful than the radiance of divine Love, for straight is the gate and narrow the way thereto.

To a Bereaved Husband

Let us rejoice with the angels today. Your dear wife, my precious student, has added one more to the glad throng and the sweet song of those who have gone up thither, having washed their robes and made them white through all they have experienced.

While in the sweet sense that she now entertains, she knows *there* is a Life in God, good, that is eternal and in this Life, no pain, no death, no parting, no night there.

Oh, my dear friend, I wish you and I knew this as well as she does, today, who has awakened as we all must in some way to the truer sense of the Love that gives us this alterative.

You have no cause for grief; there is no change in the fact and reality of your relative existence, only as the old impressions of death and parting linger in thought.

Now, dear brother, dismiss these; they are as unreal as the false sense of sickness and of sin. They do not belong to God or His creations, and you are the master of all 'that worketh or maketh a lie'. You will learn as did Jacob when he said, 'all these things are against me', that they are *for* you, and the footsteps by which God is calling you more absolutely away from the falsities of sense and flesh, into an entire surrender to divine Science; and the imperative call—'leave all for me', 'go work in my vineyard'.

I speak from my own experience of His ways that are not as ours because His love for us so exceeds ours. May His angels soothe and comfort you, for He giveth them charge over you.

Please give much love from me to your dear children, and say to them that all this that seems so severe for us all to bear, is not what it seems; but is working out for the loved one, and for her children, and her teacher, and husband, 'an exceeding weight of glory'.

To a Bereaved Family

In the midst of great rejoicing I hear a sound of loss, of heavy, worldly loss by you who have gained so much of heavenly riches.

My song seemed hushed and my harp hung upon the willow. My tears came and heart cried out, as I thought of what you had before met from demands physical and like Job, disarmed.

Then I said in my heart, wherefore is this done unto my servants, O Lord? Immediately there grew before me a sense of great gain and no loss, and such an absorbing sense, that I grew satisfied and even rejoiced, but I knew not the way our dear God was moving forward this consummate joy. Yet I can trust Him and be still, for God is Love. Now, dear disciples of the man of sorrows and the woman of grief, be of good cheer, for out of such experiences has come all the redemption of the race. And by them we may know that we are the children of Him who marks the sparrow's fall.

Be comforted and strong as I know you are under the rod, for it is and always has been His rod that refines, uplifts and sanctifies the children of men.

We know not why, but shall know hereafter, why He chasteneth those whom He loveth, that they may bear even more fruit.

MISCELLANEOUS ITEMS KNOWN TO BE EXTRACTS FROM LETTERS

Do not address the individuality, but talk to yourself as you would if you had a belief. Say to yourself, such an individual cannot deceive me as to himself and others; has no power over me. I don't believe his lies, and cannot be made to believe them. He cannot frighten me. Evil is powerless, and God is All, etc. Argue that you cannot be made to believe that you cannot protect yourself from his influence.

Mother must give you a lesson on mind of a few sentences. A real Metaphysician knows that Mind is the all and only power and the mental word inaudible more effective as a rule than the audible. Can you shelf this rule and be consistent? Do you heal the sick by physical or audible means? Do you even think, speak, act by reason of matter or mind? Do you declare all this affirmatively in your lectures? Then does right and the demonstration thereof depend on matter or *mind?* If the latter, how are you going to act rightly and cause others to do likewise most efficiently? Is it through mind-power, and how? Orally or the 'still small voice'?

I beg you will demonstrate our God in Science as the Principle that moves men's actions.... *Think* before you act and your thoughts will govern your and other men's lives more than your acts can.

God is perfecting you in His own crucial way. Continue strong in the faith; let not the shortcomings of anyone in your midst dishearten or discourage you, This has been a sad experience of mine, always to be trammelled by the errors before my eyes—if I could not rise above them. You can, I can—and the dear God knows this, or we should not have the test—so rise as to prove that all things work together for good to them that love God (good). Let us then rejoice that Love divine so loveth us as to give the experience which plumes our feeble wing for soaring.

Do not sorrow over your tasks; all things work together for good to them that love God, good. You are now learning how to meet mortal mind in all its false claims; and its evil is less dangerous than its seeming good. You have not nearly as much to meet now as when you cherished (as we all have done) its seeming good that was its greatest evil. Our Master said: fear ye not them that (would) destroy the body but rather them that destroy *both* soul and body—both the moral and physical.

Your premonitions are what will save you if you employ them. The evil always works beforehand on the minds of those in health to fear, or to believe they cannot help those it intends to slay, and if only this preparatory mental malpractice is *understood,* as I now trust it will be by you hereafter, it enables the individual to watch better and to have oil in his lamp, for each experience of this kind is a bridal that weds you to *Life* and Love everlasting.

In Truth all is right; there is no burden; there is no evil; there is no malice, hatred directed against the Truth. Handle this every day. Rise up. Do your work faithfully, and God will give you a sure reward.

The evil is at hand. God is All. Rise in the strength of Spirit to resist all that is unlike good. No one can darken or depress your thought nor take from you a clear consciousness of your Leader and her place, nor can you be made sinful. Argue this clearly every day.

Your last letter to me was cheering to my heart. You spoke of your victory over the past and of your advancing footsteps. I knew not what you had conquered; I only knew that you spake as a victor and I rejoiced with you. God grant that this again may be realized, and that you now are strong in the sense of divine Love that enables you to overcome all temptation and to rejoice in the liberty that conquers self and sense and sits at the feet of Christ, meek, strong, pure, Ask some good brother or sister to help you to overcome the so-called thorns and sins of the flesh, and I think you will see its good effects. Do not submit to the thought that you cannot be rescued from all temptation. You can awake, arise and rejoice in recognizing yourself God's dear child saved by His love.

Please read these two copies of letters, then say should we not forgive errors repented of? Did not Christ forgive even adulterous women? ... Then say whether the past should be dug up and its skeletons be on exhibition, or in the words of our Master observed, 'Let the dead bury the dead'.... If I should be called on to rehearse such dirty stuff, I should refuse to hear it.... Let all the members of my church rest assured that I love them and work and pray for the good of them all. Those who would harm me only injure themselves, and I pray, 'Father, forgive them for they know not what they do'.... Turn all your thoughts into the currents of love and let them flow on to perfect ideals.

Whom the Lord loveth He chasteneth; and afflictions work out for—us an exceeding weight of glory. These are the promises in Scripture. O may they help to comfort you in the greatest of all earthly bereavements. Remember, dear one, that Love, divine Love, guards His own. You are not alone—Love is with you, watching tenderly over you by day and night; and this Love will not leave you, but will sustain you and remember all thy tears and will answer thy prayers. Yes, this Scripture will be fulfilled, 'Thou wilt keep him in perfect peace whose mind is staid on Thee because he trusteth in Thee'. This is my *first* opportunity to write a word that I send with my prayer: Dear God, be very near unto her, bless her, console her, make her to rejoice in the consolation that Thou wilt turn her mourning into joy, and give her great reward for this parting with sublunary support and finding all in Thee.

The churches and the students must be secondary to the example of Jesus and, if he was here personally, to his call upon his students, 'Watch with me'. Had they watched with him one hour or one year and so saved losing him, you can see where the history of Christianity would be today, and how many years it will take to recover that lost opportunity. Demonstration, healing the sick and helping your Leader is needed more than all things else at this date. Unspoken influences are mentally at work to keep you and all my students from doing either of these duties aforenamed.

I cannot answer you as to the morrow. I am God's servant and know not what I shall be bidden to do in the future! If I have to call you back to me, you will haste to come. Let us wait on Him, wait on divine Love that should direct all our ways; and Love saith, take no thought for the morrow; sufficient unto the day is the evil thereof.

The healer in Christian Science carries two lines of thought, first the approximation to the truth, and second, the final truth. He argues for all the manifestations of health of body. At the same time he argues that man is God's own image and likeness. In the words of St. John, '*Now* are we the sons of God'. The healer does not discourage the thought by trying to make that appear first, which is not the beginning but the end of the desired result.

When we all shall have risen above the mentality of envy, jealousy, pride and ambition, no longer will these errors of negation seem anything to us, no seeming power and influence will. be there, the power of Love will reign supreme.

You must remember that now ' is the time to be wise as serpents. The demons of envy and hypnotism and theosophy, M.A.M.—have as subtle and various ways for getting prestige and revenge as the Cubans and Turks, and the mental field of work is at war.

Take hope, dear heart, and be strong, for spiritual strength comes to the fleshly weakness with a benediction and gives power and removes all weakness.

Now, darling, faint not—bear the cross up the *via dolorosa* and the crown of thorns will be laid off for the crown of ineffable light and love. Nobody but yourself can destroy a single belief of yours. It will return until all sin that opens the doors to palpitation of the heart, or any other lie, is destroyed.

There is no conscious or unconscious resisting of treatment or the lesson Truth. The understanding of our lesson Truth cannot be resisted, neither can error be substituted for Truth.

I go out to you in Spirit with one hope and faith—that you are God's child and He encompasses you with light and love, and in this atmosphere you are safe—saved by Divinity from humanity, and by Spirit from the flesh and do rejoice because you have made 'The Lord which is my refuge your habitation'.

Press on; you are in the line of light, thine to realize the glory of strife, Seeking is not sufficient whereby to enter the kingdom of heaven, harmony. I sorrow over the ease of Christian Scientists, They are not at ease in the pains of sense, but are at ease in its pleasures. Which drives out quickest the tenant you wish to get out of your house, the pleasant hours he enjoys in it or its unpleasantness ? I hope the teachers of Christian Science will awake to do their duty towards getting out tenants from case and pleasure in substance and life in matter. I am worn with doing the work alone.

One thing I forgot to name is this: Teach your class that the pleasures of sense material are to be overcome as well as its pains. Hence the Scripture, 'none but the pure in heart can see God'. The sexual element is not *natural*, if nature is God, and it certainly *is God*, for matter is not God, and material sense has no law and no gospel on its side. Even eating is a 'suffer it to be so now'. Sometimes we shall all learn this. Let us begin now to learn it, and to teach it, and to practise it.

We are looking towards the light and cannot help knowing that our lives talk for us and their testimony is a rebuke or an encouragement to us all. When the heart, tired of its poor testimony, turns to the head and listens, it hears the way told in this desire: 'Oh, to be nothing, nothing.' But this is not enough; so the heart answers 'Yes, but Oh! to be something, something tangibly good; Oh! to see my affections changed, detached and attached in the right direction, and being as it is, and no longer as it is not.'

What joy is ours in Christian Science! Infinite Love all our own, tireless Love watching our waiting, pointing the path, guiding our footsteps and turning them hither and thither as wisdom directs—

then when the lesson is learned, supplying the need and ending the warfare.

Do we not all understand cowardice never conquers? To get rid of temptation of any sort or to get out of a difficulty, we are not passive and let the wrong rule the right, but we struggle and thus conquer. We should not avoid the things that hurt us, but repeat them and meet them as their superior. Disease is a coward that leaves when you are not afraid of it.

(1884) Love is a mighty spiritual force,

(1887) Let the good you *can do* and the stimulation of action keep your mind from dwelling on the past, for the present demands your care, and you must go forth to meet the future calm and strong. God is your refuge and a strong deliverer. He will hide you under His wings till the storms are past and the sunlight of His presence cheers and invigorates you with new strength and exaltation.

(10/11/91) Your tender night vision and thoughts by day are indications of pure desires to be clothed in white robes.

'And not a sparrow falleth' without due observation. Your desire to be Christly will be satisfied, not in its fullest, but in its meekest want.

Yes, He who clothes the lilies will tend you and gird you with strength in Truth and Love, and so establish the labor of your hands in His vineyard. Never distrust, never doubt the All-Love, for it never faileth. As your day, so shall your strength be. Be patient, and let faith grow, stronger and stronger each day of this pilgrimage.

(3/19/00) Goodness such as yours is a sure pretext of success in all struggles to be 'better'. If a single sin remains—and who is destitute of all sin?—be of good cheer, for the victory over it is a foregone conclusion. If a supposed sensation exists that God, good, is displeased with, it must yield and neither fear nor abnormal conditions can hold it. Your good heart is the victor over it and *now* and forever you know this is truth and the Truth has made you *free.* You are liberated by divine Love from every false claim of the flesh. The law of Spirit is supreme; it dominates the flesh and you are God's own child. *Never* born of the flesh nor subject to it. Here plant your understanding and having done your part, *stand,* and God will provide for the temptation strength to overcome it.

(11/26/03) Our Cause demands *better healers;* and if less teaching classes is enjoined, more practitioners will be fitted by the book to heal. I see the need of a healer to be as excluded from other work in C.S. as for the M.D. Who would look for a successful M.D. who was a lawyer or that was a teacher by profession and practising teaching? A Jack at all trades is good for none is an old adage. I am sorely disappointed in the demonstration of C.S. and it must improve or our Cause will float into theory and we will not 'show our faith by our work'. A chatterer of C.S. is never a healer.

CHAPTER SIX

ARTICLES BY MRS. EDDY, OR POINTS FROM ARTICLES

From 'Science and Health', First Edition

The dead to personal sense are alive to Soul, and preserve all the prerogatives of being, but because personal sense buries their bodies it loses sight of this fact, showing virtually we are separated, and they no longer in sympathy with us, for there is no conscious change to themselves; hence we lose sight of each other. (p. 96)

From 'Science and Health', Second Edition

(1878) Penal law must meet the hour when he who hates his neighbor, will have no need to enter his door, to destroy his peace and prosperity, to harm his health, or to demoralize his household; for the evil mind will do this through mesmerism; and not *in propria persona* be seen committing the deed. This 'irresistible conflict' awaits us, and must be met first by law, and next by *Science,* or mesmerism that scourge of man, will leave nothing sacred as mind becomes conscious of its latent powers. The mesmeric power will attempt to gloat revenge, malice, avarice, etc., but it will rebound on itself, and send the perpetrator of the foulest crimes to 'his own place'; while metaphysical science shall pour blessings on all. (Vol. 11, p. 63)

From 'Science and Health', Third Edition

(188 1) The crimes committed mentally are drifting the age towards self-defence; we hope the method it adopts will be more humane than in periods past. The re-establishment of the Christian era, or the mediaeval period of metaphysics, will be one of moderation and peace; but the reinauguration of this period will be met with demonology, or the unlicensed cruelty of mortal mind, that will compel mankind to learn metaphysics for a refuge and defence. Then shall be fulfilled the Scripture, 'The wrath of man shall praise Thee, and the remainder thereof Thou shalt restrain'. (Vol. 11, p. 45)

(The following statement from Mrs. Eddy has also been recorded by a student: When the ability of Mind to detect what mind is doing becomes general, it will be all that is required for self-protection. After this manner the mental mediaeval age that has to conflict with this demonology will find its remedy and can deprive it of all power.)

From 'Journal', Vol. 111, p. 124

(1885) Afraid? Afraid of what? What does earth hold that can compare with God's omnipotence? Trust to His care; make faith in Him your staff—it will not bend. (Unsigned—attributed to Mrs. Eddy)

From 'Journal', Vol. IV, p. 60—Death-Change

(1886) In no subject is there more interest than in the future life, and religious believers and leaders are often asked about it. One inquirer phrased her question in this way:

> After the change called Death takes place, do we meet our friends who have gone before, or does Life continue in thought only, as in a dream?

Man is not annihilated, nor does he lose his identity by passing through the belief called Death. After this momentary belief passes from the erring mortal mind, man finds himself still in a conscious state of existence. He learns that he has but passed through an extreme moment of mortal fear, to awake with thoughts and being as material as before. Mental spiritualization is not attained by physical death, but by a conscious union with God. When we are on the same plane of conscious existence with those gone before, we shall be able to communicate with them and recognize them. When we have done our work here so well that it needs not to be done over again, the death-change increases all our joys and our means of advancement.

> (Although both the following items are signed by Josephine Woodbury, an 'open letter' in the very next issue of the *Journal* August 1886—confesses that the 'words and sentiments' therein were in no sense Mrs. Woodbury's, but Mrs. Eddy's.)

From 'Journal', Vol. IV, p. 95—Summer Communion Service

The communion can come only by regeneration, by the baptism of Spirit, as taught through Christian Science. This baptism with fire brings out the true odor of divinity, establishing the omnipresence of God, imparted to man in healing the sick by salvation from sin, and triumphing over a sense of dead and buried understanding, and revealing the Comforter which leadeth into peace. This it is to eat the bread. What is the Bread of Christian Science ? It is the strength and nutriment that God gives to the fainting heart and faltering footsteps, in the awful hours of human helplessness; yea! that power He imparts, by which we gain a recognition of Himself—that recognition which is never grasped by intellect, but by the humble heart. What is the Cup of Christian Science? It is that cup which is drank in affliction. It is the exhilaration of joy, after the triumph over temptation. It is the fruit of that vine of which the Father is the husbandsman. It is that wine-press whose seeds of sin must be crushed, and which the weary feet may not leave till each seed is in itself crushed—that out of this essence God shall distil a new creature, which shall bear witness of Himself as the Love which heals. We are bidden, as members of this church, to partake of the silent sacrament, to come to this table of His preparing with thanksgiving. To us is spoken the command, 'My child, give me thy heart'; while it is ours to answer:

Search me, oh God, and know my heart;
Try me and know my thoughts;
And see if there be any wicked way in me.

We are called to lay ourselves daily, hourly, upon the altar of self-sacrifice, of utter dependence upon God, glorying in each awful trial, rejoicing in each draught from that cup which fits us to become participants with Jesus of his martyrdom and victory. This power is given us in the same extent as we entertain the sense of the Spirit which enriched him, and we come into the fulness of demonstration as we have the same Mind which was in Christ Jesus.

Ibid., p. 97— Christian Scientist Association

This Association has great reason for congratulating itself that in the many upheavals of the last year it has rid itself of some of the mere lookers-on and drones in its busy hive of workers; while the new members, coming in such large numbers, are permeated with the desire to work—to put a steady shoulder to the wheel of progress, and keep it moving onward. Every tidal wave which sweeps over this Association purges it. It brings from the depths of mortal sense some hidden growths, washes them upon the shore, and leaves them bleaching and perishing upon the sands of time; while the great sea of thought, whose constant motion is a type of its constant power, is left clearer than before.

In this Association, laziness, lukewarmness, and vice are out of their sphere. Its atmosphere, growing purer with years, is not a comfortable inspiration to any but the lovers and correct followers of Truth. What a mighty bulwark of strength does this unity of hearts prophesy for the future!

The Seed, said to have been an article of Mrs. Eddy's recorded by Frank Mason

(Probably about 1887) For habits of whatsoever nature, destroy the (supposed) pleasure therein and you will win. Pain is but a continuity of supposed pleasure. If the hand itches, it is a pleasure to scratch it; but if this same pleasure is continued, it becomes pain. This is true of all pleasure from the physical standpoint.

Take this thought and carry it with you. God is Spirit. I am His child, made in His image and likeness. Jesus' teachings will restore to me that which I seem to have lost—the likeness of my Father.

The instantaneous realization that man is the perfect expression of the infinite would result in instantaneous heating. This is a mature, harmonious thought, and brings forth fruit after its kind. Our patients manifest health after, and in proportion to our consciousness of perfection. 'If I be lifted up', lifts itself above matter. The body is but the garment of thought and portrays the condition of mind.

The sense of dominion is the only begotten son of the Father. Allow nothing to come between you and God. Jesus recognized nothing between himself and God.

Think deeply for yourself. Muse on the allness of Spirit until it becomes a consciousness of perfection and harmony which will be manifested openly to the world.

Know that you have the supremacy of thought, and that error cannot defy the Truth, and you will win. Realize that evil possesses no power over you or your patient, and that it cannot make either of you conscious of fear. To be born into the belief of matter is the last enemy to be overcome—death—physical life. Mankind has reached the last enemy and knows it not. The divine overpowers the human and finally vanquishes it.

Put your patients in the ark into which God commanded Noah and his family to enter; that is, hold them in thought as conditions of Mind reflecting and expressing only the attributes of the infinite. Realize that they exist in Mind, and that mortal thought cannot find them, being unable to transcend itself. Having done this, 'pitch the ark within and without', that is, seal up every crevice by which the erroneous thought of worldliness can enter. Realize that God is the only thinker, and that man reflects His thoughts and can transmit only what he receives from God. Holding your patients thus, you lift them above the clouds of worldliness and, like the ark, they will always be on top of the waves above the destructive floods.

Every spiritual baptism is followed by stronger temptations. That is, each higher manifestation of Truth uncovers its supposititious opposite to be met and destroyed. Thus we rise step by step until we finally reach a condition which has no erroneous phenomenal expression. This moment must be the ascension when the senses can no longer manifest nor cognize us, we having overcome their claims. Immediately following Jesus' spiritual baptism, he was led into the wilderness to be tempted. His higher baptism drove error to a higher and more subtle temptation.

Every claim of materiality has a twofold expression and must be conquered with Truth. The first is the manifestation described in Jesus' temptation as the stones beneath his feet which Satan sought to make Jesus turn into bread. The second is the temptation which transcends the first suggestion, and which met him on the pinnacle of the temple. In these two manifestations we see the twofold power of each temptation one must meet, the lower and the higher, the physical and the mental. In other words, every manifestation of evil discerned in physical phenomenon will recur in a higher and wholly mental sense ere it is dissipated. Because of the universal belief in the existence of both mind and matter, in the present phase of existence error will manifest itself through both classes of phenomena.

Popery now openly discernible in Catholicism will be repeated in alcoholism, and similar physical manifestations must be met on the pinnacle as well as below. If we can conquer the visible physical embodiment of error, we will be endowed because of this victory with power to meet it in the higher manifestation.

Watch and strive against the senses, where you meet every class of temptation.

Poverty is just as much a disease as cancer. Jesus says, 'Seek ye first the kingdom of God ... and all these things shall be added unto you'. He did not say they were a part of the divine whole, but that they would be added. Our conceptions being yet material, the reward must come to our present consciousness. A realization of a perfect spiritual home will make our present home better. A consciousness of the purity of heavenly surroundings will bring out a more harmonious earthly existence.

We tend too much towards the physical and this tendency produces discord. Jesus said, 'Take no thought for your body'. Do not let error tell you that you are not a good loyal Christian Scientist because you are not rich. The heavenward path is only won by struggling, but you will win if you faint not. If the senses lie about this life, they also lie about death.

Electricity is the thought essence which forms the link between what is matter and mortal mind. God, the divine Mind, self-existent, self-perpetuating, and self-energizing, is the great universal reservoir, or dynamo, and the thoughts which flow from such fountains, constituting a complete expression of that infinite Mind, Spirit, are thus shown to be inseparably linked with the Principle of Life and action and to be the manifestation of spiritual force or power. All of us as individual thoughts proceeding from one central source must be communicators in some way of the flow of the divine Mind, and should recognize in each other a oneness proceeding from the unity in that source Blurred and clogged by material sense we oftentimes lose sight of our connection with the power we are to express, and in a vain attempt to externalize ourselves as an independent life, apart from God, we fail to be about our Father's business, and are thus temporarily defrauded of our birthright, for we find, if we neglect to live up to the light we have, according to the scientific law of operation, we lose our power proportionately, for that which obstructs, self-deception, pride, whatever it may be, is accumulating until removed.

Death is an illusion. It is the termination of the universal lie which declares that man was born. No person will ever be more conscious of death than he is of birth. Everything that has a beginning must of necessity have an ending. Death is not in the victim whom we say has died, but in us. It is we who are still alive—as we term it—who dig the graves. It is we who put our friends into the ground and cover them up, and forever after declare they are gone. All these phenomena are in us, not in them. Death is the culmination of the thought of physical life. In life we are in death. Our verdict of death upon our friends does not change them one iota. Jesus was the same after apparent death and burial as before. Again I say, no one will ever be conscious of death. It is absolutely nothing, and it is impossible to become conscious of nothing.

Man is a co-existent creature with his creator. He, man, has always existed, and if none of us have been conscious of death up to the present minute, it is pretty good evidence that we never will be conscious of it. The person who says, 'I am dying', is but a helpless automaton, who has unwittingly become a victim of preconceived opinions, and voices the culmination of error. If the senses lie about life, they certainly lie about death.

We lose the conscious presence of our friends by a change of belief. A stronger belief in the verdict of the world than in the presence of our friends, wipes out their presence and leaves in its place the lost belief. We still exist to them unless they otherwise accept, instead of our presence, some other belief similarly destroying their conception of us. The disciples were the same to Jesus after his apparent death as before. We exist (as matter) in each others' minds and all we know of our friends is the mortal conception of them. This concept remains until we transpose it with another, when the last becomes the dominant belief.

There is nothing gained by waiting for death, for it never comes. We must individually lift ourselves above the claims of the senses. Death brings no relief. 'He that is filthy, let him be filthy still, and he that is righteous, let him be righteous still.' 'As a tree falleth so it shall lie', substantiates this conclusion. Man still continues to live in a physical belief until he overcomes it. Death does not rid him of it, for death is a mode of matter, and does not advance mind. This is the point to be borne in mind, that, from every Eden we create in materiality, we shall be banished. The condition we call satisfactory from a material standpoint is a delusion of human sense and from it we must be exiled, 'for to be carnally minded is death'.

To successfully treat children, cut off the parent thought. Mali is the offspring of God, not man. The material birth is but the false conception. Realize that matter cannot transmit good or evil. It is inert, unintelligent, and cannot be the medium of intelligence. Seedless oranges are produced by turning the top of the parent plant back to earth, and when rooted disconnecting it. The offspring produces seedless oranges. Detach the thought of the child from the parent and the germs of erroneous seed of the parent thought will cease to impress the child.

From 'Journal', Vol. V, p. 55 — Voices of Spring[1]

(1887) What should be the voices of Spring in the human heart? Resurrected and purified desires; praise, for man's ability to seek and find the Kingdom of Heaven here—the reign of harmony that furnishes glimpses of the great Source whence cometh all earth's beautiful hieroglyphics of Love; joy, that human character may be stately as the cedars of Lebanon, and Truth thrive like the willows by the water-courses; humility, bowing down before His goodness, and peering through Mortal mind; industry, arranging with beauty each

[1]This article by Mrs. Eddy is much more changed than most of those gathered into *Miscellaneous Writings*. In the version in *Mis.* 329:32, the latter half does not appear in the *Journal* at all, and the first half is much altered, particularly the three paragraphs on p. 330, for which the equivalent in the *Journal* is as given here.

budding thought as it puts forth new glories; higher aspirations and purer pleasures, which give spiritual energy and power to work for man and in obedience to God.

Has the Springtide brought this harvest to the human heart, putting on costly wardrobes, gained in seasons of toil, defeat, and triumph? Are Christian Scientists as faithful as the seasons, birds and flowers? Do they challenge mankind as sweetly to flock to the Springtide of God's omnipotence—His power to heal and save? Will they sing in the storm? If buds of hope disclose scarcely one blossom, and birds are silent, will they yet wait and work, till the latent elements of harmonious being control earth's cold and heat, sunshine and shadow, and the heart's seedling and germ spring into freedom and greatness?

From 'No and Yes', First Edition

(1887) Does the stupid ostrich protect his life by hiding his head from the hunter? Does yielding your purse to a robber prevent his making another demand on your treasures or your life? Becoming the servant of a hard master, whose tender mercies are cruel, will not save you from his lash. Conscious obedience to the open or secret demands of evil minds, ensures moral and physical death. Ignorant submission to these evil though inaudible demands is sure doom. Your eyes must be opened, that you may see and feel this hidden influence; for if you only understood its cause you would besiege it with Science, until you compelled the city of evil to capitulate, and so saved yourself. Science is more exacting than sense; it abates not one demand. All possible progress in Christian Science is sacrificed by him who yields to the influence of animal magnetism. Knowing this, the envious mental malpractitioner, intent on reducing you to his standard, sends to you, mentally, his demoralizing arguments; but at the same moment he whispers into your thought: '*I* am not influencing you; it is such and such a one.'

From 'Journal', Vol. VI, p. 48—Comment on *Creed of the New Theology* expounded by Rev. J. G. Townsend

(1888) While this Creed lacks the steadfastness and power that understanding imparts, its intent is good, and it has, as you can see, borrowed largely ideas, without credit, from my work, *Science and Health.* A creed loosely adopted must fail signally as a basis of demonstrable Truth. Religion, separated from Science, is shockingly helpless. Science is not tentative. We may receive it on trial; but ours is the fault if it be not adopted, for it compels every human faculty to act in God's grooves. Science is a finality, or else there is no finality. My sympathy goes out to the subscribers to that creed, and returns to rest in Christian Science—much as the dove flew from the Ark in the Deluge.

From 'Journal', Vol. VI, p. 559—Malicious Animal Magnetism

(1889) One of the greatest crimes practiced in, or known to, the ages, is mental assassination. A mind liberated from the beliefs of sense, to do good, by perverting its power becomes warped into the lines of evil without let or hindrance. A mind taught its power to touch other minds by the transference of thought, for the ends of restoration from sickness, or—grandest of all, the reformation and almost transformation, into the living image and likeness of God—this mind by misusing its freedom reaches the degree of total moral depravity.

Does the community know this criminal? He sits at the friendly board and fireside; he goes to their places *of* worship; he takes his victim by the hand, and all the time claims the power and carries the will to stab to the heart, to take character and life from this friend who gives him his hand in full trust, and has perhaps toiled and suffered to benefit and bless him.

What are some of the methods of this evil, this satan let loose? What are some of the means through which these mental assassins effect their purposes? To alienate friends, to divide households, to make people sick and sinners; these are their common instrumentalities.

Their methods of operation are to infuse silently into the thoughts of those they wish to use as instruments, a false sense of the individual selected as their victim. Long acquaintance, tried fidelity, experiences that have knit hearts together, all become as nothing before these endeavors. The mind of the individual on whom they thus operate is filled with hatred of the dearest friend, is made incapable of a just judgment of this friend. Prior knowledge of him seems to be obscured, put out, annihilated, and a new image of thought to be created—one idea of individual character to be lost and another one formed, in the mind of him whom they would cause to hate his friend.

In this dilemma of thought, they get the audible falsehood into his mind, tell him how his friend has slandered him, is trying to injure him. If he is a Scientist they then say to him, 'Mr. Smith', or 'Mrs. Jones is preventing your success in healing patients, or is making your family sick, and the only way you can meet this is to take the case up, and to treat your patients against Mrs. Jones' mental malpractice; if you can destroy your patients' fear of Mrs. Jones, or can choke her off by any means however foul, you are conscientiously bound to do it, and of two evils this is choosing the least'. There may be a hundred or more operators all set at work at this very job, to kill Mrs. Jones, or to save their patients or themselves, according as the directing malevolence may dictate. The said Jones is all the while as unconscious of this conspiracy as the unborn babe. The mental assassins are morally responsible for the consequences, and God alone can save her life from the fatal effects of this malice aforethought of the first party, and the culpable blindness of the second, whom they have misguided.

When the work of the mental assassin culminates, and the victim falls, the doctors are consulted and call it heart disease or some other 'visitation of God', and thus they try to carry the age along on their deceptions.

This criminal practice, this 'wickedness in high places', has accumulated in subtilty of method until it culminates at this period in 'spiritual wickedness' and poses its power to do evil against the spiritual power in Christian Science to demonstrate good. When first denounced by me 'from the housetops', in SCIENCE AND HEALTH thirteen years ago, the revelation was received with incredulity, with derision, with pity. Today Scientists are learning, and the general public is experiencing more and more, the terrible realities of mental malpractice and assassination.

It is no longer possible to keep still concerning these things—nay, it is criminal to hold silence and to cover crime that grows bolder and picks off its victims as sharpshooters pick off the officers of an attacking force.

These secret, heaven-defying enormities *must* be proclaimed, or we become guilty before God as accessory after the fact. If a friend were fallen upon and maltreated or murdered before our eyes, should we hold ourselves guiltless—should we count ourselves men and women—if we buried the secret of the violence and our knowledge of the assassins ?

Are we such cowards, knowing the facts that we do know, as to turn and run? Shall we see the evil, the deadly danger that threatens our brother and to hide ourselves, flee away not warning him?

The Science of mind uncovers to Scientists secret sin, even more distinctly than so-called physical crimes are visible to the personal senses; crime is always veiled in obscurity, but Science fastens guilt upon its author through mind, with the certainty and directness of the eye of God himself.

Human laws will eventually be framed for these criminals that now go unwhipped of human justice. Human law even now recognizes crime as mental, for it seeks always the motive; rude counterfeit as it is of Divine Justice, it metes out punishment or pardons, according as it finds or finds not the evil intent, the mental element. The time has come for instructing human justice so that these secret criminals shall tremble before the omnipotent finger that points them out to the human executioner.

This is not an invitation to promiscuous denunciation. The time is not ripe for that, but God tells us now to uncover this wickedness, to expose its methods, to accumulate the evidence of its enormities. The human mind must be instructed by facts, taught how to recognize the signs of these secret crimes as they are worked on individuals, and also the method of self-protection, the antidotes found only in Divine Science.

God has bidden me to uncover this wickedness, and I follow His voice, Let all Scientists aid in this work, first, by bringing out in their reports on the practice of healing, careful statements of the facts of malicious animal magnetism that are daily passing before their eyes. I am not inviting them to indiscriminating condemnation, but to bring out such facts as have come within their own field of observation.

I have put on paper enough to reveal criminal magnetism, and to meet its developments for time to come, when my voice will be no longer heard. But God does not let us wait. He tells us to denounce now, some of the crimes of malicious mind, and to teach as fully as the age can bear and as the developments of this crime demand, its methods and their unfailing antidote.

I will now answer some questions that correspondents have asked me, concerning my teaching of and ways of dealing with, malicious animal magnetism.

One correspondent asks, 'Do I teach the same with regard to mesmerism to all my students?

My answer is, I do, in substance the same; the manner of expressing my thoughts may vary, but never the idea. Every student who has been through my class understands fully how to handle the ignorant animal magnetism., termed sickness, and latterly, I have taught as fully as God has allowed, how to deal with the malicious element. He tells me now to meet its growing wickedness by fuller revelations.

'Do I approve of treating personally for malicious mesmerism the offending malpractitioner, even when the malpractitioner is attempting to kill some one, and Scientists know it? Shall they treat the offender personally?'

I answer, if they do treat thus, they prolong their own undertaking. The altitude of Christian Science is Omnipotence. Truth is given us for this purpose—to destroy error and make man free in the impersonal Christ.

'Do I employ students to do the work I have not the time to do? in other words, in trying to injure fellow beings.

I could commit suicide sooner than do that; I have laid upon the altar too much for my fellow mortals, to undo my life work, and now turn to injure them. The very misguided ones, the deluded ones who would constrain others to believe this for my hurt, know better. These deceivers are under a demoniacal spell. May God open their eyes and save them from future condemnation.

From 'Journal', Vol. VII, p. 38, in reply to the question, 'Why do you approve of surgery?

(1889) Why do I approve of surgery? I did not know that I did, except as a choice of evils. If my students cannot through the power of Mind put into juxtaposition a broken bone, then they must do the next best thing.

How is a joint dislocated? Through mind. Then mind can put it back. We prove the rule of Mind-healing mathematically. Four times five are twenty and five times four are twenty.

From 'Journal', Vol. IX, p. 1—*Science and Health', Fiftieth Edition, Revised*[2]

(189 1) The long-looked-for, much-coveted volume of SCIENCE AND HEALTH, that is to mark an epoch in the Christian Science movement, has at last appeared; and will be eagerly searched, studied, pored over, by every student among us. From this date forward, the thought of all true Scientists will mount higher, and there will appear correspondingly glorious results in the wide and practical field of demonstration; yet, a full understanding of the book will come only as the ripened fruit of years of study *combined with faithful, daily effort to reduce its teachings to practice.* No adequate idea of the treasures disclosed in this volume can be given in a single article, but a few points out of many will here be touched upon.

First: Why is a revised edition of SCIENCE AND HEALTH a necessity? Does not the issuing of a 'revision' reflect upon former editions, as being faulty or incomplete? The present writer was queried only last summer upon this very point. One antagonizer of SCIENCE AND HEALTH,

[2] Although this article implies in the text that it is the work of a male student, it is nevertheless credited to Mrs. Eddy in the table of contents, and again, somewhat ambiguously, at the heading. But whoever put it in words, there *is* little doubt that the article's inspiration stemmed from Mrs. Eddy.

having heard that anew volume was anticipated—in fact was to be in press ere long—asked in tones suggestive of a sneer: 'Can inspiration be added to or taken from? Who for an instant would think of adding to or subtracting from the sayings of Jesus? And did Paul or John ever think of getting out a "revised edition" of their works? To all of which was added the statement: 'The early edition, that of 1875, was incomparably superior to any that has since appeared.'

The precise reply made is of little moment; but its substance is eminently germane to our present line of thought, *viz:* Inspiration is not a mechanical process of repeating mere words by rote, of rounding them up in just so many sentences and no more. It is not a lifeless force which can be caught and imprisoned in a word or a volume—as a taxidermist would stuff birds, always to present the same stiff, glassy appearance. It is, rather, the kaleidoscopic presentation of the beauty and wondrous power—not of some new truth heretofore unheard of—but of an eternally existing, spiritual Fact unfolding and forever re-unfolding itself to 'eyes that see'. Were Paul, John, or Jesus to return again in the flesh to teach us the same glorious Truth taught in the long buried past, would either one confine himself to the same words, the same figures of speech, the same illustrations so well known to Bible students of today? Rather would not each address himself faithfully to the task of clearing up difficulties, of removing doubts as to his precise meaning in certain passages and upon certain points that as yet seem obscure to our sense? A teacher of grammar even—one who, year in and year out, is teaching class after class the same grammatical truths or facts cannot, and does not, invariably repeat the same stereotyped expressions. Just in proportion as he combines the essentials of a teacher, in proportion as he embodies the *essence of true* teaching, will his illustrations and combinations of facts be accommodated to the needs of the learner, and attended with fresh impulses of discernment. In the days of the Massachusetts Metaphysical College, when we sat at the feet of our teacher—days that we never shall I forget!—did that teacher ever instruct two classes precisely alike? Did she employ a stereotyped form of words by which to convey to us her rich, inspired thought? Far from it! and thus, the new volume seems to take us back to the College, to gather up its fresh methods and inspired sayings, so that little stretch of the imagination is required to convince us that the teacher herself again is before us, though this time in impersonal form.

But the book itself: Is there anything new in it, does it contain any new facts and truths ? No, and yes, Certainly there are no new facts or truths presented, because there are no new facts or truths to present. Truth is never new, and never old; but is eternally fresh and living, as the author herself explains. In this sense, could there be anything new in the new book—for was it not the Truth, and the Truth only, which was told before? Her revision has, however, extended the same ideas, and made them clear; so that SCIENCE AND HEALTH shall not be misunderstood and misstated. To find in the new volume some new, grand, hitherto-unexpressed Truth, would of itself impugn the old. The student of the new, will find the landmarks of the old all untouched. God—as Spirit, omniscient, omnipresent, omnipotent, All-in-all—is taught here. Man—as made in His image and likeness—still retains his place here. Creation—as a spiritual, eternal, glorious fact from centre to remotest circumference—also appears here. The Scientific Statement of Being, unchanged by so much as a letter, is here. Evil, 'mortal mind' in the new edition, appears just as base and treacherous a liar as in the old.

All this, and more in the same vein, can be said; and yet, there is a sense in which do appear many new things. Many faces and angles never before seen are here presented to view; fresh modes or ways of bringing out practical facts are adopted, as for instance: on pages 360 to 366 inclusive, again, throughout almost the entire Chapter on 'Teaching Christian Science' (*Chap. XIII*). Also, the opening pages of Genesis, and of the Apocalypse are studded with new thoughts. Nor are these the only pages whereon gleam gems not seen before; these are simply cited as conspicuous examples of interest to all readers, present or prospective, of the fiftieth edition of SCIENCE AND HEALTH —as indicating the presence of new veins of gold which appear therein. The simple fact is, the thought of Scientists, all along the line, has mounted higher; and so treasures both new and old are given to us. Our teacher has complimented us. We can now be taken higher up toward the mountain top, until 'we all with unveiled face reflecting as a mirror the glory of the Lord, are transformed into the same image from glory to glory, even as from the Lord the Spirit'.

In regard to logical arrangement: The division of chapters is a marked improvement upon that of former editions. The chapter on Healing and Teaching has become two separate chapters, as it manifestly should; while Prayer and Atonement also, for the first time appear under separate caption. Imposition and Demonstration will hereafter be studied as Christian Science contrasted with Spiritualism; the logical arrangement being entirely subserved thereby. Many will miss the Platform of Christian Science as a distinct chapter, but it will be found at the close of the long chapter on Science of Being, where it properly belongs. The chapter on Marriage has been shortened; but, since the advanced Christian Science thought is preparing for it, the detached portions have been transferred elsewhere in a form which gives them added power. The contents of pages 411, 412, 446, 447, should be studied carefully. The chapter on Animal Magnetism also stands abridged; yet the missing thoughts reappear elsewhere in hints and suggestions whose practical value renders them of vital interest to all readers and students. Critical attention is called to the first chapter in the book, entitled Science, Theology, Medicine; especially to the ninth page, where the classification is not only scientific, but of such orderly arrangement as greatly to aid the learner's memory.

Again: Every student familiar with former editions will remark upon the change made at the heading of chapters, *viz*: the substitution of Scripture texts for quotations from classic authors; which better adapts the Work to maintain the place it holds in sacred writings. The marginal side-heads occurring throughout the volume, merit a special word of praise; ably aiding, as they do, the search for passages to which speedy reference is desired. By means of these, the eye quickly detects the page-topics, without the expense of time required to hunt laboriously through the body-text. Moreover those who have found the Index of previous editions inadequate to meet all requirements, will be rejoiced by the copious Topical Index of the Fiftieth Edition. Herein is made, not only ample reference, but double and even treble reference to the same passage, under separate headings; by which is greatly enhanced the value of an Index to a Work of this profound character.

There is here neither time nor space to compare citations, nor is it necessary to do so; since every earnest student will do this for himself, individually: moreover, such a citation would be in direct violation of our Teacher's repeatedly expressed wishes and instructions, embodied in Editor's Note Book of the JOURNAL for January last. It cannot escape notice of the student, however, that a great transformation of passages has taken place; so that a system of paging will not serve, as heretofore, for a guide to preceding editions. Forty pages of new matter are added, and yet this is far from an adequate statement; since throughout the entire volume there is scarcely a page that does not bear traces of the fresh touch of the master-hand of the author. Though favorite paragraphs and expressions reappear, they have nearly all been retouched, until they glisten like burnished gold.

'Is not the new SCIENCE AND HEALTH intended to be the teacher for the future, thus to do away with incorrect teaching, and the oral instruction of human teachers? Again: 'Is it chiefly designed for Primary, or better fitted for Normal and Obstetric students? These are questions constantly being asked; questions that are perhaps natural, and yet, if the writer mistake not, they are idle questions also. The Work is intended for all ages, grades and classes; for the child just beginning to prattle, and for the aged grandsire; for the novitiate just entering upon the study of Christian Science, and for the student who has made, as human language expresses it, the greatest advance. Without wishing to establish any *dictum*, the writer cannot refrain from giving expression to his conviction that this volume gradually *will* supersede all teaching, in the technical sense of the word; and further, that it will prove great gain for the Cause of Truth when that day arrives. Attention is specially called to what is said on page 440, in the paragraph beginning with line nine—in fact, this entire chapter merits profoundest attention.

While, as before stated, this volume is for all grades and classes, it is but pertinent to say that the most conscientious, painstaking and experienced student will advance fastest. There can be no imperative law laid down regarding John's Gospel, Paul to the Hebrews, or Revelation, to the effect that these are only for advanced Christians to study. Certainly they are for all learners—no hedges are put around them to keep any away; yet, who does not know that the experienced miner will more readily and directly delve to those subterranean depths containing the precious veins of gold! So it will be with the new volume; and we shall very soon come to realize that we have in hand a golden key with which to unlock the Treasure-house of the Bible. The author expresses it as 'treasures of Truth first thrown by revelation into her grasp, and now adjusted to be more readily seen'.

In closing, a few general observations are worthy a place.

1st. Every careful student will discover that the new volume is pre-eminently a book of the Spirit. This is not to intimate a lack in the letter; but, to claim that the conscientious student of the new SCIENCE AND HEALTH cannot long remain in the letter merely. He will be taken out of that into the unfolding glories of Truth. Especially will he be led to a realization that, to be a genuine Christian Scientist, Love must become the sole law of his being—its beginning and end. The letter is all expressed—otherwise the book could not be what it should be—but it does not appear as a skeletonized system of abstract doctrine. It is clothed in radiant grace and loveliness which cause us to forget its presence as mere letter—and, indeed, is it not *time* we turned our attention higher! In truth, the evangelistic spirit of this new SCIENCE AND HEALTH is its crowning merit. Christian

Science becomes something for practical every-day life; thus, more and more will it be recognized as being—not a mere theory—but a life of individual goodness and Truth.

2d. This new volume continues to be a rebuke to the personal senses and, as such, will prove no more acceptable to the sensualist than have former editions; in fact, it must prove less so, since it takes us upon higher ground. Hence, if any have been anticipating a treatise that should prove a bridge between the seen and the Unseen, between sense and Soul, which would render Christian Science more concordant with the testimony of material sense, or its exactments less severe, they are doomed to disappointment. Christian Science in the new volume explains nothing to carnal or mortal mind to gratify its curiosity, or to render easier a compliance with its mandates: instead, the book will be found to be arrayed against all error, and it will not be surprising if even in us many errors that hitherto have been smouldering are now, by its perusal, aroused to hostility. 'Search me, O God, and know my heart, try me, and know my thoughts', is a sentiment which will find practical exemplification in the mind of many of us on rising from study of the new Work.

3d. The new SCIENCE AND HEALTH will prove, to many, an invitation to the wedding feast. 'Write, blessed are they who are called to the marriage supper of the Lamb.' Happy, indeed, are they who having on the wedding garment come—and come as to a feast spread for all; a feast where Understanding, Truth, Joy, and Love nourish and sustain our fainting senses.

4th. A practical suggestion or two regarding study of the new edition: In the first place, *do not attempt to dispose of the earlier editions.* Some are asking, 'Can we be permitted to exchange?' Probably not; but you do not want to do so, even if you can. Fortunate is he who has all former revisions, together with the original edition of 1875! They are indicators of successive stages of growth in Christian Science; and as such, at some future day will not only possess historic value, but will be exceedingly difficult to procure. Keep them all; they will prove a *'treasure trove'.* Again: Let the new volume be studied *in connection with earlier editions.* The very contrasts help to see how the thoughts have risen only as we have been able to receive them. This, again, will reveal why the new edition could now be written for us. It is simply because the advancing thought, or demonstration, of Christian Students has ascended to that plane which makes it both possible and practicable for us to have the new Work.

From 'Retrospection and Introspection', First Edition (chapter entitled The Chief Delusion)

(1891) Animal magnetism is the opposite of Christian Science in effects upon the senses: in pleasure and pain, passion and appetite, pride and envy, malice and hate; is readily removed by Christian Science if the cause of the effect is understood.

From Address to World's Parliament of Religions (recorded by Valeria Campbell in *Sentinel,* Vol. XIII, p. 71)

(1893) As we gain the evidence in Science that man in God's image is the only real man, the evidence before the senses of man's deflection disappears, and proportionately as the fact appears to the consciousness of the mental healer, that man has his being in God, good, the reflection of this thought will restore the sick, reform the sinner, and, carried to its ultimate, as Jesus did carry it, must destroy the last enemy, called death.

Day

(July 24, 1900) It is unnecessary to go anywhere or change anything to find the glories of God. We need only open our eyes to spiritual reality; to the omnipresence of God, good, which is always available to us.

For every material sacrifice there is a spiritual blessing. Right desire is the deepest form of prayer.

I tell you truth when I say there is only one source of all good—God. The conscious recognition and acceptance of this fact acknowledged by every activity of the mind, not two or three times a day—but every few moments all day long—no matter what the outer self is doing, and this maintained will enable anyone to express his perfect freedom and dominion over all things human.

Today is my day. And my world is but a reflection of my own mental attitude. I have the power within myself to reverse any destructive thought entering my mental household. I could not lovingly entertain unwelcome visitors, therefore I shall not willingly entertain unwelcome thoughts.

Each day I shall weed from my mind all thoughts of doubt, fear, malice, hatred, revenge, petty criticism or superstition of any nature whatsoever, and shall begin today believing tremendously in the power of a constructive mental attitude.

This is the day that the Lord has made. In it I will rejoice and be glad. No man taketh my joy from me. Just for today I will know that I am God's child under His protection and, that no plague can come nigh my dwelling. Just for today I will know that God is good, and that God is Love, and that He knoweth them that trust Him. Just for today I will know that I have strength to meet and conquer every claim of error, and that under the guidance of divine Principle I will be led to throw open the door for the entrance of Truth; and know that through that same door error is cast forth. Then with a sweet sense of God's nearness I will know that yesterday has gone, and left no bitterness, and that today is big with blessings, that tomorrow belongs to God; and to realize this today eliminates all worry and pain and trouble, and brings us peace and happiness.

From 'Sentinel', Vol. V1, p. 8 (Original version of *Miscellany*, p. 347)

(1903) The Executive Members of the Mother Church will please accept my heartfelt acknowledgment of their beautiful gift to me, a LOVING CUP—presented July 16, 1903. The exquisite design of boughs encircling this cup, illustrated by Keats' touching couplet, would almost suggest that Nature had reproduced her primal presence, bough, bird, and song to salute me. The twelve beautiful pearls that crown this cup, call to mind the number of our great Master's first disciples, and the parable of the priceless pearl which purchases our field of labor in exchange for all else.

While I treasure My LOVING CUP, with all its sweet associations, who shall say that Mrs. Eddy is fond of her cups!

From 'Sentinel', Vol. VIII, p. 296

(1906) Neither space nor time can separate genuine Christian Scientists. 'Behold, how good and how pleasant it is for brethren to dwell together in unity.'

From the 'Daily Mail'—Mrs. Eddy's *Own Message from Scripture*

(1907) London, August 24—The *Daily Mail* cabled to Mary Baker G. Eddy, the Founder of Christian Science, offering to print a message from her reviewing the legal proceedings in her case, and the situation for the benefit of English Christian Scientists. Mrs. Eddy replied:

'The situation of the lawsuit is described in the Scripture, James 2:24. Our work in the future will be the same as in the past; namely, to love God supremely and to love our neighbor as ourself, to return good for evil, to reform the sinner and to heal the sick.'[3]

[3] Refers to the 'Next Friends' Suit, the virtual collapse of which took place on August 21, 1907.

From the 'New York Herald'—Mrs. Eddy's Own Denial that She is Ill (as in *My*. 275, with the following added as the third paragraph)

(1908) The Christian Science student's affection, fidelity and devotion are born in the furnace and blossom in wisdom won by experience. This is the price and reward of taking one's treasure out of material vessels.

Motive

(April 16, 1909) We think before we speak, then if our thought is right our words will be as nearly right as our thoughts; but if our thoughts are wrong and our words are right, the result will follow the wrong direction. We may deceive man but we cannot deceive God. He searcheth the heart and rewards or punishes the motive until the act follows in the right direction. Oh! Thou eternal Love, I leave my adopted children—and Thy children—to Thee who art wisdom, unfailing and unfaltering wisdom and Love, to guard them in this hour of the attempted reign of M.A.M., the reign and rule of all that is selfish, debased and unjust.

My beloved students: Enter into the closet of divine Love and there in humility ask this ever-present power to shield and to defend you from the enemies of your souls and bodies, to defend you and guard you and guide you in the paths of righteousness, pleasantness and Truth.

Be not deceived; 'God is not mocked: for whatsoever a man soweth, that shall he also reap.' God knows your motive and win reward it or punish it according to His wisdom and justice, not yours. Not the so-called human, but the divine wisdom shall reign despite your mistaken human hopes, motives or acts. Examine your motives; ask if selfish desire governs them; or if in obedience to the divine command you are taking up your cross and following Him. Self-seeking will never result in Soul-finding—in finding divine wisdom and Love apart from self, and self swallowed up in a victory of Soul. There is but one way of salvation from sin, disease and death, and this way is to take up the cross in order to follow Christ; then God, who knows your motive, will reward your act according to that motive and not according to your words. Hear O Israel! You cannot succeed with a wrong motive, for it will result in a wrong act. Cleanse your hearts, ye double-minded, and keep your account with God, for ye shall be judged according to the Book of Life that registers motives, and records the' impulses of Mind, not matter. Let thy tongue and thy pen be employed in the execution of right motives, then shall thy reward come from heaven, that overcometh the powers of earth and wherein and whereby man deals justly, walks humbly.

Logic

(July 10, 1909) If a man says, 'I lie', does he tell the truth or does he lie? The logical reply is: if he ties he tells the truth and if he tells the truth, he lies. We ask, What is a lie? It is the absence of Truth, of reality, the absence of God, the absence of good, hence evil is a lie and a lie is not real, therefore evil is unreal. An evil-doer is losing his own selfhood; he is becoming a nonentity, harming himself more than he can harm any other person. What then is success in evil? It is downright defeat. The greater its success the surer its defeat. Evil is self-destroyed. What is this destruction ? It is the loss of selfhood, the loss of the power to do good and to realize the attainable power that is good. The most selfish mortal should heed the Scripture, 'Do thyself no harm'. Selfishness is the development of sin, sickness, disease, death. Soul is unselfed; it could not be immortal and be selfish. The most selfish man or woman is the most soulless, when Selfishness consists in loving one's self better than he loves his neighbor.

Dreams

(Sept. 20, 1909) Is mortal Life a dream? Yes! Then you admit the necessity of dreams so long as you entertain the belief of mortal life. Suppose you reverse this statement, and begin your logic logically, so that one wrong statement will not include another one; and you must abandon the first to avoid the last. Admitting that mortal life is a dream is admitting that it is something. when the fact remains that it is nothing, since there is no mortal life. God, Truth, is the only Life and a dream is not Truth. The dream and the dreamer are one, even the supposition that nothing is something. Eschew that statement of life unscientific—state it scientifically and commence your solution of the problem called life on fact and not fable. Then you begin with Truth, not error; with God, not man; with Principle; not idea; and solve Life as having no beginning and no ending, the eternal now and forever.

The mistakes of a false sense of life, sensation and intelligence cease, and you are in and of an eternal Principle that has neither beginning nor end; and all paraphrase to the contrary is a fable and not the fact of existence, of God or of man.

Independence

A man has no right to do wrong. His right is to do and think right. Independence consists in his liberty and right to do right.

The misconstruction of the word independence is the offspring of malicious animal magnetism. Beware of defending your right to do wrong, and be strong to defend yourself against the right to do evil. Man's right is his power and privilege to act independently of evil suggestions or motives and he has neither right nor liberty to do wrong. Neither divine law nor human law recognizes the right of man to sin, to steal, to commit adultery, to murder; and to do these things no more means independence than no means yes, or good means evil. So long as he exercises this mistaken sense of right, he will wrong himself and others, heap up wrath against the day of wrath, and bring upon himself punishment according to his deeds. (S. & H. 23: 5)

Supply

We gather as we sow.

My income is the incoming of right ideas. It comes instantly, constantly, continually day and night. It is my God being.

(The following article is—probably incorrectly—ascribed to Mrs. Eddy.)

The Symbol Called a Quarter (25¢)

I have a quarter. It is the symbol of an idea of substance. In that single quarter ties the idea of abundance in *its entirety.* Also the means of expressing full abundance, for any idea does not have to be increased or 'worked out' in Mind. The evolution of abundance manifested abundance—from that single symbol is only held back by the sluggish action of human thought trying to account for everything through the lying elements of time and space.

If confronted by a human need, the first thing we would do humanly—would be to look at the single quarter, estimate its value according to the material standard of exchange, then look at the bills to be paid, or the human obligations to be met, *recognize and accept* mentally the inadequacy of that single symbol to meet the needs and submit right there to the human belief of finiteness and the cast-iron opposition of mortal mind to anything approaching a 'miracle'.

After all, the quarter, in reality, is not *my* idea of either abundance or limited value. If it dwells in Mind, as every idea must, then Mind fills it with limitless, infinite value, and, humanly speaking, I cannot grasp or conceive of its possibilities to meet every need, neither can I set any value—finite value—on it, for counting money in so many dollars and cents is simply one of the attempts of human thought to control a quality of Mind and circumscribe it into the finiteness of human reason. This literally takes the quarter out of the realm of reality—it ceases to be an *idea* of substance and naturally becomes a form of nothingness that fails in usefulness and disappears. On the other hand, to 'multiply' it, all human estimation and value must be set aside, and the substance, universal substance of limitless Spirit that the tiniest symbol represents, must be recognized, and then you have connected up mentally with the limitless idea and need do no more. As the electrician makes the connection and can get all the light necessary without doing another thing, so we can 'having done all, stand!' The 'mechanics' are up to God. Time and space should be eliminated. Don't keep watching the symbol—whatever its denomination according to human belief—the electrician does not expect his connections to multiply, he expects the light to increase. To grasp the universal substance *as present* would eventually make the symbol unnecessary to the one accepting this presence, for everything is here and available to man without a 'medium of exchange'; but if, humanly, it *seems* expedient to 'render unto Caesar', surely the symbol will divinely appear to the human consciousness, just as the electrician would be able to *show* the connection, but steadfastly keeps his thought centered on the less material light and the power it represents constantly.

Lack is not a curse, for there is a blessing in it when we see that it actually teaches us to turn away from the finite symbol, and grasp the endless possibilities, capabilities, and riches contained in the idea typified by the symbol when it is rightfully understood. So lack in that way is a blessing in disguise, for Love reverses it and Spirit brings its ever-present substance into manifestation to meet the human need.

NOTES IN HER HANDWRITING

From a Notebook kept by Mary Baker Eddy in her own Handwriting
(includes clippings and quotations as well as her notes)

February 18, 1890. Mrs. E. wrote notes on the Scriptures in an attic with only a skylight, for lack of means with which to rent better quarters.
She wrote *Science & Health*, 1875.

Sunday Evening, June 15, 1890. In order to destroy fear in others first destroy your own fear. This may be done in two ways. By looking *through* it, and by gaining the divine or spiritual conscious ness. This also may be accomplished in two ways, either by watching, working, and praying, or by suffering.

We cannot gain spiritual understanding except through the footsteps of faith. First faith, then understanding.

'Our faith should lengthen its borders and strengthen its base by resting on Spirit instead of matter.' S. & H.

February 9, 1892. The manifestations of the workings of A.M. on a person has three stages.

1st. Stupidity, idiocy, or frenzy, suffering or exhilaration, unconscious of the error he says or does.

2d. When told of it will deny having said or done the wrong and argue in defence of it.

3d. Will declare that there is no A.M.

January 4, 1891. Christ is the *Mind* of Christ, not the character.

I can see his way from 'take the sword', 'I came to bring a sword' to the time he said, 'put up the sword' the entire pathway and can see that it is the only way in Christian Science.

November 27, 1891. *My* present sense of heaven is to have some person that would understand me one bit.

Extracts from a letter written June 10, *1890,* from 62 N. State St., Concord, N.H., to Mrs. Lathrop:

... Love, Love alone will found, upbuild, and establish forever both the Christian Scientist and our Cause.

But envy, jealousy, or rivalry will kill the spirit of this Science in the person who possesses it and will thwart the establishment of it in this age. Oh, why is not *this* realized by every one who has the Cause at heart and *who* has labored faithfully in some directions for its advancement?

. . . A dozen Churches of C.S. in the big city of N.Y. that were harmonious and truly Christian in word and deed would tend to promote the growth and prosperity of each other. Every Church and Pastor of our denomination would be greatly supported by this *unity.* The Principle of our demonstration as Christian Scientists is *unity* and our demonstrations depend on united minds and their at-one-ment with the One Mind.

February 1, 1903. When I met with an accident in 1866 1 at first took Dr. Cushing's medicine and it did me no good; then I quit taking it. After I read Jesus' method of healing referred to in the

Gospel and it raised me from my bed, I took no more of Dr. C's medicine and when he again called I showed to him the powders he gave me lying in the drawer of the table that stood beside my bed, and others saw them there.

M.A.M. extinguishes all that is humane in human nature and utterly obscures to mortal view whatever is Divine.

July 1897. 1 wrote to Mr. Kimball that an address was proper, but not a sermon, when dedicating a church.

When traveling from the Northern to the Southern Hemisphere the Pole Star and Dipper are lost sight of; we see the Southern Cross.

The Hindu Vedas and Mohammedan Koran are what the Bible is to Christians.

Dr. Abbott regards God as an intellectual energy. I hold God to be a spiritual Energy.

Scripture Interpretations. 'You shall say to yonder mountain be removed into the sea and it shall be done.' Shall say to a belief satisfied be dissolved and it shall be done.

Opened to this Sept. 6, 1898: For if a man know not how to rule his own house, how shall he take care of the church of God? St. Paul.

France's Pasteur was a greater man than its Napoleon.

March 14th, 1897. I requested the students of Christian Science stop their teaching C.S. for one year from that date.

Next message to my church is to be CHOICE and OBEDIENCE.

Ideology, the Science of Mind. Worcester's dictionary.

Christian Science Rules. Watch, bear testimony, demonstrate.

Take notice, Healing, Revelation 21: 1 to 7.

Dickey left Jan. 14; returned in 2 weeks.

My home on Beacon St. Brookline cost $207,061.36.

(Clipping from the *Daily Patriot* Monday, December 2, 1907, re: Decoration as Officier d'Acadimie conferred on Mrs. Eddy by the French Government. 'The first woman thus honored.')

In my library is a book entitled Genealogical and Family History of the State of New Hampshire. It contains a sketch of the Baker Family, Mrs. Eddy's portrait on its first page.

Franz von Lenbach, the German artist who painted my portrait in —.

March 12, 1904, I gave as a present to Calvin A, Frye, 5,000 dollars (five thousand dollars). Mary B. G. Eddy.

Mrs. Sibyl O'Brien, of the *Boston Herald,* sought me to contribute to a symposium in this paper. February 9, 1905.

No. 172 is the number of the key to my safety box that contains my valuable papers. This key I must hand to any one that opens my box. Mary B. Eddy.

The key to my safety box in Concord, that is marked 172, opens the box that contains my *will* and private papers. I must *sign an order* for any one to open it for me, except Mr. Frye.

One thousand dollars was paid by the church for making Mrs. M. B. G. Eddy a member of The Association for International Conciliation its highest plane of American *Fondateur.*

Healing

Ask Lucy Allen of Lynn about the awful cripple that I healed on street by saying to him 'God loves you' and he rose from the sidewalk went into Mr. Allen's and told Lucy about it. The man in Chelsea, Mass., that Mrs. Slade knew that I healed....

In less than three centuries the Christianity of Christ had been legally proclaimed the religion of State of the Byzantine or eastern division of the Roman Empire (News Letter).

This gave an impulse to politicians to join the church and Christianity was stamped out, spirituality was lost and a material religion attempted to be grafted into the tree of Life.

July 9, 1899. The following Scripture came to me as if spoken in my ears when I was at prayer and anxious to know if what I had said July 6, 1899—to my students that I had called together—was just and deserved, 'Wherefore the Lord said, Forasmuch as this people draw near me with their mouth' etc., Isaiah 29. ver. 13, and our dear Master's words—'This people draweth nigh unto me with their mouth, and honoreth me with their lips; but their heart is far from me.' Matt. 15: 8. These were the words that came to me; and I looked up the Prophet's sayings also in connection with that saying of Jesus. M. B. Eddy.

December 13, 1899, 1 returned the balance of $572.45 cts on the collection taken by The Mother Church for purchasing an organ and presenting it to me for the C.S. Hall that I have had made in Concord, requesting the church to receive it from me as a contribution toward a Church Fund for indigent members.

Science and Health

The house burned where this book lay on the table and the covers burned off, but not one word in it was disfigured or gone when the book was saved. This occurred on April 15, 1891, at 12: 45 P.M. on that day.

175 Poplar St., Roslindale, Mass.

June 18, 1891

Mr. J. B. Harrington:

I address you as my student because you study the little Book that our Heavenly Father has written through me for you and for all mankind.

Your teacher was an interesting student of mine in the classroom and is doing what she can out of it I have no doubt.

You may not learn through language my feelings when I took that sacred Book rescued by the Divine hand from devouring flames, and through it saw the meaning of this rescue in the type before me.

I have received presents from my beloved students that I prize beyond all things that I ever before possessed. But dear friend, your gift to me of my last revised *Science and Health* saved from the fire that consumed all around it, but kindled not on its sacred pages, is a gift dearer to me than aught else this earth contains.

Just before the Book arrived one of my noblest and best students gave me a large diamond cross, eleven diamonds sparkling on its significant form. They said to me when presenting it: 'The cross is illumined.' Prophetic words! This Book, my book of books, taken by the finger of God out of elements of matter that would have destroyed it, illumines my life, its struggles, its victories.

I cannot thank you, for pen or tongue cannot express my thanks. But my heart speaks to you. Oh! do you hear it saying, Heavenly Father reward his life, give him victory over sense and self and crown him with what the world cannot give and thieves cannot break through and steal.

With much love to Mrs. Merriman.

I am very truly yours in Christ,

Mary B. G. Eddy.

Lord Kelvin, the greatest living scientist now that Helmholtz has passed away, declared in his address before the British Association: 'There is nothing in material science that reaches the origin of anything at all.'

The household must have light and less than 4 decades ago men periled their lives to harpoon whales for whale oil and made tallow candles dipped at home. But one day somebody noticed a scum of iridescence upon the pools of a swamp and, lo! kerosene had trickled into the world from the very heart of Mother Earth, as if to give the poor man's home a moonlight.

Jerome was fought for translating the Latin Vulgate; Wyclif and Tyndall for their translation into the English Language; Luther for his German translation.

Literary Biblical fads are to my thinking taking out much of the beauty and spirituality of the Scriptures. Eddy.

A period of transition is this: Christian Science has already made theology more ethical and more humane.

James M. Whitton says, 'The old and fmished theology of the 16th and 17th centuries will no more re-establish itself than the old Ptolemaic astronomy'. He then writes in 1897 much that is written in the textbook of C.S. Thus he writes, 'The truly human Jesus has been recovered. The divine Christ from being merely a make weight in a scheme of divine government fancied to be like that of earthly rulers, has been rediscovered as permanently indwelling in the life of *both God* and *man.'* This is a description only of my meaning in the term that I use for the Christ —namely, the *spiritual idea.*

Signs Following

When translating Scripture I took courage by reading the context that corresponded with my interpretation.

When writing S. & H. I was told nobody could understand that book, etc. I replied I have been healing the sick today with what I have written. And 30 years afterwards the sick are being healed when reading these very pages that I was writing that day.

Opposition from my students and others rather than help attended all my early labors.

I had rather have a Thomas than a Peter for a student of C.S. He doubted till convinced. I learned my way by doubting till convicted of the Truth.

'The strong soil in human nature is selfish apathy. The wayside soil is a transient laughing vain loving-ease character that never can be relied (on) in time of need. The sun struck mind is one that resists the light if this light demand the relinquishment of all that tends to darken life, dim conscience, and demand other gods. The good soil is the active honest heart. Where this exists there is energy, fidelity, success and reward gained by the individual, not a gift of God but the wages of uprightness and hard work, struggle and victory.' (From article entitled *'Soldier, Seed, and Soil'.)*

The *Christian Science Monitor* was first issued November 25, (1908) and one hundred and sixty thousand copies were sold on the first day it came out. The Publishing House was unable to fill all the orders. God is our ever-present help. When I first proposed to the Christian Scientists to have this newspaper and gave it its name I had not much encouragement from them that it would be a success....

Took the lease of the house at 569 Columbus Ave, April 25th, 1882. Rent $83.33.

Natural science (so-called) calculus shows a fourth dimension which no one understands. First is the line, next the plane, third space. The first, 2nd, 3rd, and 4th, yea, All is Spirit.

3 *C.S.* steps: (1) Not to be *idolaters.* (2) Not to fear something besides God. (3) Not to fear God.

Normal Class Subjects

1. Infinity—Mind, Spirit, Soul, Good, Life, Truth, Love, Prayer.
2. Finity—personality, evil, reversing Good.
3. Sin—serpent, lie, liar, sickness, disease, death.
4. Christian Science—a square to material sense, but to spiritual sense a sphere. The square is composed of 4 sides, viz. God, Christ, Bible, Christianity. The sphere of C.S. is without limits; it is one and all and all because one. Prayer, Watching, the Way. (Four lessons each of one hour. Tuition $200.)

Church of Christ, Scientist chartered Aug. 23, 1879. The same month Mrs. Eddy was called to the pastorate. Sept. 14th, she declined accepting the call. Oct. 16th, at a church meeting at Dorcas Rawson's, 44 Chestnut St., Lynn, it was unanimously voted that Mrs. Eddy and Mr. Eddy merited the thanks of this society for their devoted labors in the cause of Truth. At a meeting Dec. 1, 1879, held at 133 West Newton, Boston, Mrs. Eddy accepted the second call to take the pastorate and commenced preaching to this church that she had organized before she went away to prepare her revised edition of *Science and Health.* She had such tasks imposed on her that she had to go away to do this work and was employed the three hottest months of summer, when most of the church members were away to rest, to get this work ready. Then came back and saw the dead condition of the church and commenced preaching to them at Hawthorne rooms at $5.00 per week. She had lectured to them the year before 8 months without taking even the contribution or a cent to pay her fare every Sunday from Lynn to Boston, and during this time doubled the church membership and got a great interest aroused in Boston.

July 7, 1874. Paid for copyright.

1872. Commenced writing the *Science of Life* in February, 1872.

1875, *October* 30th. *Science and Health* printed.

Dissolution of Co-partnership between Mrs. Glover and her student, Richard Kennedy, was published May 11th, 1872.

September 6,1874. Sent my mss. to the printer to commence work. The work is entitled *The Science of Life.*

The material senses conflict with the spiritual sense alias there is war between the flesh and Spirit or evil and good.

Rules for overcoming animal magnetism:

1. See what it is trying to do.
2. Know that it cannot do it.
3. See that it is *not done.*

To accomplish this:

1. Be patient.
2. Be meek.
3. Be vigilant.
4. Be sober.
5. Be loving.

September 17, 1907. Let my church buy the house and rent it to me.

September 24, 1907. Terrific clouds all over the sky changed instantaneously by me and a gentle rain and *rainbow* appeared.

Book just found entitled *The Time of the End.* As early as 1571 a D.D. advanced the idea that the reappearing of Christ would occur in 1866.

Mrs. Batchelder of Boston, Mass., painted one full-sized portrait of me as I stood in my pulpit in The Mother Church of Christ, Scientist. She graduated in Florence, Italy.

S. & H. page 442, lines on sleep.

It is as necessary that I should remain at home for the central stillness of C.S. work as for the hub of a wheel not to move in the radius of its rim.

Footsteps of C.S.	1. A great light.	Matt. 4:,16
	2. Repentance.	Matt. 4: 17.
	3. Obedience.	Matt. 5: 17.
	4. Purity.	Matt. 5: 28.
	5. Less talk.	Matt, 5: 37.
	6. Perfection; resist not evil; love your enemies; return good for evil, etc., etc., etc.	Matt. 5: 48, 39-44.

Degrees in C.S.

Mr. Norcross in index of S. & H. wrote, 'Spirits that go out do not return to the body'. In correcting this Mr. Frye wrote, 'Spirits do not go out nor return to the body.'

I corrected both thus, 'Spirit neither enters nor returns to the body or matter.' (M. B. G. Eddy.)

December 19,1880. Commenced services at the Hawthorne rooms. The salary proposed was ten dollars by Mrs. Choate, but they said they would wait to see how much was collected of arrears before settling on the amount. I said I should not state my salary but leave it to them to say how much it should be, but that I should not take more than five dollars per week, and could not agree for one year as duty might call me away.

In the Margin of her 'Journal' for November, 1885, *Vol. III,* p. 149

To forgive your enemies is equivalent to having no enemies.

(This was beside the following poem, which she marked:

The fairest action of our human life
Is scorning to revenge an injury,
For who forgives without a further strife,
His adversary's heart to him doth tie:
And 'tis a firmer conquest, truly said,
To win the heart than overthrow the head.)

Title for a Compilation

Selections from the Old Testament, Authorized Version, compiled by Rev. Mary Baker G. Eddy, Author of *Science and Health with Key to the Scriptures*. Concord, N.H., 1896.

(The book bearing this title was included in Mrs. Eddy's library and contained Genesis I and II, Exodus XX, Isaiah complete and Malachi complete.)

In Presentation Copy of 'Science and Health' to Nemi Robertson

To read this book is to hear the voice of your Father. Ponder this in your heart and tell *no man*—Mother.

Pleasant View, Concord, N.H.

February 7, 1897.

In Presentation Copy of 'Science and Health' to Admiral Dewey

First in war, first in peaceful conquest; first in the love of his country; and the first shall be last to make war, last to lose an opportunity, last to surrender.

On page 341 of her Copy of 'Miscellaneous Writings', by line 19

O learn to know that you can lose nothing that is real.

On the Flyleaf of 'Mrs. Eddy's Copy of 'The Book of the Presidents and Representative Americans'

Upheld by divine Love man can make himself perfect, but he must not attempt this too rapidly with his neighbor.

(The story of this volume, of which Mrs. Eddy received the first copy and in which she is one of the four women listed, is given in *Sentinel,* Vol. VII, p. 708, quoting the *Boston Herald*. Here it is stated that the work contains a letter from Mrs. Eddy presenting in a 'few clear statements' the fundamentals of Christian Science.

(In fact, the flyleaf quotation given above may not be an inscription in the book at all, but may be simply an extract from Mrs. Eddy's letter which was printed in the book and which is understood to read more completely as follows:

(September 17, 1904. Upheld by divine Love man can make himself perfect, but he must not attempt this too rapidly with his neighbor. To so live as to keep consciousness in constant relation to God, is to individualize infinite power,—and this is Christian Science.

(Whatever God governs is not subordinate to matter, physics, or geometric altitudes, and never deprived of the light and might of omnipotence. The resuscitating power of health, harmony, and life, is God, Mind, not matter; and guided by this spiritual understanding would never falter before the infinite tasks of truth. Only by understanding that there is but one God, one power,—not two powers, matter and Mind,—can be reached correct and logical conclusions.

(Human will may trespass on divine law; corporeal sense may hide health, and truth, as the mist obscures the mountain; but Science subordinates human will and is the sunshine of Truth which melts the shadow and reveals the substance. Follow my teachings only so far as they follow Christ's in word and deed.)

Under a Quotation from Phillips Brooks in her 'Sentinel' for January 6, 1906, *Vol. VIII*, p. 294

The secret of my life is in the above.

(The quotation was as follows:

(God has not given us vast learning to solve all the problems, or unfailing wisdom to direct all the wanderings of our brothers' lives; but He has given to every one of us the power to be spiritual, and by our spirituality to lift and enlarge and enlighten the lives we touch.)

In her 'Science and Health' (found, signed, after she left us)

Whenever there seems to be a need or lack in your experience, this simply indicates the scientific fact that this seeming need is already supplied by God's gracious abundance. Then give thanks with your whole heart because you have learned in Christian Science that God's supply is ever at hand.

In her Copy of 'The Life of Jesus'

This is my book. Mary Baker Eddy.

(A student in the home was casting covetous eyes at this beautiful book!)

Pasted in front of her Bible

(A poem by Bonar which read as follows:

Where no shadow shall bewilder,
Where life's vain parade is o'er;

Where the sleep of sin is broken
And the dreamer dreams no more;
Where the bond is never severed,
Partings, claspings, sob and moan,
Midnight waking, twilight weeping,
Heavy noontide, all are done;
Where the child has found its mother,
Where the mother finds the child;
Where dear families are gathered
That are scattered on the wild;
Brother, we shall meet and rest,
Midst the holy and the blest.)

In the back of her Hymnal

Sing often in The Mother Church, hymn No. 173 (Be firm and be faithful). No. 190, Washington, D.C., First Church (Lead, kindly Light).

(At the end of a letter sent to First Church, Washington, D.C., on October 10, 1899, was the following paragraph not included in the text as given in *Miscellany,* p. 199:

(After reading this letter to your Church please unite in singing the hymn, 169, in the Christian Science Hymnal.

With love, Mother,

MARY BAKER G. EDDY.)[4]

[4] See *Journal,* Vol. XV11, p. 526.

CHAPTER SEVEN

FURTHER RECORDED STATEMENTS
(MOSTLY VERBAL) BY MRS. EDDY

RECORDED BY THE RECIPIENT

To G. C. C. (1905-6) [Gilbert Congden Carpenter]

There is no fear to prevent us from seeing the results of our labor. It is as easy to help ourselves as others, for we have a clearer understanding of God that destroys fear. We have the Mind of God. Because there is no atrophy in the Mind of God, there is none in our Mind; and as God's Mind is All and made all, there is no atrophy

We are joined by God, divine Science, to Himself, His power and love. And what God hath joined no man can put asunder. Our work does good. We have not the ability or power to do harm. There is no law that can give anyone the power to do harm. God's law is the only law and that does good, not harm, and can give man only the power to do good, not defeat, but victory. We cannot get away from God. If I ascend up into heaven, behold thou art there. Everybody loves us and everybody reflects love.

To A. H. D. (from his collection, 1908-10) [Adam H. Dickey]

Never fear a lie. Declare against it with the conviction of its nothingness, Throw your whole weight into the right scale—this is the way to destroy evil. Never weigh against yourselves by admitting a lie.

Never rant over what should be killed and put out of sight. We should never kill a serpent or a tiger; they must have their day and kill themselves—then they are dead; but nothing dies till it believes it is dead—then it rots.

Put self out of the way. Which one of these (faith, hope, love) do we lack most? Answer: love. Yes; we all lack love most, and when we have love we have all the rest. Now don't forget that! Go.

(March 30, 1908 or 1909) Now the season of storms is coming on. The enemy—mesmerists—claim they can do what they want to the weather—as they claim they can do as they will with sickness. You all know you can control a headache or a belief of dyspepsia and you are not afraid of it.

Sickness is a belief of mortal mind. Now what is a storm? Is it not a false claim of material law? Is there any such thing as material law? Then if bad weather or lightning is an erroneous concept of mortal law, can't you break it up? Now I want you to prepare yourselves to do this. I remember once when we were having a terrific storm and the lightning was around the house like chains, the students were with me and I declared to them that there was no surplus electricity and in a few minutes the whole storm disappeared. Now you know there are no thunderstorms in divine Mind. No lightning in heaven—so prepare to break up these violent storms. There is *no need* for them.

You will only learn to avoid the pitfalls by what you suffer. We learn that these pitfalls are no part of the road.

First we must see the error, then repent and then forsake it. You will have to continue with sin until you have overcome it. Then you will have another form of evil to meet—the envy and jealousy of mortal mind. That is where your Leader stands.

You can lift me out of a claim by lifting yourselves. It is error to keep your thought on me. You would heal me just as you would heal any patient by knowing and realizing the nothingness of the claim. When you have destroyed your own thought of it you have healed the patient. You don't have to do something to your treatment to help it along, or make it go somewhere. Treatment is knowing. All you have to do is to know you do not have to suffer and *you do not*. If I could know I didn't have to suffer for the sins of others I would be well instantly. Paul died and why? Because he was always talking crucifixion. We should attenuate mortal mind.

Now can't you all get out of addition? You do not have to stay in addition all the time. If you have the same principle it is just as easy and in fact easier to multiply than it is to add. You *must rise* out of the addition of Christian Science and let God, divine Mind, multiply through you

All claims are a result of a law of reversal by R.C.

Do not let the material things hinder our progress in Science; it is a trick of the devil to keep us—chasing after matter. You cannot serve God and mammon.

When you are a good healer you are all you can be. Do you understand that?

What is a good dinner or a good meal? Good devil. What is a good night's sleep? Good evil. What is a nice, new dress? Good evil. What is a sense of health in matter? Good evil. Which is nearer God—a human sense of health or of sickness? What is it that brings us into a realization of true being? Spiritual understanding. Then how do I (Mrs. Eddy) heal? By *knowing* the omnipotent, ever-present, eternal and infinite Mind is All—and therefore there is no inaction, over-action, diseased action or reaction. Spiritual understanding—a knowledge of God—makes perfect.

Science and Health 442. Important. Enemy at work on this.

Sleeplessness is an argument.

When do we need to look at disease? When our faith in God is not sufficient to destroy it instantly with the command of Truth. We only need the argument against disease to strengthen ourselves. When we can heal by knowing All is Mind, we do not need to know anything about disease.

Evil arguments and mental suggestions cannot frighten, swerve, deter, or keep me from doing the work that is mine to do today.

You cannot run away from a weakness; you must sometime fight it out or perish, and if this be so why not do it now and where you stand.

No subtlety or sophistry of evil can blind or paralyze my human capacity to apprehend and love good.

'Denial at best only brings us a human peace', Mrs. Eddy said, but she said a true treatment is 'the divine everpresence of infinite perfection'.

Life is God. This treatment is the power and activity of divine Mind; it cannot be found, it cannot be reversed, or return void; it does accomplish that for which it is sent.

God bless my enemies, make them Thy friends; give them to know the joy and peace of Love.

Hypnotism ... is not in the focal distance of God and therefore is not, for God is infinite.

If you heal yourself of self-justification you will lift yourself into the kingdom of heaven.

Everything that comes to me today brings me a blessing. There is no mortal mind to see me today or know me today; or think it can through any of its so-called laws of malpractice rob me of all good or hinder me from being conscious here and now of my birthright which is dominion.

There is no aggravation of human belief asserting itself mesmerically. The right idea once gained enables us to stand unmoved and unshaken; the offspring of Mind, the son of Mind, of God.

To M. T. D. (in a class) [Mary Tucker (?)]

Christian Scientists will have to defend the M.D.'s as the indignation and shocked thought of the public will assail them. This malpractice may be so great that they will need the aid of what Christian Scientists alone can reflect.

Christian Scientists know that M.D.'s as a rule do the very best they know according to their light.

To F. J. F. [Francis J. Fluno]

Why did Jesus have more to meet in his day than any other man? Why does Mrs. Eddy, the Discoverer and Founder of Christian Science, have more to meet than any other woman today? Why is it that as we approach the fountain-head we begin to hear the thunder as she has told us we would?

To C. A. F. (from a notebook) [Calvin Augustus Frye]

The only power there is in mesmerism is what we allow it to have.

I am so thankful that God makes me just what He would have me.

Truth reflects itself and what the Principle does its idea also does. So error tries to accomplish a certain result and its idea does the same thing! One mortal mind cannot touch another. Their thoughts meet each other part way. One never comes up to the other; that is but the belief.

All fear is formed in unconscious mind. The hidden enemy is our only enemy.

When we fail to reach the error through the silent argument, we should speak out and command and by so doing we increase our power, reaching conscious and unconscious thought; and the more formidable the error, the higher we should rise in asserting our power over it.

The bigger the error, the greater its nothingness. There shall be no more sea.

The whole rule, *February* 25, 1883. 'I am trying to rouse them with God and they are trying either to flatten them all out, or rouse them through the devil.' Mary B. G. Eddy.

Have no will opposed to God; meekness is not weakness; it is 'not my will but Thine be done', throwing ourselves into God's power.

You are one-third nearer heaven, than you were last August. They cannot make you believe you are not.

February 15*th*. You should not treat a lymphatic temperament as you would a nervous temperament. What it would take to move the former would overdo with the latter.

The anatomy of metaphysics is first to place dislocation, and secondly to set the bones of thought that are broken and cause them to be healed.

The basis of error is ignorance, superstition and fear, and they bring sin, sickness and death.

Program

1st. Turn back.

2d. Join the enemy, and so get an armistice.

3d. Press on and meet it now, for we have it to meet sometime and the sooner commenced, the sooner we get through.

The way to spring the trap and get a confession is to ask a question in such a way that they will have no chance for retrospect before answering, and they will be off guard and cannot hide the truth.

Stir them; make them either laugh or cry; move them from their foundation; make some impression on them, if not silently then audibly.

August 18, 1897. The Bible says the kingdom of heaven is already within you. Also that flesh and blood cannot enter into the kingdom of heaven. Then there can be no blood poison, etc. We must look where we would walk.

Make supplication to God daily that you may be delivered from all beliefs of sin or of sickness, and after doing this then turn to and demand of yourself to realize their unreality, and recognize your power over the temptation to yield to any such an illusion.

The three footsteps

1st. Matter over matter, i.e. the body has power to change itself and become diseased.

2d. Mortal mind over mortal mind, where all is mind and there is no matter, bringing in a harmonious belief, holding the body as an image of mind and making that harmonious.
3d. Immortal Mind over mortal mind, having but one intelligence, one Mind, one God, and we His image and likeness, and as Principle *eternal.*

The departure from God was through the Adam, which in its first statement was an intelligence separate from God; but naked, unconscious of it, i.e. holding its body unconsciously (the body did not speak); then placing intelligence in matter until the body appears to talk so much through material sense that we are almost unconscious of any voice.

Our way back to God is by retracing our footsteps, to put the body under subjection. First have a harmonious body or belief, through our conscious dominion over it, and when the last trump shall sound, to acknowledge God as the only intelligence, 'the All-in-all', Principle, we the idea.

In instantaneous healing the phenomenon flashes out at once, perfect.

Malpractice commenced first by making sick; then by calling back the old beliefs; and third by the belief in poison.

The way to gain the ear of an audience is to follow their thought a little way and then gradually lead them into your way.

Serpents were used in olden times as the symbol of wisdom but have been turned to the symbol of fear; we turn it to a staff by the benefit we get from the experience we derive from the trial.

If we have no sin, we need have no fear nor suffering.

Vegetable and mineral poisons are the duplicate of the animal poisons. Animal poison is the perversion of the love of mortals which is the counterfeit of Love as God.

Sensualism, living in the material sense, eating, drinking, etc., is an open door through which mesmerism comes in to affect us. As we cease to live in the material sense, we do shut the door upon it.

Old batches and maids will not enter heaven on account of a lack of completeness.

Sensuality is the basis of the belief of life, substance and intelligence in matter.

The first statement of error is finity. Second, intelligence in matter. Third, pleasure in matter.

There is danger of making a reality of our patients' beliefs by over-anxiety in arguing against them.

The Scientists should make error unreal to themselves that they may make it unreal to others; and sometimes can do more for others by going by themselves and meditating on spiritual realities.

Life on this mortal plane is but a dream, illustrated by sleep which at one time is a belief of oblivion (for Mind never slumbers nor sleeps); at another time a belief of leaving the body and being in another place, yet holding life in two bodies.

(From his [Calvin Frye's] Diary)

August 1890. It is so now that every morning when I open my Psalms the passage that I open will always give me warning of the experience of the day. Whenever those around me are controlled by M.A.M. and darkened, I invariably open to 'With hypocritical mockers', etc., and when I am tempted to murmur over my trials and burdens I open to where the Children of Israel murmured and found fault with God.

About *June* 8, 1884. I was sad and sobbing at the thought of how imperfectly I was demonstrating this Science in my own life and struggling to find my way, when there came a voice saying, 'You don't need to struggle, but simply to waken and see you are there'. And immediately I could see those who had passed on in belief, and they were not dead, but were right here about us; but I had not gained their point so as to be conscious to them, but as it were looked ahead to it; neither did I seem to be in an abnormal state of mind at the time I saw this and yet it seemed as real and tangible as anything ever was.

April 8, 1890. Our salvation is through Love. Call God Love always and bend all your efforts toward achieving perfect love in thought, word and deed. This is the way. All is won through it. Its presence gives me all. Its absence takes all away from me; therefore 'Love is the fulfilling of the law'. Love is heaven, and hate is hell.

Our only way to heaven is through Love; our sure way to hell is through hate.

'Woe unto you, ye lawyers, for you shut up the kingdom of heaven. Ye will not go in yourselves, neither will ye suffer any other to enter.'

When any tries to argue in justification of error to cover it up, against their honest convictions, it fills me with *righteous indignation* beyond any other form of error.

It shuts out the light from them and hinders others from seeing and walking in the light—from seeing the truth and accepting it.

What is it that argues to people, 'You do not want to practice; it is too uphill work and you can get along without it?'

What is it that sends people out of town when they are needed at home; that sends them to Europe or some out of the way place when they might be better employed?

What says to people, 'Confine your work entirely to the poor and uninfluential?'

What sends a lady, who is in a position to do well in Science, to the child bed?

What unites an unmarried Scientist, who is promising as such, to one who can destroy such usefulness and blight such prospects?

Memoranda

1. Pray God to help you awake to the claims of error, and awake to the truth that destroys them.

2. Whenever error would try to make sin, sickness, disease or death seem real, Good overrules it, and it makes them more unreal to us.

3. Good reverses every evil argument and effort, and brings out the opposite good.

April 17, 1890 When we understand the truth of a lie, then we shall understand God, and not until then.

(Miscellaneous items to C. A. F.) [Calvin A. Frye]

If you are faithful and watch with me in my Gethsemane you will learn your way through.

1. God loves all of us in this house. 2. God governs us. 3. All things are working together for our good.

To M. E. [Mary Eaton or Mary Eastaman (?)]

(Jan. 1902) Christian Science is nothing personal with me; it is a revelation from God.

You can demonstrate wealth. If you stand before the mirror your reflection is instantaneous, and just so you reflect God in all your ways. All are yours and ye are Christ's and Christ's is God. As a man thinketh so is he. Seek first God, and all things shall be added.

To E. G., and others [Eldora Gragg]

Do not shuffle by a bulldog's pen; tiptoe by.

To L. H. [Lydia Hall]

There was a time when I could rise above everything and was lord of all I surveyed, but I had to come down and teach malicious animal magnetism to my students and now look at my hands and my feet.

Lydia, did you know that the malpractitioner can argue ether, liquor or any other poison and it has the same effect upon the body as if it were taken individually?

The mental poisons: Ether, cyanide or potassium, arsenic.

Poisons the effect of which is violent pain: Calcium, hellebore and aconite.

Poisons that produce stupefaction and paralysis: Opium, hemlock, prussic acid.

Poisons that produce violent convulsions and delirium: Strychnine and belladonna.

And again:

(The enemy believes that his arguments can poison mentally and that they have the same effect upon the body as when drugs are injected physically.) The belief of canker is induced by arsenic poison mentally introduced.

They believe that they can mentally argue strychnine, mercury, morphine, liquor, ether, and other poisons mentally and that these will become injected into the thought of the patient and that he will suffer the same effects as if the drugs were injected physically. These arguments all are harmless because God is All.

To S. J. H. (from his collection, not necessarily first-hand) [Septimus J. Hanna]

Keep your eyes wide open to the fads of sin; read '*No and Yes*', beginning at last paragraph page 39. Integral calculus is no part of Science, when weighed in the balance of God. To human sense and pagan philosophy it might seem otherwise, but did Jesus teach it? *No*, a thousand times *no*. It is only a weak form of evolution harnessed to Christian Science.

Do not tell the truth regarding a lie too often. Insist on obeying the Ten Commandments, especially the first and eighth, which the Christian Scientists are most prone to disobey.

You have infinite Truth at your tongue's end. Our Cause is rushing on, on pinions of Love.

When a student loses the true sense of me, and what I do, he is at the threshold of the plunge so many make into darkness, believing that darkness is a greater light.

Will eternity be long enough in which to praise the everlasting good? God is your Shepherd. You are in no danger from aught but the 'kiss', and if you read motives as Jesus did, you will understand this, and it will lose its claim.

I have erased your verities because they are spoken *too soon*; wait for growth. The textbooks contain it all, but so arranged as to require growth before it is spoken by those who have not grown to it. *The letter killeth.* It is the Spirit, understanding behind the words which maketh alive.... There is an axe to be used and laid at the root. This axe is the first Hebrew Commandment as explained in my works. ... Wield this weapon every spare moment. Do some cutting each time, then the lie will topple down.

Wait patiently on the Lord, as I wait on students.

God bless you; God keep your eyes open to the movements of evil, so that your good will be effectual and not diluted. Every truth you promulgate, every good and ardent thought you entertain, though it expose you to the aim of evil, makes you healthier, wealthier, wiser, and longer lived—the evidence of the senses to the contrary notwithstanding. Go on in this path—and your immortality is brought to light.

Pray for divine government, divine leading. We must live amicably on earth and not a saint among us. Love your way out of hell into heaven. Be patient. Stop making much ado about little things. It is the devil that quarrels.

Sit still and let God talk—let Him do something. No family relations or human associates can dispossess me of the Truth, or interfere with my success.

To E. A. K. [Edward Ancel Kimball]

I never knew a dyspeptic who was either a man or a woman. They are nothing but stomachs all absorbed in digestion—of what? You are not a stomach! and a stomach is not talking, arguing, feeling, suffering. You are a man occupied with a great demand. He is too wise to say, 'Go to work in my vineyard' and then render you unfit to work.

(Answering a question as to how far a practitioner was entitled to go in his work after helping a patient) When they come to you and ask for your help—help them. Then if they come back and have done what you told them and wish more help—help them. But if they are not obedient to what you ask them to do, refuse to help them further; for patients such as this do not want your light; they want your oil. Shed your light upon their path freely, but do not give them of your oil.

To J. L. [John Lathrop]

Every By-law in the Manual is inspired. I did not write them any more than I wrote *Science and Health.* I study *Science and Health* constantly.[1]

Now measure yourself and your growth by your works, not by your words. All I have ever accomplished has been done by getting Mary out of the way, and letting God be reflected. When I would reach this tone, the sick would be healed without a word.

Never become discouraged, dear ones. This work is not humdrum, it is growth. It is repeating and defeating, repeating and defeating, repeating and defeating. Is not this the way a mathematician becomes a mathematician?

To S. H. M. [Sue Harper Mims]

Never leave a treatment until consciousness is baptized in love.

To M. N. (from a notebook) [Maria Newcomb]

If the heart stays young, old age can never become anything but ennobled thereby. Years do not make one grow old if one grows in grace. Decay does not belong to matter so much as to mind. Now I believe that if we kept our mind fixed on God, Life, Truth and Love, He will advance us in our years to a higher understanding and change our hope into faith, and our faith into *spiritual* understanding, and our words into works, and our ultimate faith into the fruition of entering into the Kingdom.

Concord—Thoughts. December 30, 1891. I think it has been my great aspiration that the wave of error calling itself death, should not pass over me.

I see this morning that this aspiration, this thought of itself is an error, in that it builds up the belief that there is something to fight, something to overcome, and thus it fosters fear. What if this wave does seem to engulf me, the opposite fact that it does not is the Truth,

[1] See *Sentinel*, Vol. XLI, p. 901.

and by this seeming I am not changed, not harmed, for nothing can ever have any power to affect us.

This view removes fear, and removes the aspiration, and shows me that by this means I am doing more towards conquering, more to keep off the wave. We need not take up arms against a shadow when it is clear to us that it is a shadow. I Cor. 15: 55.

February 27, 1892. The law of mortal mind that says our work, whatever it may be, will not amount to anything, must be broken. Know first that no such law can interfere with Truth.

Second—that there is no such law. All law is divine and this law of mortal mind is only the inverted image of the law of God. Reverse it and you will find the divine law that all thoughts of Truth must have an effect. Isaiah 55: 10, 11.

March 31, 1892. *Near* 12 P.M. Our work is not to change God's work, for that is finished and perfect. Neither is it to make error nothing, for it is that already; but to stand (apparently) in the midst of it, unmoved, knowing its nothingness. Isaiah 43: 2.

April 6, 1892. No mortal thought put in action by any mesmerist, or combined force of mesmerists, or anyone whom they should employ, has any power to affect.

There is no M.A.M. 'The Lord He is God and there is none beside Him.' Prov. 16: 7.

May 11, 1892. Meet every false claim with the absolute Truth, nothing short of that will answer. John 8: 32.

May 21, 1892. Mortal mind at its best only reflects the immortal and perfect Mind even as the moon reflects the sun. So mortal mind (at best) shines with a borrowed light. For it to know this great fact and have a determination to reflect Good is to turn away from itself as substance and intelligence and thereby harmony is seen in reflection, 'For this mortal shall put on immortality', &c. Ezekiel chap. 16.

June 6, 1892. A 'Judas' is necessary (as a type) to uncover evil. Evil must be uncovered in order to bring out, or prove Truth. Mrs. E. Matt. 18: 7. Luke 17: 1. John 9: 3. Romans 9: 17.

An Audible Treatment. June 18, 1892. I would bring you near to God for in Him is salvation, salvation from every ill. Sickness is an ill.

God is omnipotent, all-powerful, omnipresent, everywhere present, omniscient, all-knowing. *Make them see* every point.

God is perfect Mind. Nothing but *Mind* can know all, have all power, and be everywhere present.

Sin, sickness and death are not in this perfect Mind which is God. The universal law is that the greater must control the lesser. Then perfection must rule over imperfection.

Prove to them the fact that the body is controlled by Mind.

Show the utter powerlessness of the body as matter.

Prove it to them by illustrations that they can lay hold of. Use smiles, tears, a blush, action of the body in coming or going to different localities. Show them that the eyes have no power to weep, the face no power to smile, the arm no power to lift itself, the limbs no power to walk. Prove by inaction during sleep and death. Then show the condition of the body in sickness, paralysis and death to be its response to the fear which is produced in consequence of the ignorance of the fact that mind governs instead of the body. Show them that this discordant action is unconscious to them until they are awakened to it.

Bring to bear the fact that death has many times come by fright. Use page 45 top and 378 *Science and Health*. Read chapter on medicine.

Body and mind are one, in action, or the visible manifestation of an invisible power. The *I* and body one. The *I* must be changed in order to change the body.

Let them see that the perfect Mind which is without these discordant conditions, fear, ignorance, &c. must govern.

Make them *see all* this, and in proportion as *you see it*, can you make them. Isa. 10: 15.

July 10, 1892. To the senses a pain is present. Now this pain is a condition of (mortal) mind, which we call mesmerism, a condition which would say, *I am something*.

We know that the true, or real condition of Mind, which is perfection, freedom from all pain, is ever-present.

The intermediate condition of mind is one which has the knowledge that the false, or condition of pain, has no power to hold or perpetuate itself, because of the ever-presence of the true condition which only needs be recognized. To recognize it, is to call upon God for help.

'And it shall come to pass that before they call, I will answer; and while they are yet speaking, I will hear.' Isaiah 65: 24.

August 1, 1892. See all false claims as conditions of (mortal) mind entirely distinct from the person.

Handle each one as it appears to your thought.

Watch your own thought that you be not tripped and used as a channel to prevent the good work you are trying to do.

This is most important, as the subtlety of evil is to prevent Truth from appearing.

Another subtlety is the claim that to 'handle the serpent' will not do any good. *Look well to this.*

August 6, 1892. The intermediate condition referred to in note of July 10 is the 'Jesus thought'. This is the mediator between God (perfect Mind) and man (mortal mind) or the 'link between the human and divine'. This condition recognizes all evil as evil, and as nothing, and destroys it by so doing, and by seeing the opposite Good at the same time. Evil would crucify this condition but cannot.

Give the 'Jesus thought' its rightful place and know that it cannot be moved, then success must follow. It will do its work without fail.

'For he must reign, till he hath put all enemies under his feet.' I Cor. 15: 25.

Taunton. August 17, 1892. Ignorance is the one great error, and this is only another name for the unconscious mind. When this is removed Harmony or the conscious Mind governs.

When *teaching* music or mathematics we remove the ignorance on the subject.

When healing a patient we are correcting the errors causing the disturbance even as we solve a problem for a child bringing out the right results. We should be able if *necessary* to heal without teaching, even as we would solve the problem before explaining how it was done.

But mortal mind *claims power* to rise up and rebel against being corrected; but let the understanding prevail that it has no power so to do, then that ignorance which alone gave it power to rise in rebellion is removed. Ps. 92: 7. Isa. 54: 17.

See nothing but conditions of mind.

All is Mind.

September 1892. Mortal thought awakened is startled at its own shadow.

While it slumbered the shadow was unperceived. It must needs learn the nothingness of itself and its shadow, then the fear which in its ignorance was unconscious, and became conscious at the awakening will pass away, for mortal mind will see that it need not be afraid of itself. II Thess. 2: 8.

October 16, 1892. Sometimes I seem to hear the voice of the Father like this—My child, there is nothing in mortal mind to fear, not even the educated thought that knows what it is doing. But these different claims must needs remain until thou art not afraid. They are here only for thee to learn that they cannot harm. When that is learned their mission is accomplished and away they go. Ex. 4: 4.

October 25. The way to learn their powerlessness is through the constant recognition of God's power to dislodge them.

November 22, 1892. When a discord is present, *remember* that when Love is pushing upon the sense, evil is aggravated and is forced from unconsciousness to conscious thought. Then be not afraid at such times. Darkness should be seen as the forerunner of great light. Then we may rejoice at such times, instead of being filled with fear. Zech. 14: 6, 7.

January 22, 1893. The condition that sees another condition as one that is 'bound of Satan', and bows before it, or fears it, and thereby gives it power is the most dangerous of the two and needs more to be looked after and rebuked. All conditions have their individuality (or claim to) and stand distinctively apart from every other condition and yet there are links connecting them with each other.

June 27, 1892. (This copied from slips)

1. Ever keep the fact of the Allness of God and the nothingness of error before us, then begin at home and root up every sin or belief of A.M. Destroy them with the Truth of Being. Let them learn first to show piety at home. Then we are fitted to heal or apply the Truth to error which disappears as Truth appears. Harmony of belief (the body) will appear before the understanding of Truth comes to the individual whom we are healing, one of the signs of Truth.

'Error is a *coward* before Truth.'

2. May Jesus Christ's baptism of the Holy Spirit cleanse you from sin, sickness, and death.

3. How to handle M.A.M. Love is all-powerful. Love is omnipotent. Love is All. Thy kingdom has come. Thy will is done on earth as it is in heaven, and earth is heaven.

(Notes taken in a class taught by Mrs. Eddy)

The rod that Moses threw down, became through God, the power of good. The rod Moses had, God did not give him, but God commanded him to throw it down, and it became a serpent, his enemy.

Then God spoke to Moses (who fled in fear) and commanded him to pick up the serpent (demonstrated the nothingness) and it became a rod.

He could not expect to throw away the rod power at once, but must take it up as a staff, let it become the power of God, see it (sickness, error) work in us unto salvation.

Jesus bore our infirmities. He took every step of the way before us. He demonstrated the whole problem and left us the rule. We must expect to take all the steps ourselves, and I tell you this, not to pronounce sentence upon you, but that being forewarned, you may be forearmed. When passing through the belief of sin, sickness or death, are you going to make a reality of it, or are you going to pick up the serpent and have no fear; but know that the serpent once handled becomes a *rod*, a staff? If made a reality it becomes a stumbling block.

Expect to suffer through every belief of mortal mind; but once settled upon, give it no thought, as you know when these problems are worked out, you not only believe, but know and understand, that man is perfect, and cannot suffer. You must understand the nothingness of every phase of the dream in order to realize the somethingness of Truth. But we must not flee from the serpent. God's word is, pick it up, and we can prove to ourselves that as soon as our fear of the serpent is overcome, so that we can stretch forth our hand (power) and pick it up, the serpent changes into power.

Higher understanding always brings with it submission and humbleness. Take the stand today, *God is All*. Live it. No thought of mortal mind affects; there is no mortal mind. The fire of Truth destroys all error in consciousness, and God is All.

When you hear a Scientist speak the lie or live it, never mention it, as you double the lie by doing so. When seeing such, declare for Truth, and so destroy the lie.

Go slowly, take each step, and feel content. Do not let ambition to go beyond another influence you. Lay aside ambition and pride. Put pride beneath your feet. Never care for popularity, or covet praise, and never let words of praise delight you, but rather rejoice in rebuke in that it takes out of your way obstacles in your path.

The difference between Science and faith-healing: one makes the healed *know God*; the other simply heals the physical. Faith-healing is not really healing, or else the patient would be one with God. So do not think because you heal you are a Christian Scientist; as medicine heals as regards the senses, and so does error. A Christian Scientist heals the morals as well as the physical. When carrying a case, and having used the arguments for some time and not healing, depend upon it, they are implanting the belief in the patient's thought. The arguments must be dropped. But when one is teaching a child to walk, they give the child a finger to hold by; but they do not withdraw the finger until the child can walk; then the finger is removed. So with arguments; they are the finger.

Rise to a sense of the omnipotence of God. Know that God is All. It is not sufficient to *say it*. You must realize it. Destroy fear with Love. Remember God's law is the only law. Do not ask the patient's belief; you are perpetuating as long as you take account of error. Never expect to win without drinking his cup, and carrying his cross.

How to treat sin? To treat sin when understanding the unreality of sin, to cast your net on the right side. Do not treat for sin; declare for God, realizing His omnipotence. It is the only safe way. Touching sin is dangerous, as it cannot be unreal to you until you understand its nothingness.

Now what of those who make a claim such as this: declaring the Truth harmonizes matter, that Truth will heal matter, or in any way making matter a reality to be healed? If we admit there is matter, then we must admit all the causes and effects, all the beliefs; there is no other way. Then never admit matter. Never for one moment admit a claim of anything to harmonize.

And what of those that admit God knows sin? If He knows it, it is in Principle, and man is the expression of Principle; then man must sin, as he expresses Principle. Sin *is not* in Principle, and there is nothing else. Now learn the lesson that sin is nothing, so to you, until you understand its nothingness, you must uncover it and handle it; let the serpent turn into a rod.

Let your prayer be daily: reveal to me, O God, my secret faults, every error, every sin. Earnestly desire to know thyself, to have thy heart searched, to let thyself be humbled, and the man of God stand revealed. Never for one instant say, 'Thank God, I am not as other men'. There is no I. If you are a personality, you are as other men; but if you are the *idea* of God, there is but one I, God.

Stand alone. Never allow anyone to help you: as sure as you do, you cripple yourself; you weaken your power. Remember what it means in Jeremiah 17: 5. The arm of strength is in God and nowhere else. Trust then in God and when you have all you can bear, and even more than you think you can bear, go and say, 'Watch with me one hour', and then once more take your stand.

You have but one Leader and your allegiance and trust belong to but one.

The seed must remain quiet; it must not be disturbed or it cannot grow. It must not be worried. Do not stir the ground. How sad a thing it is to see the fowls of the air come and scratch away the seed ere it has a chance to grow; but how sad to have seed worried and stirred, and then grow stunted and distorted, unfit for fruit. Now, remember, let the seed have a chance. Watch that the fowls of the air cannot scratch it; care for it tenderly, and then after that, take heed that man's hand disturbs not the soil; let the ground remain protected; this is your work and the result is sure.

Never let the world come in. Now you know the material universe is the expression of mortal mind and that it is powerless (but until you realize and understand this, it is not powerless) so watch lest ye enter into temptation. When you once understand the real, then you have dominion over all these things, but until then, *watch*. You shall have dominion over the whole world, but only when you have conquered.

Remember God never gave man dominion over man. Man was told by divine law to 'bear one another's burdens', to uplift the hands that hang down; but never to rule or have dominion over man.

In teaching, all reform has been a *stir*, so you must stir the mind, move the waters and then go in. The pool of Bethesda, the waters were stirred before they went in, so you must stir the waters, then go in and you can expect to win.

Treat yourself before you treat your patients.

Be a law to yourself. Remember you are a law to yourself anyway, so be one on the right side. Let it be understood, and never let it be neglected.

When battling with mortal mind, stand firmly on the side of right, that God is All, and if you have a sense that you cannot win, lay the problem aside for a while; then once more take it up, as you would when a child in mathematics, and never ask for help except you come to the agony of the garden. Science reveals the necessity either before or after death to quench the love of sin. The remission of the penalty due for sin would be for Truth to pardon error. Escape from punishment is not in accordance with God's government, in which justice is the handmaid of mercy. In the undoing of the errors of sense here or hereafter, one must pay to the uttermost farthing in order to bring the body into subjection to Spirit. Unwinding one's snarls, learning from experience, dividing (through pangs unspeakable) between Truth and error, these are the divine methods of paying the wages of sin.

The mists of error sooner or later will melt in the fervent heat of suffering. Mortality will burst the barriers of sense, and man be found perfect and eternal.

Your Holy City called salvation will we have for walls and bulwarks, Isaiah 26: 1, 2. 'Open ye the gates that the righteous nation which keepeth the truth may enter in.' 'Violence shall no more be heard in thy land, wasting nor destruction within thy borders; but thou shalt call thy walls Salvation, and thy gates, Praise.' Isaiah 60: 18.

'Behold I lay in Zion a foundation stone, a precious corner stone, a sure foundation. Judgment also will I lay to the line, and righteousness to the plummet.'

The divine mystery of Godliness was the rock of Truth on which he built his church of the new-born, against which the gates of hell cannot prevail.

God is All. The law of Life and Truth does more than forgive the false sense named sin; for it pursues and punishes, and will not let it go, until it is destroyed, until nothing remains to suffer or to be punished. Forgiven thus, sickness and sin have no relapse. God's law is in three words, 'I am All', and this Gospel is ever-present to rebuke any claim of another law. God pities our woes with the love of a father for his child, not by becoming human and knowing sin; but by removing our knowledge of what is not.

Divine pardon is that divine presence which is the sure destruction of sin. So the only proof of sin's pardon is its destruction. The belief in sin, its pleasures, gain, or power, must suffer until it is self-destroyed. 'Whatsoever a man soweth, that shall he reap.' 'As a tree falleth so shall it lie.' As death finds mortal mind, so shall he be after death.

Heaven is within man, when all is harmony. God is the same yesterday, today, and forever. Our mortal idea of Him is progressing, growing, expanding.

Moses from a high realization talked with God. But to the Children of Israel he could only forbid sin, not deny it.

The difference between imagination and belief: Imagination is thought in solution; belief is the gathering together of the vapors into a solid conviction.

We must not rely too much on the thought, 'By their fruits shall ye know them', 'Not every one that saith unto me, Lord, Lord, shall enter into the kingdom of heaven'.

Animal magnetism is the malicious or unconscious action of error, the direct opposite of Christian Science. It exists in mortal mind. It must be met, recognized and mastered before it can be destroyed by Christian Science. To do this it is necessary to recognize that all is Truth, God, and there is none beside Him. Deny all else. To do this we must attain a high realization of Truth.

Remember what Christ said to his disciples, 'This kind goeth not out, but by fasting and prayer'; prayer that enables us to silence the claims of sense, to deny all sin and error, and to let our lives attest our sincerity; fasting that enables us to deny the claims of appetite, learn that we live to eat, *not* eat to live.

Learn to see only in spiritual discernment, and learn that hearing is the *all-knowing*; that touch is the divine consciousness of all.

Never treat without the consent of the patient. Deny all sickness and discord, but do not restrict it to personality. Treat yourself for a higher consciousness of God's power. Deny *all* but Him, and realize there is none beside Him; then you will reach not only the one case, but all error. Rebuke discord in every thought and by your very presence. In treating error, realize that you are treating nothing; then it will disappear before you. We sometimes make it such a reality to ourselves that we hold it over the patient, even when we would leave it,

We do not heal by faith, but by conviction, based on understanding. The steps are improved belief, faith, and understanding. The sooner we realize the utter nothingness of all the evidences of the senses, the sooner we arrive at the true Science of Being, God. This must come by prayer and fasting, prayer that is one constant desire for something higher, whose earnest sincerity will work its own answer.

Contradict the evidence of the senses all the time, in all ways. Be willing to surrender all affection, all worship that is merely personal. Do not make the mistake of refusing to admit the belief of error. There is a belief, a strong one, and it must be met and denied. Flee from it, and it will follow faster than ever. Suffering is the gospel that will bring man to a knowledge of his real estate. Better to have pain than pleasure. The greater the pain, the nearer its own overthrow. We should not wait for perfection in our work before demonstration. That would be to admit the reality of imperfection, the very thing we are trying to overthrow.

Christ said, 'Come ye that labor and are heavy laden, and I will give you rest'. To come unto him is to show our acquaintance with Him, to demonstrate. We do this while we are weary and heavy laden, and we find rest.

To be sick, does not always prove we are sinning, any more than to be well proves we are not sinning.

Remember man's extremity is God's opportunity.

Christ was the first and greatest Scientist. He overcame the world, the flesh, and evil. He came, not as a Saviour from the consequences of sin, but to teach us how to overcome sin with understanding. He spares us nothing of suffering, but to him who strives and overcomes shall be given a crown of Life. He died a man in the flesh, and he rose a man in the flesh. As a tree falleth, so shall it lie. He explained this to

Thomas before he demonstrated the unreality of matter and disappeared from his disciples.

Probation, progress, goes on, until there is no life, substance, or intelligence in matter.

Before each meal, deny the existence of any power or intelligence that can interfere with our conscious oneness with God.

There is within us a divine selfhood that recognizes the genuine, good and true; a reflection of the divine perfection and intelligence, that enables us to lay hold of the Truth when it is presented to us.

What is meant by the Trinity? Father is supreme being; Son, the divine reflection; Holy Ghost, the Saviour, divine Science.

Do not go into the ways of the Gentiles: Follow not after the ways of the world. Help them, salute them, but do not follow their customs. Do not urge your views on those who do not wish to listen.

Heal the sick: Help those who need it, whether in sickness or sin. Do not say you *can* heal; say you will *try*.

The kingdom of heaven is at hand: Wherever God is, is heaven, and He is everywhere, omnipotent and omnipresent.

Provide neither gold nor silver nor brass in your purses: Does not mean money, but what it might attain in worldly sense, position, power, or whatever might bring you into prominence, or gain the world's approval.

No scrip: Anything which seems to promise advancement.

Neither two coats: A semblance of worldliness, to gain the world, or to win the Pharisee. Always and above *all be honest* and *true*. Be yourself as God made you.

Neither shoes: Shoes are a protection over rough places. There are no rough places, only as we make them. Have no fear, and they will not appear. God makes straight paths; trust all to Him.

Neither staves: No support, nothing to lean upon but the conscious oneness with God. The workman is worthy, and is worthy of God's sustenance, the Bread of Life.

And when you come into a home, salute it: Knock at the door of human beliefs, wait for permission to enter. Speak gently, decorously; make no onslaught upon doors and windows, demanding entrance, or you will get a rebuff, and deserve it. Neither try to gain an entrance secretly, against the owner's will; that is worst of all. God has given each one certain rights no one has a right to invade.

Justice is man's highest mortal belief.

Study to be quiet. In quietness and in confidence shall be your strength.

Mind is the quickening power. Let the same Mind be in you that was in Christ Jesus, Spirit, boundless freedom; for the law of the

Spirit of Life has made me free. Life: to know God. Understanding: to know God is Life eternal. Truth: power, demonstrated law of God Bread of Heaven: that which nourishes and sustains.

To N. R. (items from a notebook—not necessarily first-hand) [Nemi Robertson]
Animal magnetism can always be detected in thought by (1) a confusion; (2) forgetting; (3) refusal to do one's duty; (4) moral illness. The declaration of *one Mind*—and no power or presence beside God will destroy these effects. Mind is all action.

Giving lectures and teaching classes is not Christian Science. Healing the sick *is.*

The only time is *now;* the only power is Love; the only Mind is God.

To build a church requires more than money, stones and talk. The world will give you plenty of money. M.A.M. will stone you. Talk will not be lacking. But demonstration—one Mind—one God this is necessary. See Matthew 7: 21-3

I have taken you up into the mountain and shown you the Promised Land, but you will have to walk every step of the way there yourself.

As a child puts her hand in the hand of a parent, so I have put my hand in the hand of God—and He will never let me go!

Students expect more and more teaching. This is the work of the evil one. God alone teaches. He says something to us all every hour. When will they all awake to hear *His* voice and stop looking to me?

Watch that M.A.M. does not dull your thought to the clear Word of God. I gave so much to your class—my last class—and *so little* has been done with it! Why? Because sleep overcomes the thought. Students must be watchers against the 'thief that cometh in the night'. (Also recorded as a specific 'watch'—see p.37)

One God. One Mind. All is Truth, Life and Love. This is the path, straight and narrow, leading to the Father's secret reward. You must follow every step of the way. I alone know what that means!

When the storm of A.M., Catholicism, Theosophy, demonology, blows upon our house, *Truth* will sustain it. *We have to know this.* It was this that saved the Cause after Dr. Eddy was taken away.

God bless you my dear, I know He does. *You* must know it too!

Anatomy is the sign of the dragon. Knowledge of God is the reward of diligent seeking. One God. One Mind. Love is the *only power.*

Our Father sees us in secret. Do you know what this means? Only God can give you the answer. Divine Love will lead you if you *trust.*

Theory never built a church, never taught a class, never wrote the Christian Science textbook. Healing the sick is done by practice, not profession—by prayer and fasting from material sense. Mortal mind claims otherwise, but God is All, and there is no evil. Love rules, and you know it.

When you lean on divine Love as a staff—as David did—then you are safe.

God wrote the textbook. Study it; let God speak to you!

Love controls the weather. No electricity of mortal mind. No thunder, no high wind to blow. Divine Mind governs all. (Given to the workers at Pleasant View.)

Many minds are at work at this instant to stop our work for humanity and for the Cause. Yet their effort will fail. Why? Because God speaks to me as He has spoken from the earliest days when He guided me to the founding of this Cause. He speaks, and I must follow. This is my cross. How I wish I could explain to you what this means!

(Between 1904-6) It was when I could turn to God *completely*—leaving all thought of family and friends behind—even the nearest and dearest—that He could lead me into the land of Christian Science. I do not know how others find this path, but much was demanded of me in the first years; much giving up. Yet divine Love has more than compensated me for it all!

Students do not understand animal magnetism for what it is and for what it *is not*. When they do, they will raise the dead, and *not until* then.

I have told you that evil has no power, yet I have told you to handle evil as though it had power. This is because of your place in growth spiritual. When the Allness of God is seen, the nothingness of evil is evident—hold to that.

(In reply to a remark about the beauty of a spring day at Pleasant View) You would not believe the storms of evil that rage and roar round this house. Yet within, all is calm and serene with the light of His presence.

Jesus understood his spirituality; hence his success in healing. If you all understood as he did, you would not need me to teach you, and to correct you. I am amazed when I see how little Christian Science healing is done. So much is faith healing, little more.

Students love the explanations of Christian Science: God is Love, God is good, God is Mind, etc. This is the crown of Christian Science. But they dislike the cross of Christ—the patient, slow bearing of the cross they shun. They will not handle animal magnetism. All the cross-bearing they leave to me, while they love the crown. Yet this lesson they will learn.

The work of many minds attempted to stop the building of The Mother Church. Now that plan of M.A.M. was defeated. It is up to the students to protect that demonstration—from the enemy *within our gates*.

Mortal mind says, 'Trust in me!' God says, 'I Am'. This is the answer to error.

When students rise in the consciousness of *God alone* as reality, then error, animal magnetism will disappear. Why? Because it never was.

My angels are exalted thoughts (S. & H. 299). (Mrs. Eddy said that this passage *understood* would raise the dead.)

I do not understand students when they speak of difficult cases. When I first practised in Truth, *all* my cases were difficult. Mortal mind never gave me an *easy* case. But all this is M.A.M. You must rise to see only *one Mind*, and the mists will disappear. Rouse yourselves! *God is here*!

Animal magnetism is powerless—but you must declare against it as though it had *all power*.

The Weather

God governs all, is All-in-all. God is our constant Guide and Guardian. No mortal thought, known or unknown, seen or unseen, can interfere with the manifestation of Love's presence with us. The weather manifests God's government, and no evildoers can change this fact. The devils of human thought—all the powers of *many* minds, are powerless in Love's presence. God is All. God is Mind.

To C. S. [Clara Shannon]

God did not send Christ because He saw the evil, but our need brought the Christ. He sent Him in afar higher way than our material thought could see. He was the effect of our need.

God's pity. He hears our cry and sends more love. We are conscious of a need, and reach out to God and become capable of taking in more of God.

Astrology: Belief in a horoscope is a mortal thought, and it does actually affect human lives until it is overcome by Christian Science. Every human being comes under its influence, unless, and until, we meet it with the truth. Astrologists believe that a man can improve on his horoscope. (Mrs. Eddy said we were to know that there was no solar, lunar or planetary influence.)

Palmistry: Human thought is reflected in the lines of the hand just as clearly as in the face or in the head.

Evolution: Basis cannot be lesser than that which it evolves. The lesser cannot contain the greater. This does away with evolution; 'the invisible becomes visible'.

Theology—the worship of personality: Christian Science theology is: reality of good and the unreality of evil. Theologies are opinions of men *about* what Jesus did; also, *about* the teachings of the Scriptures and the prophets. In Science we understand all the teachings of Christ, which include all good and exclude all evil. And we can prove it.

Animal magnetism, I acknowledge your claims, but I denounce your power. When error speaks, nothing is said. Stop justifying yourself in error.

To A. S. [Augusta Stetson or Allison Stewart]

Self-depreciation is not humility but the meanest kind of pride because it admits a sense of self apart from God.

To L. S. (from his collection) [Lewis Strang]

A RULE AT PLEASANT VIEW. No student can eat at my table who does not say a few words for God before he or she leaves the table. I was early educated to this. I always do it at my table because I CANNOT AVOID doing it.

To M. W. (from some notes—including indirect quotations) [Martha Wilcox]

Mrs. Eddy said that sometimes a sense of a personality arises before your thought and leads you to believe that a personality is something outside and separate from your thought, that can harm you. She showed me that the real danger was never this threatened attack from outside my thought where the personality seemed to be, but that the real danger was always within my thought. She made it clear that my sense of personality was mental—a mental image formed in my so-called mortal mind, and was never external or separate from my mind. This supposititious mortal mind outlines itself as a belief of a material personality, with form and conditions and laws and circumstances—in fact, with all of the phenomena that are embraced in what is called material life and personality. And then she showed me that not one solitary fact in this whole fabric of supposititious evil was true. She showed me that I must detect that all this mental phenomenon was only aggressive mental suggestion coming to me for me to adopt it as my own thought.

She showed me that, because mental practice is mental, the only place that I could meet it was within what seemed to be my own mentality, and the only way that I could meet it was to give up the belief in a power and presence other than God, or Truth. She showed me that this seeming *within* enemy could never harm me, if I were awake to the Truth and active in the Truth....

This lesson on mental malpractice was quite apropos for one entering the household comprised of never less than seventeen and up to twenty-five personalities. After this talk on mental malpractice, Mrs. Eddy opened her Bible and read to me from Luke 16: 10, 11, 12. She, no doubt, realized that at my stage of growth, I thought of creation—that is, all things—as separated into two groups, one group spiritual and the other group material, and that somehow I must get rid of the group I called material. But during this lesson I caught my first glimpse of the fact that all right, useful things which I had been calling 'the unrighteous mammon'—were mental and represented spiritual ideas. She showed me that unless I were faithful and orderly with the objects of sense that made up my present mode of consciousness, there could never be revealed to me the 'true riches', or the progressively higher revealments, of substance and things.

The two lessons that I received that first morning were fundamentally great. First, I was to handle mental malpractice within my own mentality. Second, the 'objects of sense' when correctly understood, are really 'ideas of Soul'. There are not two groups of creation—but just one.

When she had finished, she said, 'Now, take your young child down into Egypt and let it grow up until it is strong enough to stand alone'.

One night after I had tucked her in bed, I said, 'Mother, I did not forget once nor make a mistake, did I? She smiled up at me from her pillow and replied, 'No, you didn't. Nighty night.' At about midnight she rang my bell. I went to her and asked her what she wanted. She said, 'Martha, do you ever forget? I replied, 'Mother, Mind never forgets'. Then she said, 'Go back to bed'.

The next morning after she was seated in her study, she said, 'Martha, if you had admitted last night that anyone can forget, you would have made yourself liable to forgetting. Whatever error you admit in yourself as real or in another, you make yourself liable to that error. Admitting error as real produces error and is all there is to it.'

At one time, I was under her personal instruction and was a mental worker for seven weeks. One evening she gave me a problem to work out, and I had a great desire to prove the reality at hand. So I worked the greater part of the night. In the morning she called me to her and said, 'Martha, why did you not do your work?' I replied, 'Mother, I did'. She said, 'No, you didn't. You had a good talk with the devil. Why did you not know God's allness.' I said, 'Mother, I tried.' Her reply was, 'Well, if Jesus had just tried and failed, we would have no Science today'. Then she had a card hung on the inside of the door to my room on which was printed in large letters, 'Faith without works is dead'. I had to look at it for two weeks!

Another time she said, 'Now, Martha, you go upstairs and write out a treatment for rain. We need rain.' On that special day, while it was very sultry, the sun never shone brighter. I had hardly seated myself to write out the treatment, when my number rang, and I had to go to her. She said, 'Well, give me your treatment'. I said, 'Mother, I did not have time to write it out'. She said, 'Well, just tell it to me'. So I started in to show God's allness, but she soon stopped me and said, 'Now, Martha, come down from sailing around up there. It's rain we need. Let's have rain.' With the greatest feeling of humility and in tears, I said, 'Mother, I can't do it'. Then she said, 'It took Calvin and Laura a long time to do it, but you can see that it must be done, and learn somewhat of how to do it'.

Then she talked to me about the weather, and when she had finished, I went to my room and wrote down as nearly as I could remember and had understood, some of the things she had told me. 'God does not make sultry weather, and if we, through belief, make weather sultry, we must unmake it. God governs the weather. He governs the elements and there are no destructive winds or lightning. Love always looks out from the clouds. Beliefs about the weather are easier healed than sickness.'

To the Christian Scientists' Association (as recorded by William B. Johnson, Secretary)

CAUSE OR PROFESSION—WHICH?

'He anointeth my head with oil, my cup runneth over' means, the action of Mind on our consciousness. Water corresponds to unconscious mind. All unconscious thought is in solution, when it comes to the surface it is dry land. The Red Sea, spoken of in the Scriptures, is the figuration of fear in unconscious mind. Error, sin, sickness and death, is sown and commences in the unconscious mind of your patients, and yourself; your patients, through ignorant fear; your own, through neglect, or wilful sin. 'Baptism by fire' corresponds to fear in mortal mind. All our suffering is from fear. We have got to pass through the furnace heated seven times hotter than it was wont to be. Man's extremity is God's opportunity. The remedy for the trials of the hour, hatred, fear, etc., is love. How shall I meet this heated hatred, this envy, this malice, this poison of thought? is the question with the Christian Scientist. The answer is, by the exercise of Love, which chasteneth the evildoer. Evil hath its own reward. The law in Israel today is—What you say or do to cause another to suffer, shall cause you, not them to suffer, and we do not succeed because we do not observe this law. That the spirit of revenge in mortal mind may not prevail, students should see the necessity of, and strive to attain a clearer understanding of the law of Love.

There is only one way to meet this rule of sin. Would we entertain a guest that was spoiling our house? Now, instead of entertaining the guest that says, 'you cannot heal!'; old beliefs are re-established; you feel your patient's beliefs etc., it is your duty to eject this guest at once. No man can enter into a strong man's house and spoil his goods except he first bind the strong man; and then he will spoil his house. You can make your house—the body—just what the mind is. The discouragement brought to you, you are able to expel as an unwelcome guest. This is the ground on which all must work. Watch just what your thoughts are, and labor there until success greets your efforts. If you think you haven't time to attend to it, say I have; or if you think you need help, prove it otherwise. There is no one who can help you like yourself. There are no *conditions* hindering. They are only what you admit. Whenever you take this position you go up higher. The opposite position is that of 'I don't care'. Let me tell you something for your encouragement. The one who has met the most, and conquered it, is the nearest heaven, harmony. Students are morally responsible to meet any error in themselves, and then it will disappear from the patient. It is not the patient. It is some moral wrong in the student. Never allow error (the use of medicines) to be used indirectly, not merely from fear that they injure your patient, for they have no virtue, but for the reason that God would not get all the glory of the healing. (Delivered at meeting of February, 1889)

To a 'New York Herald' Correspondent (extracts from the newspaper's further account of the interview with Mrs. Eddy, supplementing the first record which is given fairly fully in *My.* 341-6)

(*May* 5, 1901) The problem (of the government of the Church) is not so much as to the form of the government as providing an authority that will ever keep its spirit true to the Christian Science doctrine, a monitor more than a master. I have made rigid by-laws for the government of the Church, and every one has been necessary, but they need to be administered in gentleness and forbearance as well as in firmness with the erring. I have always been motherly to my Church, instead of dictatorial, as has been falsely said....

Woman has the finer spiritual nature. She more readily takes the impress of Christian Science. If, as you say (I leave all statistics to the publication department), there are 13,000 women, against 5,000 men, out of a book total of 18,000, it shows that their minds are more receptive; their enthusiasm greater at the beginning of a struggle, but in the strength of man lies the power of carrying it on.

I look on man as the designate of the Word, but, to my view, the idea of race is superior to the idea of sex. Indeed, may we not look forward to a human condition, when perfection is nearer, wherein neither male nor female shall be known, and the race may reproduce itself otherwise than now? ...

We are not indifferent to forms of government, but we support the best in each. A church to be universal must in many things be neutral about forms of government and at the same time support what is right to support.

When all men are one in the Church of Christ, the perfection of life and the perfection of government under the application of the Golden Rule will come. It will all be simple, natural, without clash or combat, all over the world in a divine brotherhood.

PRESERVED BY OTHER STUDENTS

By A. E. B. [Alfred E. Baker]

There is no anger, hence no pain; there is no hate, hence no poison; there is no fear, hence no death.

By C.

(2/10/95) 1 walk right up to death, and I don't find anything more.

(1/28/98) The only trouble is we limit God's power. We could even raise the dead from the grave if we did not limit Him. Jesus would not have passed on if the disciples had watched with him as requested.

(2/2/98) There is no overaction, inaction, stoppage or clogging to the heart, for the heart is Love.

(2/7/98) There is nothing to change of life.

(11/13/10) Manna must fall from your lips everyday to help some mortal mind for time and eternity.

O! May you feel the touch of the spiritual idea that is the light in your path!

By L. C. [Laura Conant]

Now my students, you go from this class with the intention of doing right. You will not wilfully err. Let me tell you, only one of two things can hinder this intention or disturb you; that is fear or malice. When you follow my rules these cannot touch you. When you have treated a patient and have removed all envy, hatred and pride from your own thought, stand in the Truth, not a treatment but an *attitude.* Some say they have treated and *worked* and gone their way when in reality they have not given one helpful thought to their relief. Do not work, *seek.* Do not be anxious, knock and find and stand in the consciousness of Truth. *Do not look to matter to tell* you your success but look *up, for your* harvest is right at hand. You *know* the Father's love, *trust it.* Then when you hear a whisper, 'Now you are a sinner and so and so is your punishment, this suffering is the consequence', *put it out; put it out.*

Animal magnetism says you are a sinner when you know *you* are not going deliberately to work to sin. Then empty your thought of fear and say, 'I look to God, my Father to see what I am. He alone shall tell me of myself.'

In the presence of death declare Life is spiritual, that Life *is present,* that Life is my life. Life is God, so life cannot lapse, collapse or relapse, for God is divine Principle.

The qualities of mental malpractice: a stolid moral sense; great lack of spiritual sentiments; the desire to subjugate; unsurpassed secretiveness masked by innocence and youth.

Never notice publicly an error if it can be avoided. Never rejoice in victory over it nor lament. It gives power where it does not belong. Evil is not *something.* Then wherefore give it the honor of noticing it further than to remove it? Then let the dead bury their dead. Have no funeral knell or trumpet blast over nothing, otherwise you will make it something and consistency is especially most desirable in dealing with nothingness. To talk of evil is as inconsistent as to talk of sickness unless it be to untalk it and put it out of mind forever.

There is no fatal mistake; there is no unforgivable wrong; there is no unpardonable sin; there is no permanent injury; there is no incurable disease; there is no such thing as too late.

Adhesion and cohesion are qualities of Mind and work together for good. In weather conditions these properties cannot be reversed to harm or retard man.

To the sore question, 'What are the workingmen's rights?' Science answers, mercy and justice, wherein the financial, civil, social, moral, and religious aspect of all questions reflect the face of the Father; and this question will not rest until both the employer and the employee are actuated by the spirit of this saying of the meek and mighty Son of God, 'Therefore all things whatsoever ye would that men should do to you, do ye even so to them.'

I cannot answer you as to the morrow. I am God's servant and know not what I shall be bidden to do in the future. Let us wait on Him, wait on divine Love that should direct all our ways and Love saith, 'Take no thought for the morrow. Sufficient unto the day is the evil thereof.'

God moves in a mysterious way—to the human sense, but to the spiritual it is plainly Love that guides and directs in obedience to Love all that we commit unto Him.

(Regarding patients) Walk with them to Emmaus, but treat them from the housetops.

In treating a claim never become discouraged if it reappears; but go to work and keep on treating it each time, and each time it will appear in a milder form; finally it will disappear forever.

Trust in God and He will direct thy path. God is beside us at all times and in our daily work. Realize the ever-present Love and rejoice. Error cannot rob us of our abundance; the demonstration of this is abundance of light and love and intelligence even for an our material needs. I CAN is the son of I AM because I AM is I CAN. I can express love, patience, truth, because I am. Declare against the sense of limitation and realize that nothing can hinder my progress in advancing and getting employment. There is nothing to hinder my success or progress. I am honestly ready to see what God wants me to do.

If we do not control our possessions with the understanding that they are spiritual, they will control us with the belief that they are material.

Love is the uric acid solvent. *Materia medica* says uric acid is poison. It is identical with the venomous poison of the snake. An claims of disease are the result of vegetable, animal or mineral poison, and act as cancer eating away, having the quality of irritability, or fretting and vexation. Poison affects mainly the nervous system, having principally the quality of irritability or ugliness, we learn in Science founded on self-righteousness. The vegetation of Mind win express life and beauty. The minerals of Mind will reflect brilliancy and utility. The animals of Mind will change into sublimity and pure affection of Life, Truth and Love.

Baptism is mental cleansing. Bread is the true idea or understanding of God. Ascension of thought reveals infinite and eternal progression. Ideas fitly joined together are never severed. What God bath joined....

God, good, Spirit, is ever-present and man is His image and likeness. This is a rule that will solve any problem.

If we live the truth we talk then this we can give to another, but if we talk beyond what we have lived and demonstrated, this darkens both us and those that hear us.

(Or again: We talk beyond what we demonstrate; stop talking and demonstrate what you understand of Truth. If you talk beyond that, it darkens those who hear.)

You think you bury the body. You will sometime resurrect it to your own damnation or to its utter destruction. Paul says if you build again those things which you destroy, you are making yourself a transgressor.

I find the way by *experience;* hence I am a Christian Science weather vane constantly veering with the winds of Truth.

These verdicts are what mortal mind argues and must be handled in giving treatment:

1. The pre-natal belief, deep-seated and remote.
2. The parental.
3. The personal and professional.

Always look for dependability and stability in a thought.

Hold sacredly to your joy, your gratitude. It will keep the door of spiritual revelation open and unfold to your receptive thought the white Christ light of unselfishness, or joy and activity, for ministry is gratitude and compassion.

(After remarking that we need to go back and pick up all the beliefs we had under *materia medica* and see the unreality of them) When we are healed in Christian Science we are healed to the practitioner's understanding, but only to our belief; then we must go back and gain the understanding that the practitioner had in order to be really healed.

In the presence of death always declare the presence of Life, Life, Life, and never let your thought rest on or in the negative for one moment.

Striving to be better is being better. When you are fitting yourself to go up higher, you are going up higher.

There is nothing about me that attracts, corresponds with, or responds to, any form of error or evil. In proportion to your realization of this are you immune to the mesmeric and hypnotic influences of A.M.

First temptation (i.e. turning stones into bread): turning to material pleasure for satisfaction. The temptation regarding the pinnacle of the temple: Jesus could have been at the top of the priesthood, as he was of the order of Melchizedek. He could have sought the power of the world if he had compromised with the Pharisees and Rome.

'Father, if it be possible': i.e. possible in any other way to prove this truth.

Short Isolated Items attributed to Mrs. Eddy and preserved by L. C. [Laura Conant]

I feel like telling my students to hurry up.

Man reflects the divine perception, intelligence and memory.

Pray that your flight be not in the winter or the sabbath day; that is, pray for divine energy and watch against human apathy.

We awaken in others the attitude which we hold of them.

Any claim that says you cannot do it is self-mesmerism. *Go and do it.*

Whatever my need is it is met now,—God rules.

(Said of *Science and Health*) Great power comes from opening this book.

I speak to the whole of human consciousness and if you do everyone will hear you.

Humility—yielding to God, willingness to learn all things rightly. True rest is refuge from the elements of earth, Love-giving Life destroys the last enemy, death.

Body is the embodiment of right ideas. Watch your beliefs rather than your body.

The problem may be universal, the solution is individual. Hell is a state of forgetting or neglecting God.

In the real organization of work there is time for everything, rest, work, play, study, etc., etc.

Be not a self-appointed judge in Israel. Supply we gather as we give. Mental power is the Saviour. To know is to be.

No belief of transference or mental suggestion through a manometer can touch God's child with a belief of sensuality.

Material birth. Handle universal belief and universal consent.

Electricity is the counterfeit of the descent of the Holy Ghost.

When my students need me I will come to them.

If you do not have patients come to you, you can treat the birds and plants; they need treatment.

We may have tears for gladness but never for sorrow. (Similarly: Stop your blubbering. God works through strength, not through weakness.)

If we speak from the heart it will reach the heart.

The Golden Rule is the unchangeable law of God.

Every treatment we give will go on and on forever.

Know that divine Love is All and because it is All I cannot be robbed of my love and made to forget.

No intellectual disqualifications from poison.

Love flows through every avenue, fills every channel and removes every obstruction.

By A. H. D. [Adam H. Dickey]

(To A. F. [Alfred Farlow]) Shall I do wrong for taking your eggs by not paying for them? Or shall you do right by accepting what is just?

(To L. S. [Laura Sargent]) There is no evil, but you are in the sense of evil and your problem is to work out of it.

(To J. W. [John Willis-?]) They are telling you because there is but one Mind that you have not any mind. You know that you cannot lose the divine Mind or any of its faculties. (She told me to work on poison and hatred from revenge.)

By M. E. [Mary Eaton]

(To friends at Concord) Go about and all over the house within and without, but you will not then have seen the house wherein I dwell—but you will see it. (See *Journal*, Vol. XV, p. 532.)

By G.

He, Jesus, healed the young man then and there, and he neither prayed nor fasted as men interpret those words today. Is it not reasonable to suppose, therefore, that the fasting (denial) meant the denial of the reality of any such thing as fits (Mark 9: 7, 9, 25-9), or lunacy, and that the prayer meant the affirmation of the all-presence and the all-power of God wherein there is no possibility of either fits or lunacy? These are the essential features in the Christian Science prayer of today, and by it thousands are being healed every month.

By R. G.

What you have to meet is a fear; and what pacifies fear does not destroy it. Take your weapon that kills it, the First Commandment; and with that cut off its head.

Forget your own beliefs in thinking of what others endured and are silent, with no help nor man, and all the heathen can do to man daily. But 'all' is nothing that they can do. Love lives, rejoices and triumphs, and all that seems to be, is not.

Our Cause is rushing on; its chariot wheels are heard before the lips can speak its coming. Let us have on our wedding garments, for purity and peace now await our bridal.

The dear Love that knows all is Love, does all things well; hence whatever else appears is not His heaven, but the wrath that must, will praise Him sometime, and in some way.

The only manner whereby wrong is met scientifically is first to see it; next to be sorry for it; and lastly to correct it. This being the fact, the divine order is too important for me to forget or deny by admitting that wrong is not wrong, or that wrong can be forgiven.

Jesus said, or rather implied, that a Christian Scientist is not a reed shaken with the wind (is not an unreliable man) no matter what the influence may be, any more than he is one in soft raiment; i.e. a king or tyrant.

The unity of Love to its expression, man, can never be discontinued, as it is sustained by ever-operating, now operating divine law. There is no mortal law to destroy divine law.

God alone can handle M.A.M. The divine idea, alone, can handle it. God knows there is nothing to hate.

If human belief handles A.M. there is a fight, but divine Love knows there is nothing to fight. God is all that will handle A.M. When error appears, it only appears to disappear.

One has no pain. It is the soreness of fear, the inflammation of fear, the irritation of fear. Do not let evil deceive you. You have not these things. A.M. is the only thought that can have them.

Take this thought earnestly twice each day: There is no evil thinking and no evil argument; the lie and liar are a lie, an illusion; there is no such person nor thought. *God is all there is.*

Always remember that error in the individual is the result of a long line of mortal relationships with its prejudices, doubts, fears, etc. This is all there is to a mortal personality.

There is no opposite to Love. Hate claims to be; see that it is nothing. Human hate has nothing on which to operate. It claims to degenerate, consume, and disintegrate. One's protection against hate is the realization that divine Love flows through every avenue, cleanses every channel, and removes every obstruction. In fact, the law of Love is the law of elimination and the law of destruction to everything unlike itself. There is no mortal selfhood to be touched by hate. 'Human hate has no legitimate mandate and no kingdom.'

My future is locked up in the secret of my God, and He will direct my path on, on to the bright realm of the real where we may meet to part no more.

I have no desire to rule, possess, or control men, or their kingdoms on earth—because what I am, every child of God is also, and my rights are the rights of all others, so I cannot court a sense of material power or influence.

God is speaking to us all either in commendation or rebuke through the things which we experience. If we are doing strictly right, we shall be blessed for all we endure; if not, and we continue to justify ourselves, we shall suffer more and more and gain nothing by that suffering.

My prayer is for all who learn by suffering, and for all who learn by enjoying, to enter into the rest of rightness; for every experience human is met, compensated or punished by divine Love.

Selfishness is sin. Sensuality is disease and sickness. Sexuality is death.

Selfishness is the father of the lie. Sensuality is the mother of the lie. Sexuality is the child of the lie.

Selfishness is the predisposing cause. Sensuality is the remote cause. Sexuality is the exciting cause.

Selfishness is the old theology. Sensuality is the *materia medica.* Sexuality is the old natural science (so-called).

Selfishness is the old mortal sight. Sensuality is the old mortal hearing. Sexuality is the old mortal feeling (touch).

OVERCOME selfishness and you bring out unity. OVERCOME sensuality and you bring out purity. OVERCOME sexuality and you bring out the God idea.

These are the laws of sickness, sin and death, which war against the spiritual laws of Life, Truth and Love.

'Science lays the axe at the root of the tree.' You must go back to overcome the root, *cause*. Selfishness is the cause of sensuality.

What is God? God is Life, Truth, Love. What is man? God's idea, perfect, made in His image and likeness. How many men are there? One, the perfect man. How many bodies are there? One. How many ideas can there be of this man and body? Just one. Does this idea admit of disease? No. Can that body have a diseased eye? No. Is that eye diseased? No. Then what is the matter? You believe it is diseased. Do you believe this? No. Why? Because you are God's perfect man—and believe only what is true about man. Then what is this that talks belief and disease? Error. Can error make disease? Did it ever do anything? No. Can it ever do anything? No. Has it any power? No. Why has it no power? Because God is all-power. Is there any other power than God? No. Then is error anything? Error is nothing because God created all things All-in-all.

With this silent argument, you have silenced—entirely destroyed the false type of man, and put him in his own true inheritance, and what was belief has become truth, and he is transformed by the renewing of his mind. And his body, which is not apart from him, but part of him, takes on its true likeness, and the Christ is made manifest in the flesh.

Short Isolated Items attributed to Mrs. Eddy
and preserved by R. G.

The trick ecclesiastical is to conciliate the students of Science. Look out for wolves in sheep's clothing.

God loves you; He will finish and furnish all that remains to be felt and known by us and all poor sinners.

God bless you, gird you with courage, faith, health; know that divine Love does all this for you.

I must be affirmative and positive in my work, and know that all is spiritual and Christ.

My true self cannot be conscious of pain or disease. These are false beliefs.

We should rejoice always. Truth sweeps out all error with certainty and assurance. Error has no power of action—no abiding place.

Every good treatment is God manifested actively in the flesh through the activity of the right idea about the false sense of belief.

Every good treatment is God manifesting the law of good to man. It knows fear is nothing.

Do not treat a man for his belief—but as a belief without a believer.

Recognize all limitation as mesmerism. Hit it squarely in the face.

A Christian Science treatment is the transformation of consciousness. Handle the law of reversal.

One man cannot furnish consciousness for another man. Christian Science is a state of individual consciousness of knowing God.

Love means Life. It is the only corrective equal to every emergency and conquers every condition of discord.

Cling to God, good, the true idea about the false claim, and it will save from error.

Everything is—but the trouble is man has a false sense about *isness.*

Error says, 'I cannot'; Christ says, 'I can'.

Never argue all on one side. But handle the serpent; then claim the real, the Love.

God must be reflected. His goodness, His care, His love, His substance, are reflected by His ideas.

God is supreme. He reigns, and evil *is not.* The only *is* connected with evil, is that *it is not.* See this and take courage.

Calling or thinking of error as *lie* relieves it of any personality whatever.

God, good, is with you always. M.A.M. has no power. *Know this* and you are safe.

Prayer without ceasing is to live in the consciousness of one Mind, one God.

(Mrs. Eddy said if we were really conscious of the meaning of the synonyms of God, this would heal every case. Then she defined them as follows:)

Mind—Infinite knowing—not thinking. It is reasoning.

Spirit—The presence of omnipotence. Nothing else is going on.

Soul—Consciousness. We are the children of Soul. If we knew this, there would be no dimness of sight, no dullness of hearing.

Principle—The presence of infinite law.

Life—The reflection of activity. No weariness.

Truth—Infinite inclusion of all facts.

Love—Infinite giving. Jesus gave on the cross-gave comfort to those hanging with him; compassion to mother; blessing to disciples.

By E. E. N. (A student's notes from the class of 1889) [Emma Easton Newman]

I give you nothing new; there is nothing new under the sun. It is only the application of an eternal Truth in a new and practical way. I cannot answer all your questions for I cannot answer all my own. There is an eternity for us to learn in, if we patiently wait. If you cannot understand my terms, wait and see what they mean. Do not misconstrue them by your old interpretations. Come empty of all preconceived opinions, creeds, prejudices, doctrines or isms, to receive the Truth, and with charity of open minds receive the Truth I give you; then test the reality of your own by it. Except one is empty he cannot be filled.

No one ever learned a truth by argument, for any falsity can be established by the reasoning of the natural mind. Spiritual Truth is only spiritually discerned. I give you but the key to knowledge. You can only unlock by living it in your own life; otherwise it will be only theory. There is no salvation in theory,

I will never say a word I have not proven. If I theorize I will tell you so. I can only show the way I have gone. I am only an Ambassador, a voice, to lead you into your own kingdom where God, the Truth, alone illumines every one according to his own degree. The system of Truth I am teaching when reduced is simply, the bringing the Christ to you, or the Way, the Truth, and the Life to your whole being.

I wish as an act of justice that you hold sacredly in your memory that I assume no good or power of myself, that to God alone I ascribe all *love*, wisdom and power, the All-in-all, the all good; that I am absolutely nothing, a mere instrument in God's hands to be used as He will. This is the only position for any one of us to be in.

This is my wish that you do not talk of or discuss this Truth outside the class while studying. You will have questions enough of your own to settle without wrestling with those of other people; but when you have come into the clear understanding of Truth, you have no right to withhold it from those who *seek* it honestly, for it is God's truth, not yours—but be sure and give it out more in your life.

A study into the nature of Mind itself, its powers and laws, and the application of its laws to the wellbeing of mankind, has been heretofore considered among things mysterious and intangible, because dealing with the unseen. Nothing can exist which is not created, and nothing is created which is not an expression of its source, cause, creation, Truth, Principle or law. Truth is not seen merely because it is Truth. To be received it must correspond to some awakened knowledge of love in the heart. Truth is loving our neighbor as ourselves. Truth is purity, justice, tenderness.

To know anything, there must be some response within to the thing known. Perfection cannot contain imperfection. Good cannot contain evil, else it would not be perfect good. The *infinite is all.* No sin. Then where is evil? A belief in physical causation produces fear, and fear acts directly and indirectly upon the body. Fear is also the remote (or latent) cause of all disease, as a race belief held throughout the whole history of mankind. It is the open door through which the enemy can at any moment rush in and bind the strong man.

Prov. 29: 25. The fear of man bringeth a snare: but whoso putteth his trust in the Lord shall be safe. Very many forms of disease are well known to be results of immorality, and consequently of purely mental origin. A momentary thought of sensuality, avarice, or revenge distorts the face, impairs respiration, retards or quickens circulation and goes tingling through every fibre and nerve of the body, but if long enough continued, it results in disease of some form or permanent deformity in the face, if not of the whole body.

What is the difference between belief and understanding? Belief is a decision made from reasoning in material things. May be a false conclusion. Understanding is a demonstrable knowledge obtained from a clear perception of the real and eternal. 'Now we see through a glass darkly; but then face to face: now I know in part; then shall I know even as also I am known.'

Our identity is eternally fixed in infinite Mind. We cannot *realize* our absolute identity in this dream of life, but we have eternity to work it out in. Our growth is orderly; there is nothing sudden.

A falsity does not hold me. I hold it. Truth holds me; I do not hold it. Every true and noble thought helps raise humanity and lets the light in, Put aside self, and there is perfection and fullness. The normal condition of man is that he should know his relation to God and know that the body, his expression, is subject to the law of his Spirit, which is the light of life within him, where there is no darkness, discord or disease. Spirituality is the normal condition of man. Christianity is not a state for a man to get into. Materiality is the state for man to get out of and then he is in his normal condition, the condition in which we were really created, in the image and likeness of God.

Darkness is merely the absence of light. Who says that darkness has power? Self. What is self? Absence of identity, the *not* Spirit, shadow, error, myth, a dream, an apparent thing. Empty yourself of natural sympathy. Natural sympathy means suffering with a person; be full of the divine sympathy. Disease exists as feeling only; all we have to destroy is the belief. We do not dream dreams; the dreams dream us.

By M. P. [Mary Plunkett (?)]

Can you all hear the wonderful tone that has just been struck—a tone never before heard in human consciousness? Could you, my dear ones, but see the grandeur of your outlook, the sublimity of your hope—and the infinite capacity of your being—you would do what? Let error kill itself. It comes to you for life and you give it the only life it has—in belief.

My life is a manifestation of divine Life from which I derive all moral and physical health. Therefore, my life should be beyond the reach of accidents as the divine Life is.

Statements in Class

Can our errors be met and overcome other than by crucifixion? No, there is no other way, else Jesus could not have been crucified. Each one must pass through Gethsemane and up Calvary's height to the cross....

After the crucifixion the resurrection.

Duty never points in two directions. (See *Sentinel,* Vol. VIII, p. 765.)

The Coin of Christian Science

GOLD —The silent thoughts of Truth and Love which heal the sick.

SILVER—The spoken word of Truth and Love which casts out evil and heals the sick.

CURRENCY—The written word of Truth and Love published and distributed throughout the world healing sickness and sin. But this currency must be backed up by a gold reserve in human character.

(To the class of '98) You shall run and not be weary; to run—to rise higher spiritually and not to react, and not be weary. but rest in divine Love and not relapse.

MISCELLANEOUS STATEMENTS ATTRIBUTED TO MRS. EDDY

Read *Science and Health* 562: 29-568: 7, before reading this article. To know that the dragon is in truth but a mythical creation, saves us from it. If we make something of it, and attempt to destroy it, we will be vanquished every time. Only Truth and Love can destroy the dragon. What is it to love? To always see the man of God's creation, and nothing else, and to separate from our thought of man any belief of fear, sin, or disease. This is love. Let us strive more and more earnestly to reflect this love in our homes, where little errors so often tempt us to lose sight of the real child of God.

We each dwell in our own world of consciousness. We look out through the windows of this consciousness and behold the passing procession of mortal mind. Day after day we have been lured forth, have been pressed into the whirl, lost our individual peace and poise in divine Mind, and found ourselves dragged through the uncleanness, the pain of the procession. We seek to regain our own home of consciousness, wiser for the experience, thinking we will not again become part of error's pageant: but here let the newer understanding of Love guard well your door. Stay in your own home of demonstration. Keep your peace, for idle curiosity, criticism, or even false sympathy may lure you forth.

Wherein lies the wisdom of the serpent? To hide itself. Therefore hide yourself in the understanding of Christian Science, be it great or small, We have all in some way needed the experience we have had. Never be found as a Christian Scientist mourning over an experience. It is a thing of the past, but not so the manifold power and presence of God resulting therefrom.

Mortals may have a big belief of brain, but according to Christian Science the claim that somebody thinks blinds man to the fact that there is but *one* Mind, God, and consequently only one real *thinker* and one *thought.* Isa. 14: 24: 'The Lord of hosts hath sworn, saying, Surely as I have thought, so shall it come to pass; and as I have purposed, so shall it stand.' When man begins to see himself as the reflection of God, Mind, and recognizes that he has within himself the capacity to act as possessing all power from Him in whom we live, move and have our being, he has reached the highest of all endowments and fruitful of all good works. *He who is obedient to Truth has immense power for service.* The Truth frees him from ignorance of his capacities and privileges, It fortifies and sustains him under all circumstances. It is here and now. Pentecostal power is always present. It is the power of Mind enabling man to do the will of wisdom, for God's biddings are always enablings. It is the power to think, to act, to speak so that life will be fruitful and joyous. It is the capacity every man possesses to act in harmony with divine power and this is to preserve a scientific sense of being. Nothing is *truth* but the absolute. We do not know anything. Mind is the only source of power. Thought is the only force. Therefore those who have turned to the fountainhead of being for the solution of any problem, have brought such titanic force into intelligent activity that the results may seem incredible. Principle does not require time to become itself and find its true expression. Mind is causative. We reflect the ideas of Mind, interpret them to ourselves and objectify or bring out the fruit of thought. Therefore the word of God spoken into consciousness is the seed bearing fruit after its kind.

The earth is simply what we recognize with the material senses, hence it is in reality mortal mind, and the declaration, 'I give you dominion over the earth' means, I give you power to control your mind.

Jesus taught and I teach that there is in mortal mind a perpetual force impelling wrongly.... Constant watching is required in order to see it and then be able to put it down.

Sometimes when a man has made a mistake, he insists upon that mistake until the mistake looms up to him more clearly than God.

The first thing I do in the morning when I awake is to declare I shall have no other mind before divine Mind and become fully conscious of this and then adhere to it throughout the entire day, and then the evil cannot touch me.

Marriage, birth and atonement are one. They express unity. Unity of Principle and idea is the only marriage. Birth is revelation. The *one* child *is* born—*is* created.

All mortal thought is *mis*conception. Because *God is all,* the belief of birth is only a belief and does not affect us. Birth is getting rid of mortal mind and its paraphernalia. To destroy the belief of death, we must first destroy the belief of birth, for the first enemy is sin and the last enemy is death.

The Christian Scientist who is faithful to this Cause and its Leader will reap rewards spiritual, and blessedness beyond the power of human thought to conceive. Will you join your Leader in this, refusing sensuality, animality, lust in any of its forms? Oh, dear ones, I know the cost and I know the joy. Will you, can you, rise in this moment important for Truth?

Who in your midst can instruct you into higher spheres of influence? Can a student teach another of my students beyond what they find in my books? Your closet is the best place whereby to learn from divine Love your duty to yourself and to others. More silent prayer and watching is the need.

Work half done is not yet done at all. Wholeness is the rule in Science. Continually going half the distance to a place will never get you there. An error half met is not met at all, for 'an error in the premise is an error in the conclusion'. As long as we believe that dying brings good to us, we will continue to die. Death is an argument of evil to keep us always dying, Evil is not eternal. Life is. We will die as long as we admit that we must.

Renegade students and mesmerists make a law that old beliefs shall come back. And we must know that if these seem to appear, it is mesmerism, not disease. Their laws also cause an irritation of the mucous membrane.

These laws have not yet been broken, in belief, for students. In cases where death has been imminent, the error has been met when it was understood that it was mesmerism and not old beliefs that was killing.

God is invaluable in every emergency. He leadeth not into temptation. How unspeakably blessed is the deliverance from the fiction of error that has deceived mortals! Just think of it! Within the entire range of all that is or ever was, you are now, and are included in the infinity of consciousness, imperishable, undisturbed, and you win be satisfied when you awake in that likeness.

Christians all have to learn their way to heaven through much tribulation, but when we get to harmony of being—the only heaven—we shall see and understand the need there was for all this.

Christians suffer in this wicked world insomuch as they oppose it, and are helping to destroy it before it would destroy them.

When we realize our own helplessness as mortals, then 'His strength is made perfect in weakness'; we look up to divine Love and Love meets the need.

I am not the door through which to enter, nor the rock whereon to build; but what God has spoken to this age through me, is the *way* and sure *foundation*, and no man entereth by any other way into Christian Science.

The law of God cannot be made flexible. I am relying on that for a correct decision (in a suit at law). What has the law of God to do with the case? *Everything.* In contradistinction to so-called material law, spiritual law is inflexible. It is never two-sided, nor can it be made to conform to human desire or will. It is the law of divine Principle, the law of absolute Truth, the law of immutable Love, the law of eternal Life. There is no physical or moral ill too insidious or too deeply rooted, to be made to yield to this immutable law of God, good.

How do we see God? Through a perfect man—the divine ideal—by having no other mind but God, good. How shall we see man? By reaching the perfect idea of God.

Yes, our Cause is getting its rightful chariot wheels. The world moves, and towards heaven if it only knew it. The wrath of the 'evil one' is but the sign of the one evil getting its death blow.

The origin of evil is the problem of the ages, it confronts each generation anew, it confronts Christian Science; the question is often asked, if God created only the good whence cometh the evil? To this question Christian Science replies evil never did exist as an entity; it is but a belief that there is an opposite intelligence to God. This belief is a species of idolatry. The admission of the reality of evil perpetuates faith in evil and the Scriptures declare that to whom ye yield yourselves servants to obey, his servants ye are. This leading self-evident proposition of Christian Science that good being real its opposite is necessarily unreal, needs to be grasped in an its divine requirements.

When you argue on all subjects that should end well, be a law to your own consciousness that what you say cannot be reversed and inverted and made to produce the very opposite of what you argue for. This is a late phase of theosophy and M.A.M. that needs to be met.

Three stages
1st. Good resolves.
2nd. Continual asking forgiveness.
3rd. Hardness of heart, resolve to take own course. 'Did not bargain to be a Christian.'

When animal magnetism has done its worst, it has done nothing. When animal magnetism has howled and howled, it has done nothing.

Truth cannot be reversed; it bears the fruit of health and holiness.
Life cannot be reversed; it bears the fruit of immortal harmony.
Love cannot be reversed; it destroys all fear and heals the sick and the sinful.

What is the atonement? It is self-sacrifice that finds the way for others through the experience that meets and overcomes error; then shows this way to others who have slept, to save them from a similar experience.

Mentally treat yourself that nothing can govern your actions or come to your thought that is not from the divine Mind. Be strong there. So many sinister suggestions come to mind, watch! and each day commit yourself to the care of our one Parent, trust Him, turn to Him in all your ways for light to direct your footsteps and wisdom to enable you to separate the tares from the wheat—so that you can judge well between the human or the evil 'suggestion' and the good or divine impulse.

To make too little of error is to ignore, evade, endure, excuse, and conceal it. To make too much of error is to love, hate, fear, honor, and drive it. Then error is not to be ignored, evaded, endured, excused, concealed, loved, hated, feared, honored, driven.

The 'liberty of the sons of God' is for each one to desire God and for each one to desire for his mortal neighbor just what he desires for himself.

All genius is sad in its youth. It is the precursor of mortal mind that discords-never harmonizes-with Life, Truth or Love. So dear young friend, cultivate joy, hope, faith. Life lies before you glorious. Banish the shadow, seize the substance thereof and God, good, is with you alway.

Be wholly absorbed in the work of gaining daily more understanding of God. Then personal ambition, envy, desire to be in this or that place cannot use you. Personal ambition has no place in a Christian's thought or life. He is wholly occupied in the loving, humble purpose to do good, to be good, and to prove that good is all that can govern thought, action, condition, or being.

I have only to trust in God, for Love is destroying disease. I can't do it. Truth and Love are at work and error and hate can't stand before them. They are destroying sin, disease and death. I know this and my faith in it cannot fail and I cannot fear.

No one is loyal to Truth, to himself, to his God, or is worthy of heaven, who has not faith, pluck, and patience enough to endure, without fainting, apparent defeat and delayed rewards.

It is not self-hardening, but humility under trouble, that makes us ripe for deliverance. They who are conscious of integrity never shun a trial, It is a hard task to forgive injuries without reluctance. But to rejoice in the fall of an enemy is malicious and murderous. The greatest provocation will never justify our revenge.

Trust in God—God is Life—God is infinite, therefore if we are the image and likeness of infinity, we have no beginning and no end, and are His image and likeness; that is my life insurance.

Because I have put my trust in good, I have no responsibility whatever. My home is in God. I partake of the bounties of God's table, spread with the milk and honey of His kingdom. I give no heed to what I shall say, to what I shall wear, or wherewithal I shall pay my debts. Whatsoever I shall speak, God speaks through me. His word is for the healing of the nations. He clothes me with white garments of His own weaving—the robe of righteousness eternal and indestructible. Truth is my income, is ever-present, and has wiped out all my indebtedness. Truth and Love flow freely without price.

O God, I have taken hold of Thy hand, of Thine omnipotence. Thou hast taken my feet from the mire and clay and established them upon the rock. I am not afraid for I know thou hast lifted me above the world, its erroneous illusions and temptations. I know them henceforth no more forever.

If you rise spiritually, you lose your sense of 'I' in matter and gain your selfhood in Spirit. This brings the divine health which is not dependent upon the body, but is of the Father, forever the same.

Malpractice is the wrath of man, and it is being made to praise God by driving you out of the tenement or belief in body. If it does not drive you out of it, it will kill you in it.

Keep your joy! This is the hour of demonstration, dominion and power, gratitude and glorification; for even with faults man is still Love's idea.

I love to be where God wants me to be; I love to do what God wants me to do; without asking how, when, or why. I have my place in Principle; I have my work in Principle; I have my reward in Principle; and there is no law of mental malpractice that can act through any condition or circumstance to hinder or obstruct the perfect and complete manifestation of God's plan for me here and now.

The Science of Mind uncovers to Scientists secret sin, even more distinctly than so-called physical crimes are visible to the personal senses: crime is always veiled in obscurity, but Science fastens guilt upon its author through Mind with the certainty and directness of the eye of God Himself.

Error wants to be let alone, but we are not going to let it alone. Rather will we continue our effort at right thinking until the absurd and illegitimate argument that man is flesh and bones—organized matter—is met and the ideas of God manifested.

Put away all selfishness out of your thoughts such as thinking you have been wronged or any sense of ingratitude or injustice from others. Bury it out of sight forever and let love pour in where that has seemed to be. Forgive as you expect to be forgiven.

Remember to keep your own doorstep clean. Always keep your medicine chest in order. The greatest blessing you can bestow on any one is to know God governs him. It is more difficult to demonstrate over the personal sense of a patient than to heal the disease.

Definition of spiritual senses

Sight—spiritual discernment.
Hearing—spiritual understanding.
Feeling—divine consciousness.
Smell—intuition of character.
Taste—relish of Truth.

Abide in the 91st Psalm and know that such abiding is treatment and protection. There is nothing that can make laws or influence you. There is but one Mind and that is Love. Do not give life to evil by attaching it to a person or thing. It cannot live without a body. Man is immortal, one. There is but one infinite manifestation. No error can attach itself to man and why deceive ourselves by thinking it can do so? Every manifestation of life is ever-present and omnipresent good and this carries within itself all healing, sustaining. Know that the kingdom of heaven is within you and this is your armor.

If a person has a belief of consumption, the treatment should go far enough to destroy, or uncover, the belief in the reality of sexuality and the existence of material creative organs. Man is not a creator; he does not even assist in creation. The supposition that he does, or that any of the conditions or supposed facts that pertain to the subject of sex are true, is purely fictitious, a fragment of the dream from which we are awakening.

God made them male and female from the beginning but His creation was not physical. He made qualities, and formations of character shall ever remain thus, as the reflection of God, the Father and Mother of the universe; not that God is male and female in person, two in form, but as including in Himself all qualities of Mind. When we understand this, we shall have no outlined personality but shall have mental individuality all the same. This is absolute Science, wherein there is but one Mind in the unity of masculine, feminine and neuter as Mind, as infinite Mind and not finite; here is the union again of man and woman, not personal but impersonal, not physical but mental, not finite but infinite. This must be so in the reflection of God, for He is neither finite nor physical and if we would reflect God, we must become like Him in our consciousness.

S. & H. is changing the belief that heart is matter and sustains life, to the understanding that 'God is our Life', that, 'In Him we live, move, and have our being'. This change of heart would deliver man from heart disease and advance Christianity a hundredfold.

There is another heart in us that needs to be changed; namely, the human affections. Changed from selfishness to benevolence and love for God and man; changed so as to have but one God and to love Him supremely, and our brother man as ourselves. This change of heart will have its effect physically as well as spiritually, and heal disease sooner than burnt offerings or drugs. It is a good thing to mentally remind yourself daily that God is the only law-maker for man, morally, spiritually, and physically.

Do not attack hypnotism; do not take Scriptural authority for its identification, but allude to it briefly when you do speak of it, as you would to a ghost story. This will check its spread more than any other way would.

Have you had much experience with malpractice? There is none. The way I meet it is by keeping the First Commandment. Know there is no evil mind to intercept God and you.

No one can hurt me nor take from me anything that is good. I know no such thing as sin, suffering, want or disease, for I am a reflection of Life, Truth, and Love. I am never disappointed. The harmony of my being cannot be disturbed, because I live in the Infinite.

We would better suffer for another's wrong-doing than to misjudge a person, and the student cannot (does not) always know who is sinning; but he can make sin, through Science—divine Science—to *himself nothing.*

Faith lifts up the aspirations to Principle for more light and spiritual love, and with the unfolding of Truth to the understanding which comes from desire and research, cross-taking and cross-bearing, to belief comes a return of blessings from Principle which controls all and will control it so as to be found right when judged by wisdom. For wisdom will restrain error when the time cometh for its solution by the understanding.

The real Christian Science compact is love for one another. This bond is wholly spiritual and inviolate. It should never be violated in thought or action even for the sake of maintaining the purity of the letter of Christian Science. For the spirit, the reflection of divine Love, is always more important than the letter. (See *Miscellaneous Writings* 91: 10)

I saw the love of God encircling the universe and man, filling all space, and that divine Love so permeated my own consciousness that I loved with Christ-like compassion everything I saw. This realization of divine Love called into expression the beauty of holiness, the perfection of being (S. & H. 253: 2) which healed and regenerated and saved all who turned to me for help.

My body is not a toxine factory; it is the substance of Love, the reflex of Soul. This omnipresent Truth is an antidote, antitoxin to all poison, both internal and external.

What is the scientific realization of which sexual intercourse is the counterfeit? It is the recognition and realization through communion with God of man as a perfect, complete idea, masculine and feminine. That which is true of yourself as a complete reflection of Father-Mother God, is true of every individual in the universe and reveals God and His creation, perfect and eternal. Mortals are struggling for completeness and hope to find it through sexual intercourse; when in fact this desire is simply the divine idea, struggling to express itself in completeness. A recognition of this brings compassion, tenderness, and love for the poor struggling heart and conviction that there is no sin.

Oh, may the light that is never dim so encompass you, that no night is there. May His angels hold thee in their power, and Songs of Science be heard in the intuitions of thought, till your life is in tune with the rhythm of God.

There is no mental, moral, physical, or financial paralysis in God's kingdom. The world is mentally and morally paralyzed to the Truth of being and this must be handled in every case. Our treatments must be universal as well as individual.

To teach students in class without teaching them how to handle animal magnetism, is like sending soldiers into battle with brass buttons and braid but with no ammunition for their muskets.

This is a mental age. Malpractice would dominate, and unless Christian Scientists are awake to it and alert, it would hold back Christian Science for centuries.

If students come to me with their thoughts full of worldliness, self, pride, hate, materiality, etc., although I have so much to give them, it all stops here (she said, pressing her hand to her throat); but if they cleanse their thoughts of all these things, then I can just pour it out upon them.

It is good to be afflicted, to drink in the experience by which we are made meet for the Master's crown; Love is in itself a purifier, and if we reach its glorious behest we must be purified in the process.

Thirty years I have been in the fiery furnace and the dross has dropped away from the gold through agony. But 'if we suffer with him we shall also reign with him'.

Your Father is rich and will not deprive you of one good thing, but will add continually to your storehouse of blessings; everything belongs to God, then it is yours now as His reflection, for there is no debt in divine Love.

Oh! that personality and materiality were made the point of attack by all who desire to be Christian Scientists. Pull down the strongholds and we would have healers worth having. Spiritualization of thought is what the cause demands and I see little growth in that direction.

Could we but fill our consciousness with the thought that every individual idea of God is as fixed in its place in divine Mind as the steadfast stars in their orbits, it would help to dispel the illusion that any of God's children is out of a position, displaced, out of line with the source of supply. No one of that universe, which is unseen and eternal, is ever out of place, for God is without variableness or shadow of turning, and His ideas reflect His stability.

Malicious animal magnetism cannot through any claim of business necessity or policy move me either internally or externally. It cannot change my habitation, for I inhabit infinity, eternity. I dwell in the realm of unending bliss, in a house—not made with hands high in the heavens of Life, Truth, and Love. I live in the atmosphere of purity, peace and plenty, and in the sunshine of Love and joy. My home has an everlasting foundation. There is no limit to its beauty and pleasantness; and infinite Love conducts my home. There is but one home-maker; one home beautiful; one builder; one habitation. 'For in Him we live and move and have our being.' Principle gives every good and perfect gift. Principle gives all; is the only source and cause of all good.

Exclude time and place from thought—think only of here and now. Whatever is mine, is mine now; nothing can come between me and that supply—neither time nor space. Supply is, therefore, here and now. God cannot be impoverished; man cannot be impoverished. Nothing can come between me and my perfect supply; there is nothing that can take it away from me, for there is but one power, all harmonious, beautiful. I know poverty is an error that Truth destroys.

Declare continually your own perfection and freedom, and let the true and divine idea destroy the mesmerism that argues that you are sad and unhappy, This idea is your Saviour.

To know that 'all things work together for good to them that love God', even when every material evidence points to the appearance that evil is in control of a situation or condition, is to abide unshaken in a spiritual composure that the world cannot take away.

Through faith and patience we inherit the promise of Him who cares for us as a shepherd does his flock. We do not have to look forward to the end of an erroneous experience; we do not have to say, 'When? When?' for evil is nothing, and has no power, activity nor representative NOW.

There are no hindrances, interruptions, personalities, conditions or circumstances that can make inactive or suspend the law of Spirit. I cannot be mesmerized to doubt the power of Truth over this and every other error. I know that I have confidence in all my treatments; I know how to handle all error and handle it instantly. All that I need to know in handling error is revealed to me, for it is God who handles the case, and it is God who gives all right ideas.

Do not repeat the lies, Return good for evil. Let us forgive and love our enemies. This is our duty; this is the rule in Christian Science. Oh! let us keep it inviolate, and be on God's side. Remember this, dear ones.

Human nature is a keyboard; animal magnetism plays upon it. If there is a silent key, there can be no sound. If we faithfully handle error we shall be a silent key.

The divine law of Life, Truth and Love is a law of instant and complete expulsion and elimination of all poisons and impurities from the system. Why? Because the floodtides of divine Life, Truth and Love are pouring and surging through consciousness, uplifting, purifying, nourishing, healing, elevating, sustaining and energizing mankind.

Everything that comes to me today brings me a blessing. There is no mortal mind to see me today or know me today; or think it can through any of its so-called laws of malpractice rob me of all good or hinder me from being conscious here and now of my birthright which is dominion.

A Treatment for Supply

The power of divine intelligence gives you a business capacity without limitation, an acuteness and comprehension, a perception of character and clear-cut systematic knowledge which leads to success. Truth reflected by you attracts to you trade from all channels of good. There is no fear, sickness, envy, doubt, anxiety, hate or jealousy. The discordant conditions of business have no power over you. You have no power to attract them. The divine Mind is yours to draw from and execute with, to bring out in your business harmony, success and prosperity. There is no unrest, discord, fear or friction; no weakness, discouragement, uncertainty or failure. You have an inexhaustible supply. There is no avarice, greed, trust in money, or love of money. You have abundant proof of God's loving care and His law of supply. You live in the land of promise. God has called you out of any sojourn in Egypt (in darkness), to return to your own country and inheritance. The days of hunger, famine, thirst are past. God is substance, Principle, Life. Man as His image reflects the capabilities and possibilities of Spirit. You live in Mind, in the atmosphere of plenty. There is no power or presence that can resist good or prevent your prayer being answered, from being effectual. While you remain in this frame of mind you are obedient to the Principle of your being and naught can hinder your healing the sick and the sinning.

You all heal. You all have demonstrations. Now with regard to long ones, have patience. Keep on and on, living the Truth and declaring it. *Never give up.* Be patient and patience will have its perfect work.

Be vigilant. Be wise. Store your mind with deep treasures. Learn to talk just the inspiration of Truth. Spiritualize your whole being let this be the outcome of your growth.

Nothing can come to me but what comes from God and nothing can go forth from me but that which goeth forth from God, good, divine Love.

Mother, clasp thy nestling tenderly, rear thine offspring wisely, for thou knowest not when the mantle of Christ's presence shall fall upon thine own dear one.

Remember that there will be nothing come to you that you cannot overcome. The victory is yours by inheritance; claim it and use it as yours. There is but one law, the law of God. All true active thought, motive, and purpose are in divine Mind.

There is no power in evil; the reverse is true, God is the power. He is infinite; then your work is the Christ power against nothingness; hold there, know it and there is nothing else; know it is with power and what else is there? Nothing; then the work is done, God did it.

God's child can never make a mistake; can never lose an opportunity, never cause a regret. His life is bright with abundant goodness, hope and promise. Love has a plan and purpose for everyone to fulfill and none can escape it or fail to perform the will of God.

There never was one thousand years ago. Man is divine and has nothing to do with time. You do not say that two times two *was* four. There is no was, no past, present or future—just NOW.

Never resent a wound from anyone, but always leave it to God to avenge and heal. He will rightly reward; you cannot. Forgiveness is forgetfulness of sin, disease and all error in others and in ourselves. No wrong is forgiven until it is forgotten. If this is not done, it works like remembering disease; it makes you a sinner; it grows chronic and incurable. If we do not do this, it does us more harm than our enemies.

I cannot harm myself; I cannot be made to harm myself. I cannot harm another; I cannot be made to harm another. Another cannot harm me; another cannot be made to harm me. Because we are all God's children, we all love each other.

The kingdom of heaven is God's government of His ideas, His wise and compelling enforcement of law, His unerring jurisdiction. I am a citizen of His dominion, governed by His laws and protected by these laws; my affairs are administered justly and harmoniously by these laws. The laws of divine Principle operate because infinite power and intelligence are back of them, not because we invoke them—and they no more stop working than the laws of this country.

You are the child of the loving God, surrounded and protected by infinite Love. There is no hatred or evil to frighten you. You have no disease, you have nothing to fear, you are not in danger, you are entirely well, and continually held in the presence of God.

God is always with a good desire, giving it power, activity, energy, intelligent action and rich fruition. He brings every right endeavor to its fulfillment, and gives more blessings than one has sought.

Possess yourself of good and dispossess yourself of any other mind, and all the mystery of iniquity beateth in vain against your house.

Abide in Love. Nothing can touch or harm you in Love. Know that you live in Love. Love is God as Life itself. Take this understanding with you and bless others with Love.

To know there is but one God, one cause, one effect, one Mind, heals instantly. Have but one God, and your reflection of Him does the healing.

When Truth first comes to the consciousness of a mortal, it usually heals him physically. Then comes the demand to commence giving up material idols, and to digest, assimilate, and demonstrate Truth for himself. At this period the conscious and unconscious efforts of evil strive to obstruct, to continue the bondage, and to cause the individual to simply handle his new-found treasure, talk about it perhaps with fervor or emotion, but to go no further.

I advise you to do what you think is right, and never lose an opportunity of doing good. Ask wisdom of God and He will guide you.

Originality and versatility, infinitely expressed, mean that you will forever express the boundless, new ideas, ever broadening into revelation of all the facts of Mind, clear and fully understood, spontaneous, without effort, with perfect freedom, increasing clarity, unrestricted mental growth, forever more and more. There are no channels in infinite Mind; man is one with it. Channel is merely a term to explain something.

God, good, is 'jealous' in our sense of the word. It admits of nothing unlike simple honesty, goodness, truth and love to be put into good's foundation or superstructure. This I have seen *proven* beyond cavil over a half century.

A true Science treatment does not consist of treating a disordered body or person, but does consist of destroying the error which is wholly mental.

2 x 2 = 5 illustrates how unscientific it is to look at a blackboard and see 2 x 2 = 5; and then realize that 2 X 2 = 4; then turn to the blackboard to see if it has changed on the board, ere we believe the manifestation is complete. Never look at the body to see if the error has disappeared. If we do, and see the error as physical, or belonging to the individual, or see that man has a material body, then we do not treat scientifically. Now, you know that one and one are two, two and two are four, three times three are nine. You know that much of the truth of numbers, and it is all-powerful, no matter how much error you know. As it is with numbers, so it is with Science. The little you do know is real, and reflects God, no matter how much error you know that you have not worked out of yet; for as you know more and more of Truth, all error disappears from thought. No error can bind us beyond our belief in it.

I ask that you awake to resist the tempter that would cast you down from the pinnacle, and resist the power unseen of *mental malpractice* that would lure you back to the flesh and to evil.

What is the perfect Principle of perfect manhood? To be pure physically, beautiful morally, harmonious mentally, and perfect spiritually, for this is our relation to God, Christ, heaven, eternity and infinity.

Treatment Against Mortal Mind

No shadow of mortal mind can touch me, there is nothing to fear. God works in me to will and to do, and I shall perform my work. No cloud can touch me, or my patients. We must not fear for the struggles that come, for they must be met. All that is within me is the spirit of victory. Awake, spirit of Truth; cast off these shackles of mortal fear and distress. Come forth and be manifest in me. Faith is the substance of things hoped for, the evidence of things not seen.

For Patients

Now you know really and truly there is nothing to fear and you have no fear. You are as free as the birds that fly, for the body is the smallest part of you, and no part of your spiritual being. You are greater than your fears, so put them down forever.

No good thoughts are ever lost; all good is eternal and ever present. We do know the Science of being, and nothing can disqualify us for demonstrating it. When we turn for power from matter to Spirit, we can move mountains, surmount obstacles, and achieve every success and overcome fear and sin. The claiming of our rightful heritage as God's children is the true mental culture and spiritual education. In the reality of being is all we want or need, or can possibly have or wish for. It includes more than we can discern in the measure of happiness and the completion of every wish or prayer that is wholesome or right for us to have. I must know that the definition of man in *Science and Health* applies to me. I am that spiritual man, I am God's image and likeness, reflecting a full, perfect image of Life, Mind, action, etc., not under material laws or limitations. God's law is life-giving and life-sustaining eternally. Doing good and thinking good sustains life. Love is the very nearest thing to us all the time. It is the nature of God to bless and care for us all the time. We can always bring God to us instantly by declaring He is with us. We never reach out for Him in vain. God has ordained for us all good, and He will remove our sins from us as far as the east is from the west, when we want to give them up. Hold steadfastly the thought of yourself as good only, as spiritual only. The belief that there is two of me is where all the trouble comes from. Every treatment must include the understanding that it is the Mind of God; it cannot return void, and it cannot be reversed by any so-called law of malpractice or human belief. *Error* says we are sick or discouraged; we don't say it. It is error talking about itself. If we admit it we have accepted a lie. Truth says, I have perfect eyes, perfect heart, perfect limbs, etc.; all there is to me is like God, like perfection. We should discard mortal mind judgment and pray for the Christ Mind. It is our human will or judgment that argues we can't do so and so. There is no reason why we may not always demonstrate truth and be well and happy. We must break the general claim of fear, by knowing it has no effect or purpose, no power, control, or action; fear is senseless and sinful, and obedience to God breaks the claim and casts it out; fear itself is without foundation or reason; therefore no part of my consciousness. When God governs, there are no reverses or failures, no temperament or qualities, or disposition that can disqualify us for demonstrating truth. Our trust in God and our understanding is sufficient to extricate from any inharmonious conditions or predicaments or disease in which we may seem to be.

Health is the law of God, unchangeable and perfect, the result of perpetual harmonious action. C.S. works from the standpoint of a well man. The understanding of man's perfection is the true medicine and meets every case. There is no material body or man to need healing. I am the man that knows health, harmony, peace, etc. A treatment is knowing the truth and claiming it; the letter of it must be concise and to the point; do not waste words; the knowing that it is true is the right mental action, and is the source of health, of all good. It is necessary to know the facts of God's omnipotence, and what He has ordained for me. There is but one Infinity and that includes all. The action, force and power of truth is self-evident, self-sustaining; nothing can interfere with it; it is perfection, and life. Infinity includes only man that is well, that is perfect, and harmonious. All things are possible to Mind and right thought. Every C.S. treatment is accumulative; the work goes on to bless all mankind. Error is non-scientific thinking and scientific thinking is all that is needed to destroy it, A treatment must include the realization that it goes forth with power and truth, and cannot be reversed by any law of nature or of *materia medica*; no form of error can make a Christian Science treatment produce an opposite effect, nor can I be made to overlook or forget anything in the treatment that is necessary for its certain accomplishment of good; we must go ahead of error, and keep ahead of error all the way. Error is nothing but erroneous thought, and we must never give in to it or go down before it. The law of God includes a law that annuls every false claim, and we know it and must use it. Mental activity must be tranquil—not lazy; it must express force, be exact and it must know the reality of man's oneness with God, and the utter unreality of evil in all its forms of beliefs. Know there is no mental or material poison; no substance or mind to contain or manifest poison, irritation or inflammation; no organism or substance that can give forth impurities; no impeded circulation or imperfect action. We cannot be made apathetic or forgetful, for God is our guide and instructor. Know that your treatments are good ones, and have no fear that they are not; fear cannot abide with you. A Christian Science treatment is never afraid it will not work.

Spiritual Interpretation of the Ten Commandments

1. True creation. One God, one Mind, one cause, one creator.
2. False creation. Mortal mind forms its own concepts and fears or loves them.
3. Creation. Scholastic theology takes God's name in vain by believing His creation is both material and spiritual. As there is but one creator, there is but one creation.
4. Reign of harmony.
5. Reflection.

6. Christ. By reflecting our Father-Mother God, thereby uniting in one consciousness the male and female, the Christ is born, which reveals man as eternal.

7. Unity. Knowing that we reflect the male and female, we must not adulterate this idea by supposing that each of God's children is not complete, infinite. Seeing this purity, we are partakers of the marriage supper of the Lamb, the unity of man with the spiritual idea.

8. Individuality. Mortal mind cannot steal from our individuality by making us suppose personality, or any phase of matter, has power to give to, or take away from God's idea, anything.

9. Love. 'Love thy neighbor as thyself.' See the spiritual idea.

10. Fulfillment. Love gives us all things.

Every pure thought falling silently and gently into human consciousness does its part in cleansing the whole world, just as every falling snowflake does its silent share in transforming the noisomeness of the grimy earth into a soft white blanket of purity. We must remember that the smallest truth is mightier than the greatest lie the world has ever known. The one is as enduring as eternity; the other is as transient as a shadow. Take from a lie its power to deceive and it becomes nothing, for its very being depends upon its ability to mislead. A lie must have two willing accessories—one who is willing to be deceived: one who is willing to deceive—the victimized and the victim; if either is wanting, the lie can do nothing.

Take the First Commandment for your medicine. It cures all disease. There is but one Mind, and no person can, or is, harming you. It is a dream, a falsity, an illusion. You have no material head, heart, back. There is no electro-magnetism, no nerve centers for fools or demons to play upon with glamor.

The hour has struck that God forewarned me of. That I may help you at this time, I send these hints: (*Be sure to remember this*:)

The ministerial league growing out of the religious congress whereby to strengthen their failing prospects, include among other things, prayer for the heretic. This combined mental force is in belief *the one* that to the religious mind brings more anguish and hopelessness, and hatred of me, than any other power let loose. Take in your mental defense the strong consciousness, that only the prayer of the righteous availeth anything, etc. You can but faintly conceive the portion that this brings to me, the one mark and target. 1895.

What thou needest to know is that mortal mind has translated the body and its functions into matter, and immortal Mind gives back the original with the functions, preserved and harmonious, but no as not in matter, but as and of Mind.

Short, Unidentified, Isolated Items Attributed to Mrs. Eddy

Be careful not to use human will but speak in the power of divine Love that is a law to human hate and destroys it.

This is the second coming of the Christ and it will be the last.

We must recognize the claims of error and oppose it, or we are in danger of being blinded by it and becoming its victim.

One Mind, and loving others as we would be loved is the panacea for all our wrongs, trouble and strife.

When holding no hate in thought and only Love we are doing good to all and this continually.

Vigilance and victory are in Truth inseparable.

Be wise, calm, slow to judge, patient, *pure, loving*. These are the graces of Christian Science.

Heaven in the heart of one means heaven in the heart of all.

Defeat is to acknowledge defeat.

If you have so much to meet, just think how much you have to meet it with.

God bless you and every day show you a little more of *infinite Love.* Just your daily bread; more you will not digest.

The time will come when Christian Scientists will not have offices downtown and sit and wait for sick people to come and be healed.

God never leaves us without light enough to take one step. Do not stop walking until the light gives out.

The irresistible law of God puts me in the right place at the right time, maintains my success and gives me individual freedom.

The more spiritual one is, the more conscious to him is an error of belief.

We experience a recurrence of evil and suffering because we do not forget them. We are often deterred from undertaking things because of the remembrance of past failures.

Self-knowledge gives us a knowledge of others.

Depersonalize self. To personalize thought limits spiritual growth.

The right thing done at the wrong time ceases to be the right thing. There is as much in when a thing is done as in what is done.

If you fight, you make a fight.

What you are doing is not sacrifice but offering.

The strongest tie I ever had, aside from God, was love of home.

Every leaf of every tree declares perpetually that God is Love.

Demonstrate your way out of wanting or needing money, and you will have it.

We lose nothing by giving. God pays back a scientific giver.

Let us wait on God. He will prepare the thoughts and minds of men for whatever He has to reveal.

Every working Scientist ought to handle the claim of mortal mind attraction between man and woman every day of his or her life.

The temptations that beset all Christians, are either to feel too sharply the burdens borne, or to try to lay them down.

Live Christian Science; mind your own business and keep your mouth shut for God's sake.

Do not say to error, 'You cannot harm me', but declare that God protects me from all attacks of error.

Laura, remember I shall still work in this same chair.

When I see a student grateful I know he is safe.

Mortal mind has not been kind enough to me to cause me to want to loiter in it.

Error never shoots dead men. Error minds its own business.

Divine Love breathes deep and long to accomplish its divine purpose.

The Christ must be lost as something to be followed and gained as something to be embodied.

A formula is an effort to gain an instantaneous healing without the Holy Ghost.

There is no rebound of hatred after the baptism of Love. Destroy hatred.

God knows that I live; I am not in the body, and the body cannot talk to me.

If we obey God's law, our affairs come under His immediate control.

I know and see God only in His reflection.

Life is not eternally prolonged; life is forever spontaneously self-renewed.

Supply is continuous, ever-present and available; prove it. I could no more stop my income than a straw could stop Niagara.

Criticize yourself, open your thought so you will become a receiver. This is the preparation for giving.

A realization of a perfect spiritual home will make our present home better.

We the lever. GOD THE POWER.

Do not go on past work, Each day is God's unfoldment.... Make it a spontaneous unfoldment of God's idea.

There is no discordant claim that you cannot love yourself out of.

Strive to work from God, instead of up to God.

May God give you the sweet peace and wisdom of impersonal love; and there is none other.

If it isn't right, I don't want it; and if it is right, I can trust God's law to establish it.

Love yourself, error and all. Love is, no matter what else seemeth to be.

Do not feel too much God's dear methods of unfoldment as a rod, but make them a staff.

When others hate, oppose, ignore,
Help me, dear Lord, to love them more.

Love unselfed, love of one's enemies, humility, moderation, strength, are the cardinals of Christian Science.

Love contains. Love maintains. Love sustains.

This hour is the acme of hate against Love, and Love alone can meet it.

Be yourself as God made you.

Oh! keep me ever seeing Thee and seeing as Thou seest—my Life, my joy, my All.

God takes care of us all. *He is all* and there is no other mind, presence, or power.

God does not demand a half of the heart, but the *whole heart*.

I beg of you to lay up your treasures —thoughts—in heaven; earth has *nothing* worth loving.

I would that I could bear the burden of life without a scar.

Life is not rest, it is action; doing good is life, rest and action.

It is a shield to mentally remind yourself daily that *God* is the only Law-maker for man, morally, spiritually and physically.

I am at my wit's end to express what is the fact relative to the fable.

To be overanxious regarding our own spiritual progress, is to acknowledge a person apart from God.

The seven devils to be overcome are self-righteousness, self-condemnation, self-pity, self-love, self-will, self-praise, self-justification—and make it all God.

Talking does not do any good. You must live the Truth and demonstrate it. (When a student asked if they could give it to another then, she replied: Yes, you can.)

You do not feel love enough. Feel love! Feel love! (Said to a practitioner whose patient was not being healed.)

Dear, don't go back into the house. (Said to one who had been healed but had a tendency to rehearse the error.)

It will become as easy and natural to heal as it is to breathe.

Nehemiah 9: 36, 37—her definition of animal magnetism.

Christian Scientists have a better remedy than material means for error.

When we realize that discord is unreal, then comes out the human sense of immortal harmony.

Beneath, around, about, above, surrounding, are the healing currents of Truth and Love.

Neither person, place nor claim of circumstances can stand between me and God.

When the thinker is lost in the eminence of Mind, the healing takes place.

CHAPTER EIGHT

RECORDED EVENTS

STUDENTS' VERSIONS BASED ON MRS. EDDY'S OWN ACCOUNTS

From A. H. D. [Adam H. Dickey]

When our Leader was called to the meeting in Chicago[1] she thought that they were to speak and take entire charge of the meeting. She did not learn that she was to speak until the last moment. She was so 'outdone' that she did not know what to do. She had made no preparation, but she let God speak and that is how *Science and the Senses* was given. She made the remark, 'If I did not give it to them! It was a caution!' She then referred to 'The Mother's Evening Prayer'; and said it was enough to *melt a heart of stone.*

(Other records of the same event)

When Mrs. Eddy found herself called to make her speech in Chicago, not knowing that she was to be the only speaker, Laura Sargent undertook to comfort her by saying, 'Mother, God is with you.' Mrs. Eddy turned and said, 'I know that better than you do.'

When Miss Robertson visited Mrs. Eddy at Pleasant View, Mrs. Eddy said to her, 'Do you know when I had most evil in my life to meet?' Then she said, 'It was when I spoke in Chicago on *Science and the Senses.* The newspapers said it was a triumph for the Cause. For me it was a trial and tribulation. I, and I alone, had to carry the whole burden. All the Christian Scientists were happy, but I fought with animal magnetism all night after that talk.' Miss Robertson said, 'But Mother, God was with you right through it all!' Mrs. Eddy said, 'Don't you suppose I knew that?'

After the Chicago address when Mrs. Eddy was greeting people at the Palmer House, Mrs. P—(who had started teachings at variance with Mrs. Eddy) got in line to shake hands with her in order to show her students that Mrs. Eddy was friendly toward her. When Mrs. Eddy was at the point of shaking hands with her she

[1] June 14, 1888.

suddenly wheeled about so that she passed her right by, ignoring her completely, and shook hands with the next person.

(Approved, August 3, 1910) It seemed even from infancy that there was a fight against her, but she would always hold her own in contending for the right until she was justified. Only eight years old when she did this and her mother used to counsel the rest of the family never to oppose her.

From C. A. F. [Calvin Augustus Frye]

(Related April 9, 1890) During my first preaching in Boston I (Mrs. Eddy) had this experience. K—[Kennedy] influenced young men to go to church where I preached, Dr. Williams' church, comer of Shawmut Ave. and Madison St. (Baptist Tabernacle), and disturb the service. As soon as service had well begun they, having taken seats in front, would get up one at a time and go out of church just to disturb the meeting. Finally Dr. W. seeing their intention placed himself inside the door, and when they began to go out he rose and locked the door, and ordered them to their seats threatening them with arrest for disturbing services.

After that stopped, one day as I was preaching a stone came through the glass crashing through the glass and fell at my side; upon which a venerable gentleman arose and implored me not to attempt to go on with the service. I replied that I feared no harm and called upon them to stand still and see the salvation of God. Then of a sudden a heavy thunderbolt burst which shook the house and members of the audience say that they saw the lightning playing all around me. At the same time my voice was heard above it all saying, 'He uttered His voice, the earth melted'. During this time there were no clouds to be seen in the sky. We were never more troubled with any attempts to thus disturb the meetings.

The first encouragement Mrs. Eddy received after issuing the first edition of *Science and Health* was from A. Bronson Alcott, who called to see her and said, 'I have faith in you'. She afterwards healed him from a severe form of rheumatism which had confined him to his chair.

(1909—probably August 3) Mother heard an audible voice from God saying: 'Leave alone successor contention before it is meddled with.'

From I. C. T. Collection [Irving C. Tomlinson]

In the early days it was hard for Mrs. Eddy to find patients to heal and one day she went out on the street to see if she could find some one. She saw the doctor's gig tied in front of a house nearby. When the doctor drove away, Mrs. Eddy went to the door, and asked a tear-stained woman who came to the door if there was anyone sick in the house. The lady said her daughter had just died. Mrs. Eddy asked if she could go in and see the daughter. The woman at first demurred but finally let her go in where the body lay. In a little while the mother heard voices, and looking into the room she saw that her daughter was sitting up in bed and talking to Mrs. Eddy. Mrs. Eddy said that 'a wordless flood of Life filled her consciousness and the girl was raised from the dead'. Mrs. Eddy asked the mother to bring the daughter's clothes, and the amazed mother asked why. She answered that she wanted to take the girl out for a walk.

The mother said, 'You don't know what you are asking. My daughter has been ill for months with consumption and could not go out if she wanted to.' Mrs. Eddy reassured the mother and told her that no harm should come to her daughter through anything that she should do, and finally the mother brought the girl's clothes. She then took the girl out and walked her up and down for about half an hour, the mother and father following behind to see what was being done. The girl's color came back as she was not only alive, but healed of the disease. When they got back to the house, the mother took off her diamond ring and gave it to Mrs. Eddy, and this ring she always wore.

(ANOTHER VERSION: Mrs. Eddy once went into a house and saw a woman weeping in the hallway. The woman said, 'My daughter is dying of consumption. The doctor has just left and he told me he could not do more for her.' Mrs. Eddy asked if she might go up and heal the daughter. The mother consented and Mrs. Eddy went upstairs to the bedroom. The father, who was very antagonistic to Mrs. Eddy, was standing by the bed; but Mrs. Eddy felt that, having the mother's permission to help the girl, it was right for her to go ahead, so she said to the sick girl, 'Get up and come for a walk'. The girl got up and Mrs. Eddy helped her dress and they went out of the house for a walk together. The father followed them, secretly as he thought, dodging behind trees and watching around corners, expecting every moment to see his daughter drop dead. Mrs. Eddy knew that he was following, but that did not interfere with her demonstration, for when they returned from the walk the daughter was completely healed.)

Mrs. Eddy was living on Columbus Avenue and enjoyed seeing a little baby who lived across the street. She missed the smiles of the little one and wondered what had happened. One morning she noticed the doctor's carriage leaving the home of the child. Mrs. Eddy went over to the house, spoke with the mother and asked to see the child. The mother said the child had passed on while the doctor was there. Mrs. Eddy went and sat beside the child, realizing the truth of being as no one else has since the time of Jesus, and the child was healed. Instead of gratitude being expressed by the mother, she took the child and expressed ugliness toward our Leader. The child remained healed.

There was in an asylum, past which Mrs. Eddy used to drive, a mentally deranged man who had a sore on his leg. Every day when he saw Mrs. Eddy's carriage coming, he would run to the gate and pull down his sock so our Leader would see his sore. One day when Mrs. Sargent was at Pleasant View she heard Mrs. Eddy tell her sister that this man had been healed of the sore and of the insanity.

One time a mother brought her dead baby to Mrs. Eddy and placed it on her lap. Our Leader asked her to come back in an hour, and began to treat the child. She realized that Life is Love, and that Love is right here, and Love is Life, and kept on realizing this more and more clearly. After a while she felt something moving on her lap (she had forgotten the baby); she looked down and saw the child looking up at her, smiling and kicking its feet.

Mrs. Eddy drove into Concord one day and stopped at the Christian Science Hall and Mr. Frye went in with a letter, leaving the carriage door open. A gentleman was standing in front of the hall who had called at Pleasant View earlier in the day to see Mrs. Eddy but was told that she could not see him and that an appointment or an opportunity might be arranged later. As he went away from the house he was very discouraged and said, so that a worker heard him, 'There may not be any later'. This man stepped to the carriage, took off his hat, and said, 'Mrs. Eddy?' Our Leader said, 'Yes'. 'May I ask you one question?' he asked. 'Certainly!', she said. Then he said, 'Can you tell me about God, who is He, where is He, and what is He?'

Mrs. Eddy told him that God was his Mind, his Life, and continued talking just three minutes. Then the man looked at the clock which they could both see, and said, 'I have learned more in these three minutes about God than I have in all the rest of my life.' He raised his hat and said good-bye and the carriage drove off.

Mrs. Eddy afterwards told her students that she saw he was suffering from jaundice and that as she talked with him she saw the unhealthy color fade from his face like the shadow of a cloud vanishing away, and his face become perfectly normal. She added,

'He was healed, but he did not recognize it while we were talking.' Next day the man wrote he was completely healed and that he took the train home that same night.

From a Student

One day when Mrs. Eddy's father came upon her grandfather in the fields watching a snake, he saw that the grandfather's head was moving to and fro just as was the snake's. Mrs. Eddy said, 'If you watch error long enough, you will find yourself doing just what it is doing.'

ACCOUNTS OF HEALING WORK BY MRS. EDDY (GATHERED FROM VARIOUS SOURCES)

From J. B. [Julia Bartlett]

Mrs. Eddy's eldest sister, Abigail Tilton, was very much opposed to Christian Science; but when her little daughter lay dying she called Mrs. Eddy, or told her what the situation was by messenger, and permitted her to see the child. Mrs. Eddy asked her sister to leave the room and in a short time healed her niece, got her out of bed and dressed, and had a romp around the room with the child, thus getting the child's thought back to normal, as it were.

When the mother came in and saw them playing she said, 'It is the work of the devil'.

From C. A. F. [Calvin Augustus Frye]

Jerry, the horse, was limping; and Mrs. Eddy called for the carriage to stop. She put her head out of the window and said to Jerry, 'You go right along about your own business and do not pay any attention to anything said to you; you listen to me'. And that was the end of Jerry's limping.

From I. O. K. [Ira Oscar Knapp]

One of the early cases that came before (the Directors) was a charge of immoral conduct against a First Member who was a student of Mrs. Eddy's. From the evidence submitted, the Directors were convinced that the charges were sustained. They, therefore, removed the individual from membership in the church, and took his practitioner's card out of the *Christian Science Journal*. That punishment in no wise healed the individual, but made him so rebellious that he threatened a lawsuit in revenge.

When Mrs. Eddy heard of this case, she asked the Directors to restore her student to full church membership, including his office as a First Member, and to replace his card in the Journal. This resulted in a complete healing of the individual.

From N. R. [Nemi Robertson]

This student wrote a letter to Mrs. Eddy at a time when she was exercised in her mind about a patient who showed great resentment toward Mrs. Eddy. Although she had not actually mentioned the patient, the reply from Mrs. Eddy contained the advice: 'Turn your patient's thought *to God*, and let *Love* show me to him just as I really *am*!' The patient was healed.

From I. C. T. Collection [Irving C. Tomlinson]

In one of Mrs. Eddy's classes there was a woman who had a strong sense of resentment and condemnation toward her husband, who was very immoral. Mrs. Eddy said to her that Jesus healed the Magdalen by condemning the sin, but not the woman. The lady answered, 'Yes, but I have not the consciousness that Jesus had'. Our Leader instantly rebuked this by saying that she could claim the Christ-consciousness, for otherwise she could not heal a single case of sin or sickness.

The student's consciousness was so illumined that her state of mind completely changed toward her husband, and when she returned home, she found him healed.

At the time the church at Concord was being built Mrs. Sweet went into the building and slipped on a board and hurt herself. Some workers at Pleasant View tried to help her, but without much success.

Mrs. Eddy asked them what was the matter with Mrs. Sweet. They answered that she was all right. Mrs. Eddy said, 'She is not all right'. She then asked Mrs. Sweet what the trouble was, and the latter replied that it was being met. Mrs. Eddy said, 'It is not being met'.

Then our Leader asked her how she was working. Mrs. Sweet answered that she was knowing that there was no accident in Mind. Mrs. Eddy replied, 'That would not heal you. You were brought here to help me. You are one of my best workers.' She then pointed out that the only trouble was an argument to interfere with her usefulness to the Leader. By the time Mrs. Eddy finished talking to her, Mrs. Sweet was healed. Mrs. Eddy said to her, 'I will say for your comfort that if you were brought here with every bone broken in your whole body, you would respond to my treatment'.

Mrs. W. went with Mrs. Eddy to a furniture shop to help her select some chairs. The clerk who was waiting on them wore a bandage over one eye. Mrs. Eddy seemed absorbed in thought while they were being shown the chairs, paying very little attention to them, and when pressed as to which she liked best, she said, 'Any that we can sit on'.

Mrs. W. was annoyed at Mrs. Eddy's indifference, and told the clerk that they would come back the next day and give a decision about the chairs.

They were on the second floor of the shop, with two doors opening out, one into a stairway, the other to a chute for sliding boxes down to the sidewalk. Mrs. Eddy opened one door and went downstairs. Mrs. W. in her perturbation opened the other door and stepped on the chute, and slid down to the sidewalk, where Mrs. Eddy arrived in time to see her picking herself up. Mrs. W. reproached our Leader for her lack of attention to the business in hand, and Mrs. Eddy replied, 'Could I think of chairs when the man was suffering?'

When Mrs. W. went the next day to see about the chairs, the clerk said, 'Who was that lady with you yesterday? I had an abscess on my eye, and when she went out, I took the bandage off, and there was not a sign of it left.'

One time some of the workers at Pleasant View were sitting in front of a window working against a storm which was approaching; suddenly Mrs. Eddy came up behind them and said, 'You are not meeting it because you are mesmerized by the appearance'. Then she swept them aside, took up the case herself, and in a short time they saw the blue sky appear through the center of the storm cloud.

In one of Mrs. Eddy's classes a clergyman who was very elderly had a partial belief of blindness, and asked our Leader if it could be cured, She answered, 'Yes, if you only touch the hem of *His* garment'. And the man was healed during class.

A well-known actor was healed physically and his testimony appeared in the *Journal.* Afterwards, one day he was walking along a street in Concord with a big cigar in his mouth. Mrs. Eddy passed in her carriage and looked at him. He took the cigar out of his mouth and threw it away, and was healed of the desire to smoke then and there.

One day Mrs. Eddy was going out for her afternoon drive when a tall, gaunt man, who appeared far gone in consumption, came up to her gate, held out his hands to her and shouted, 'Help me!' Mrs. Eddy said a few words to him out of the carriage window; talked to him for about two minutes and then drove on out of the gate. On her return she exclaimed, 'What a need that man had!' Next day they received a letter from the man telling Mrs. Eddy that he was conscious he had been healed as soon as the carriage drove on.

From L. C. [Laura Conant]

Mr. Frye fell down the stairs. The students worked for him, but they were frightened and believed he had broken his neck, because his head wobbled so. Mrs. Eddy sensed the situation and appeared on the scene. She declared in a commanding way from the top of the stairs, 'Calvin Frye, come up here'. After calling him three times she turned her back on the situation and he rose up and followed her.

(A similar episode has been described by members of Mrs. Eddy's household and is reported at length in Adam Dickey's *Memoirs of Mary Baker Eddy*[1], pp. 107-12. It is related that one evening Laura Sargent found Calvin Frye reclining awkwardly on a couch in his room. He showed no signs of life. When she failed to get any response from him, she went for assistance, and two other students came and tried to rouse him by various means, but without success.

(It soon became obvious that Mrs. Eddy must be informed. Accordingly, Mrs. Sargent went to the room where she was already in bed. While preparing to dress, however, Mrs. Eddy seemed suddenly to sense the urgency of the situation. Rather than waste more time, she had the unconscious form of Calvin Frye brought to her. He was dragged along in a rocking-chair and remained slumped there within Mrs. Eddy's reach beside her bed.

(Adam Dickey calls it 'an interesting moment'. She laid her hand on Mr. Frye's shoulder and called on him vigorously: 'Calvin, wake up. It is Mother who is calling you. Wake up, Calvin, this Cause needs you. Mother needs you, and you must not leave. Calvin, wake up. Disappoint your enemies, Calvin, and awake.'

(The first words which Calvin Frye uttered when, after a long while, he began to come round were: 'I don't want to stay. I want to go.' Mrs. Eddy now turned to the others, who had remained passive onlookers, and said: 'Just listen to that!' A little while later the students took him from the room; and the following day he went about his duties as usual. No one felt inclined to rehearse

[1] Copies of Adam Dickey's *Memoirs* were recalled by the Board of Directors shortly after its publication in 1927; only a few originals remain in existence. The story of the raising of Calvin Frye can be read, however, in some other books about Mary Baker Eddy where the Dickey account is reproduced in varying detail.

the experience in front of him. In Mr. Dickey's words, however, 'the fact remains that Calvin Frye had passed through what mortal mind calls "death", and the grave had been cheated of its victim by our Leader's quick and effective work'.)

During the building of The Mother Church one of the key workers passed on and a group of students set to work to restore him. They met with no apparent success. One of the students records that Mrs. Eddy later told him never to work to bring a man back. He then understood that one would never correct the belief that man dies in the material body while holding a belief that he has lived in it and must return to it. There is also this reported statement by Mrs. Eddy: 'Discord comes from looking away from all—thinking there is something else. You heal disease by knowing there is none. You heal sin and death in the same way.'

A student once told Mrs. Eddy that she had restored a horse that had passed out. Mrs. Eddy replied encouragingly, although she corrected her as follows: 'There is no life in matter to pass out; so do not put any into it.' Again, she said, 'If you argue "there is no pain, no catarrh" and so forth, you are putting your weight on the side of error. Take the side with God and put all the balance there. That is what is needed.'

An interesting lesson on the need to start with life and health as the facts of being—rather than believe that ill-functioning physicality has to be made to function more smoothly—has been preserved by a New York student. In the early days of Christian Science the recognition of health came to Mrs. Eddy so immediately that she began to fear Christian Science would scarcely get the credit it deserved. People were saying that the improvement had already taken place before Mrs. Eddy had arrived on the scene. Consequently, on one occasion, she deliberately asked God to delay the healing of a dying man until at least she had reached him. But this time, when she arrived at the house, she could do nothing. As she put it to a friend: 'I couldn't do a thing. I went home and put my face upon the carpet, and there I stayed, until I found Jacob's ladder, from the bottom to the top. Then I saw that God, in His own time and way, would take unto Himself the glory, and it was not for me to say!'

A member of Mrs. Eddy's household had an appointment with the dentist and Mrs. Eddy needed her just when the appointment was scheduled and would not let her go. She said that if she had, she would have been allowing mortal mind to rob what should be sacrificed for the whole world's good.(?) The need was met without the dentist and the tooth filled with substance.

Mrs. Eddy passed a drunken man in Lynn and turned to the one with her and said, 'If that is the man I see, that is the man I am and I refuse it because it is not the man I wish to be.' The man was healed.

An old school friend of Mrs. Eddy's, who was down and out, called on her one day and she talked with him. Before he left she gave him a prayer that she had given the students and asked him to say it each day. After two weeks he came back completely healed. Then Mrs. Eddy gave him $500.00 to set him up in business. [Equal to $12,000 today—2006.]

The prayer was: O divine Love, give me higher, holier, purer desires, more self-abnegation, more love and spiritual aspirations.

A reporter once asked Mrs. Eddy for a brief definition of Christian Science treatment. She thought a moment and said, 'Absolute acknowledgment of present perfection'. The reporter was not a Christian Scientist and did not become one. Yet many years later he found himself on what he was told was his death-bed, and these words came back to him and restored him to health.

Mrs. Eddy went to a case where the patient was dying with pneumonia and the room was filled with relatives and friends. She was propped up in the bed with pillows. Mrs. Eddy went to her and yanked the pillows out from under her and said, 'You are not going to do what these people think you are going to do.' The patient was healed.

A student told Mrs. Eddy of a case of bronchial trouble that she had been endeavoring to heal without success. Mrs. Eddy leaned over the desk and shook her finger at her saying, 'What are bronchial tubes for?' Then she answered her own question, 'They are to be used to sing praises to the Lord, and for nothing else'. The student's patient was healed in that hour.

One, of the students who lived at the Metaphysical College in its early days on Columbus Avenue had had difficulty in walking upstairs since childhood. One day she was struggling up to the third floor, and when only halfway up said out loud, 'I know I'll never get to the top'. At this moment Mrs. Eddy (then Glover) appeared at a door nearby. 'Run up those stairs', she commanded, 'run up those stairs'. The student obeyed, and found out that from then on she had no difficulty in climbing stairs.

One of Mrs. Eddy's students had worked for herself without success and had had another student work for her without success; and she was nearly passing on. Mrs. Eddy sent a message to her which read as follows: God gave you an abiding sense of Life that needs not to be fought for. Remember this and you will live forever.

She recovered at once.

OTHER RECOLLECTIONS BY STUDENTS (FIRST-PERSON)

By H. C. [Henrietta Chanfrau]

One day Mrs. Eddy asked me, 'Henrietta, do you keep a copy of *Science and Health* in your bedroom?' When I told her that I always had a copy on my little table by my bed, and had had one there from the first, always carrying it with me wherever I went (traveling, etc.), she said, 'Give it up from now on. The textbook does not belong in the bedroom. Take God into your bedroom!'

During one of my visits at Pleasant View, Mr. Ira Knapp, one of the first Directors of The Mother Church, came to see Mrs. Eddy. While he was waiting to see her, we spoke a few words together in the lower hall. He was very much upset, and finally told me it was because of some talk that had been going about Boston among the members of the church concerning him personally. I said what I could, but just then word was brought that Mrs. Eddy would see him.

When he came downstairs after his talk with her, a smile lighted up his face when he saw me. I did not like to ask what her words to him had been, but he told me without a word on my part. She said, 'When you have tasted gall and wormwood, you are ready and able to take manna, and *not until* then!'

Frequently during my visits with Mrs. Eddy, she would give answers to questions I put to her. One day I asked her, 'Mother, where will we be after we pass on?' She quickly answered, 'Why, right here, dear, only we shall be much freer because we are freed from the necessity of handling material sense. After we pass on, the moral laws obeyed here will count as blessings in spiritual sense.'

One afternoon Mr. Stephen Chase, Director of The Mother Church, called on Mrs. Eddy. She asked me to stay with her, and I did so. The conversation was a lengthy one, and Mr. Chase was very earnestly trying to tell Mrs. Eddy of some of the problems the Directors were having to meet, while Mrs. Eddy constantly made little pleasant jokes. This surprised me, because I had never seen her in such a light, jovial mood before in the presence of so many tales of difficulty. Finally she sent me away on some little errand, and when I returned, Mr. Chase was gone.

She said, 'Henrietta, I *know* how upset he was, but I wouldn't add fuel to the fire! The Christian Science Directors are not the best Scientists in the world, but they certainly are *steadfast* to their duty. And I know how to value that!'

Another bit of valuable advice I heard our Leader give was in a talk she had with Mr. Ira Knapp, one of the Directors whom I have already mentioned. He brought some papers to Mrs. Eddy one day, and I was in her study with her while she signed them. Then she turned to him and looked straight at him, as though studying him. Then she said, 'How long do you talk with your patients? He seemed very much surprised, and said, 'Why, I don't know; perhaps half an hour or maybe an hour'. She said, 'That's what's the trouble with you. Now just stop all those long visits. They come to you and pour out all their troubles on you, and that gets stored up inside you. Make every one of your patients limit their time to ten minutes, and you will be better for it, and they will, too.' When he had gone, she said to me, 'The successful Christian Science Practitioner is *not* one whose office is full of people from morning till night'.

One morning Mrs. Eddy was examining us in her study, putting various questions to us. Finally she said, 'Dear ones, you have answered well. Now that you have been so patient with Mother, what can she do for *you*?' We were all surprised at the question, but Mr. Strang, I believe it was, spoke up finally, 'Mother, will you prophesy for us?' Her face clouded for just an instant, and then she said, 'To perform the demonstration of prophecy always includes a temptation of animal magnetism. Now I have always found this rule of help: When you are about to prophesy, always handle animal magnetism first, and then you will find the times are in His hands, and all need for prophecy will be gone. Why? Because *faith in God* will have taken its place!'

But next day she referred to this again, and said, 'My dear students, God has told me this much for you: At the end of this century, Christian Science will be the only universally acknowledged religion in the world, because the other religions have no demonstrating basis. But much work remains undone, much self-denial waits for us all before this end can be fulfilled. The main thing is for us to handle

M.A.M. that would make us fold our hands till this manifests itself. But Truth demands work, work, work! Never forget that!'

One day Mrs. Eddy was looking at the current issue of the *Christian Science Journal,* as I entered the room. She showed me several advertising cards of the practitioners, and pointed to their statements, 'Absent treatments a speciality', and the like. Then she said, 'Just look at that! Students calling themselves Christian Scientists specializing in absent treatments! It's all a lie of A.M. and can be one of the greatest obstructions to the worker.' I asked her why she did not require them to stop publication of such cards, and she said, 'All in time, dear. I must suffer it to be so now, but in God's way they will be shown what to do. Meanwhile Mother must protect them for they know not what they do. They know so little, oh, so little!'

By A. H. D. [Adam H. Dickey]

Two men were fighting; one was choking the other (she said), and she asked us, 'Which one would you work for?' She then said the one that was doing the choking. (She explained that malicious animal magnetism was the cause and in destroying that you freed the victim.)

Someone in the room was speaking. 'Instead of speaking of joints, I should have said', this one said, 'locomotion and action is perfect'. Mrs. Eddy said: 'Yes, in declaring the perfection of all things begin with God, not with matter. You do not arrive at perfection by thinking of material organism. Begin with Mind and keep your thought away from all things material.'

Mrs. Eddy called all the workers together and made them promise to keep their watch. In explanation she said, 'To keep your watch does not mean only to be awake at that hour and be working mentally. It means to do the work and succeed in breaking the mesmerism for the two hours assigned. If you don't succeed, you haven't kept your watch.'

(In his *Memoirs of Mary Baker Eddy* Adam Dickey devotes three pages, 126-9, to explaining the importance which Mrs. Eddy attached to *watching*. He shows that by this practice Mrs. Eddy meant the 'handling', not ignoring, of the animal magnetism which would misinterpret or distort the picture God presents and requires us to watch. He records that on one occasion she told the whole household that the students she called to her home were those who understood how to watch. If they kept a good watch they were retained: if they failed on that score they were sent away.

(Among the illustrations which she gave of the mesmerist's claims or 'laws' were: ability to catch a worker unprepared—for, just as the goodman of the house would watch if he knew the hour in which his house would be assailed, so the mesmerist claimed to fix an hour in the distant future when the assault could come unexpectedly; ability to prolong the assault indefinitely—to 'cover every hour in the night'; ability to 'produce suffering asleep or awake'; and so on. It was about this time, 1908, that Mrs. Eddy included her statement in *Science and Health,* 'Christian Scientists, be a law to yourselves that mental malpractice cannot harm you either when asleep or when awake', and drew attention in the periodicals to its importance. As she told the workers, 'If you can defeat the mesmerist in this, you can defeat him in all things'.

(To complete her lesson Mrs. Eddy explained that she had met mesmerism's attack over many years and the time had come for the students to do so themselves. Otherwise they would be mesmerized into believing that the revelation of Christian Science was concerned with a mortal, or sickly person, instead of being the statement of Truth; and they would have no Cause. Indeed, Mr. Dickey reports her as saying that if they did not handle mesmerism, 'the Cause will perish and we will go along another 1900 years with the world sunk into the blackest night'.

(She further implied that the mesmerism which pretended that health is not a divine fact would prevent healing—for just so long as the false mesmeric pretence was accepted. Likewise, the mesmerism which produced acceptance of the belief that there was a person to die or be dead was the only way death could seem to come to pass. The belief, for example, that the revelator of Christian Science was mortal constituted mental assassination of the one voicing the revelation, and the only way in which Mrs. Eddy's death could appear or be witnessed by any particular individual. It is in the above-mentioned pages that Mr. Dickey comes closest to keeping his solemn promise to Mrs. Eddy that if she 'should ever leave here' he should write a history of what transpired in his experiences with her and say that she was 'mentally murdered'.)

By J. M. [Joseph Mann]

John Lathrop told Mrs. Eddy he had been reading the lesson sermon and getting 'more out of it all the time'. 'Do you call that watching?' she asked. Then she told him the story of the Union soldier on guard duty (see p. 12, l.40) and added: 'Don't be a soldier who only walks back and forth.'

Mr. Kimball asked Mrs. Eddy what would happen to the Christian Science Movement if she should pass on. She replied: 'It would degenerate into material prosperity.' He then asked what would happen if she ascended. She hesitated, before answering with a beatific smile, 'The Mother Church would be dissolved'.

By N. R. [Nemi Robertson]

(8/12/05) Today I visited our Leader at Pleasant View and she spoke with me for about a half hour. She seemed distressed in regard to two of the Boston officials, and kept saying, 'God will reward them; they will see me *as I am*!' Then she turned to me and said, 'Dear, do not be distressed at what you see and hear here. Love cares for us all, and I am old in God's service. I long for heaven.' Then she sat silent for quite a time, looking through the window. At last I said, 'Mother, are you ever lonely?' She turned and looked at me, and then said, 'Alone, child, but never lonely!'

MISCELLANEOUS RECOLLECTIONS

(THIRD-PERSON—ARRANGED IN ALPHABETICAL ORDER OF NAMES OF STUDENTS CONCERNED)

Miss Julia Bartlett recalled that in the early days the Scientists had no trouble in healing. They could sit and work at their knitting and think of their patients and heal them. But after a while it got so they could not heal and the people in Lynn said they were losing their healing power. Mrs. Eddy saw that it was K—[Kennedy] and others with him who were mentally interfering with them, so she called them together, told them what the matter was, and showed them how to protect themselves against it.

When Mr. Dickey was telling our Leader of Mrs. Dickey's healing work in Kansas City (she was there and he was at the home), she said that she wanted to tell him something and said that she could not give it out and cautioned him not even to tell Mrs. Dickey until he thought she was ready for it. She said, 'When any practitioner puts *Science and Health* in a patient's hands, it is *Science and Health* that does the healing'.

She said she hadn't attained one millionth of what the book calls for. 'It is a wonderful book and covers eternity', she said.

One day Mrs. Eddy touched Adam Dickey's hand with her finger and asked him, 'What is this?' He replied, 'Matter'. She said, 'It is *not*; it is Spirit'. Then another time she looked at him and said, 'You are Spirit'. And he said, 'No, Mother, I am spiritual'. She said in a very emphatic way, 'You are Spirit'. And he said, 'Mother, I do not see that'. She said, 'You are Spirit', the third time, but he said he could not see it. When he was going to his room he met Mrs. Sargent and he told her of the conversation with Mrs. Eddy and she said, 'Oh, Mr. Dickey, why did you say that! Mother was trying to give you her highest teaching.'

When Mrs. Dunbar's sister died, Mrs. Eddy said, 'So the saintly sister has gone higher. She is not dead but lives. Consumption never killed her. Today she is free from this belief. When we are on the same plane of consciousness we know and can converse with another.'

Mrs. Eddy detected a false sense of theology in her dress-maker, Miss Eveleth. In order to break this she got her to make a dress for her on Sunday. When she tried it on on Monday the hooks and eyes were one-sixteenth inch out of the way. Mrs. Eddy declared vigorously, 'This is sin. Your thought was not right in doing this. If it had been it would have been correct.'

Judge Ewing was sent by Mrs. Eddy on a lecture tour that took him around the world giving his lecture CHRISTIAN SCIENCE, THE RELIGION OF JESUS CHRIST. On his return he found himself called on to give a lecture in Lynn, Mass. It was a stormy night and when he got on the platform he immediately felt he was up against an antagonistic audience doubtless composed of the then very large, active body of Spiritualistic sympathizers in that town who were strongly opposed to Christian Science.

It seemed useless for him to try to give his regular lecture to such an audience; so in his usual friendly way of taking an audience into his confidence, Judge Ewing decided the only way was to get nearer to them. He got down from the platform and stood right in front of the audience. He began to talk to them about Lynn, assuring them from his own recent travel experiences that their town was well known all over the world for its wonderful footwear that for years had been sent out everywhere. After enlarging on this for a while, he gave them the real reason why Lynn would live forever in the hearts and minds of men—it was the place in which *Science and Health* was written by Mrs. Eddy.

Then, allowing Spirit to speak through him, he told in beautiful, sympathetic language of some of Mrs. Eddy's struggles, privations and difficulties in bringing forth her book, and emphasized that it was only her deep love for mankind that enabled her to stand and overcome all that she had to meet.

By the time he was through talking about Mrs. Eddy there was hardly a dry eye in the place; and so he knew that the opposition was broken and he could deliver his regular lecture on Christian Science. He got back on to the platform and did so.

The following morning he took the first train for Concord, N.H., where he had an appointment with Mrs. Eddy. Immediately Mrs. Eddy began to thank him for all the things he had said about her the night before and assured him how true they were. She quoted whole statements he had made and the Judge began to puzzle how she could have gotten hold of them, because he himself had come in on the train that brought the newspapers; so she could not have read the reports yet. How was she able to repeat his own statements in his own words?

Finally he burst out with, How do you know what I said? And Mrs. Eddy replied, 'Suppose I told you that I heard you?'

Mrs. Eddy rebuked Calvin Frye on one occasion for being too 'plethoric'. She said, I cannot understand why you students become so plethoric when each day you deny matter; it is because Science brings you a human sense of harmony.

Mr. Frye told Miss Robertson that Mrs. Eddy called him from bed one cold winter night to dictate the words that she later used for the motto on the Christian Science Souvenir Spoon.2 He said that she seemed very happy when she spoke the words. But she never mentioned it again until someone, nearly a year later, was speaking with her about the proposed spoon. Then she turned to Mr. Frye and reminded him of the words she had dictated to him. He managed to find the paper on which they were written and brought it to her.

She said, 'When God told me that, I didn't know what it was for. Now I know.' The motto is: 'Not matter but Mind satisfieth.'

Mrs. Eddy was showing Mrs. Gragg and three other students a beautiful quilt that had been made for her by loving hands. She turned to them saying, 'I thank you for it'. Mrs. Gragg said, 'But Mother, we were not privileged to help make this for you.' 'Yes you were, dear, yes you were', was the reply.

Lydia Hall showed Mrs. Eddy a motto called THE HOUSE BEAUTIFUL. She asked her where she got it. Lydia said a friend had bought it for her. Mrs. Eddy replied, Do not buy another and tell the lady not to buy any more. It is all contained in my books and what is the thought behind it? To make money.

Described in *Journal* for January, 1899.

A lady came to the door at Pleasant View with a box of American Beauty roses and begged Lydia to accept them and give them to Mrs. Eddy; and say that she would call in the afternoon to see Mrs. Eddy. Lydia waited until the midday meal before bringing them in and showing them to Mrs. Eddy, who gave a wave of her hand and said, Take them away; what a mockery!

Lydia took them to the kitchen and all day long suffered severely. As night drew on and she was tucking Mrs. Eddy into her swing on the front veranda, no amount of tucking in seemed right and she had to come back constantly to do it over. Mrs. Eddy finally said, 'Lydia, you are suffering and have been suffering all day'. She replied saying, 'Yes, Mother'. Then Mrs. Eddy said, 'What have you done with those roses?' 'I took them to the kitchen, Mother.' 'Are they destroyed?' 'No.' 'Go to the kitchen immediately and take the roses and put them in the fire.'

Lydia said that this was a most difficult thing for her to do. However, she complied with Mrs. Eddy's instruction. Immediately she was released from the pain and was her normal self again.

As she came in about an hour later to make preparations for the night, Mrs. Eddy said to her, 'You are free?' 'Yes, Mother, I am.' 'Lydia, do you know what that means? That was theosophy. They believe that if they can get something into your hands they can use you as an avenue. Now be on your watch.'

Lydia Hall's father was jealous of Mrs. Eddy because Lydia preferred to live with her Leader rather than stay at home with him. When he died and Lydia went home, she suffered greatly. Mrs. Eddy later told her it was the sense of jealousy that had not been met, and which was still present to be met, even though the father had passed on. She should have gone to work right then and there to know that the good would neutralize it and destroy it.

Mrs. Eddy told Lydia Hall that she always started her handling of error by the following method: 'There is no animal magnetism; there is no hate, no electro-magnetism, no esoteric magic, black art, hypnotism, etc., for God is All-in-all.'

Once when Lydia Hall was with our Leader her bell rang calling her to come down to Mrs. Eddy's room. When she got there Mrs. Eddy told her to arrange a doily on the table. Lydia did not think that it needed arranging but she went through the motions and returned to her room. When she was first called she had been reading a newsy letter from home, and when she got back to her room she continued to read it. The bell rang again, and again Mrs. Eddy directed her to arrange the doily. As she went up the stairs she said under her breath, 'The old fuss'. Then when she reached her room she resumed reading the letter.

The bell rang a third time. This time Mrs. Eddy said, 'Lydia, did you say *the old fuss*?' She said no, although in later years in relating the incident she said this was not true, but she was afraid to confess to Mrs. Eddy. This time after she returned to her room she did not resume reading the gossipy letter, but took up her copy of *Science and Health* and began to study it.

The lesson of this incident was summed up in words which Mrs. Eddy used at the third time of calling: 'Lydia, if when you are doing a thing your thought is not right, no matter how perfectly it is done outwardly, it is not done rightly.'

Mrs. Eddy received a letter at Pleasant View from Christian Scientists in Concord asking her to congratulate them over the birth of a Christian Science baby. She read it aloud; then with apparent indignation uttered: 'A Christian Science baby! A crime! Just as much a crime as a murder would be!' She paused a few moments; then raised her hand and shaking her finger declared with great emphasis: 'No loyal Christian Scientist will ever marry.'

> (In later years, when these remarks were repeated, they ran head-on into official opposition; and the recorder was finally driven to recant. On her death-bed, however, she confessed that her recantation was erroneous and that she had stated the above remarks exactly as she had understood them to have been spoken.)

(From the Bliss Knapp book, p. 11) Mrs. Eddy possessed the ability to read the unspoken thoughts of her pupils. For example: A student called at her home for an interview and was told that Mrs. Eddy would see her in a few moments. While the student was looking out of the window as she waited for Mrs. Eddy, she saw an intoxicated man across the street. She began to ponder the case, and asked herself, 'Where is that seeming error? Am I drunk or is that man drunk? Is the error in me or is it in him?' Immediately Mrs. Eddy, who had entered the room unobserved, said aloud, 'No, that error is not in your thought'.

(From the Bliss Knapp book, p. 135) Mrs. Eddy ... detected mentally that Mr. Knapp was still grieving for his wife. She immediately rebuked that condition, and speaking sternly to him, said, 'Mr. Knapp, are you still babying that lie about the loss of your wife?' And then she handled the error so completely, that the grief was entirely removed from Mr. Knapp's thought; and ever afterwards he could think and speak of his wife as naturally as when she was with him.

One morning when Mrs. Carpenter was with Mrs. Eddy in her study at Pleasant View, our Leader mentioned that she was writing a letter to Mrs. Longyear who had requested advice regarding a Christian Science practitioner. She then read out what she had replied to Mrs. Longyear. It was: 'I cannot advise you regarding a Christian Science practitioner, but I most earnestly request that you select one who knows Christian Science history.'

Mrs. Linscott asked Mrs. Eddy if it was right to kill chickens for food. Mrs. Eddy replied, 'You do not take life, do you?'

When Frederick Mann was a boy he was in the room when Mrs. Eddy asked her students where evil came from. They thought and thought and endeavored to give scientific answers, When she asked him, he said, 'I don't know'. Then she said, 'He is the scientific one'.

Mrs. Eddy sent Joseph Mann out to hoe potatoes. He thought it was a form of punishment and let his thought drop. Soon she sent for him to come in to do some very important mental work. But he had let his thought drop and was not prepared to do it.

The lesson he learned was that he should never let his thought drop because of the outward task he was called upon to do, no matter how menial it might seem to be.

(7/28/06) Mrs. Eddy sent a copy of the *Sentinel* to Archibald McLellan (Editor) and wrote on the right-hand side where the torch then appeared: 'What if you put here the figure of a woman with a lamp in her hand? This would illustrate Longfellow's lines in verse, see page 763.' On the left-hand side she similarly wrote: 'The same on this side also.'

(On page 763 she had pencilled the last four lines of the Longfellow poem, thus sponsoring the words that appeared a few weeks later on the front page of the *Sentinel* with the new, approved design. Although there have been changes in the design since 1911, the verses remain.)

(From *An Historical Sketch* by B. Tatham Woodhead) Lady Victoria (Murray) asked Mrs. Eddy how she healed the sick. Leaning back in her chair Mrs. Eddy smilingly said: 'I will tell you. I heal the same way today as I did when I commenced. My original way was instantaneous. The students did not understand any more than an English scholar could understand a foreign language without learning it. They, therefore, put it into their language. The argument used in healing is simply tuning-up. If your violin *is* in tune it is unnecessary to tune it up. Keep your violin in tune.' This last sentence was repeated quite imperatively and much emphasized. 'There is no disease', she continued. 'If I dream there is a table in place of that chair, that is only a belief. The patient believes it, he does not *feel* it. God is All, and God is infinite, precludes all else. Keep your violin in tune.'

One time when Mrs. Eddy was speaking with Miss Robertson, word was brought that Dr. Alfred Baker was downstairs. Mrs. Eddy rose and went down to see him, telling Miss Robertson to remain in her study. When she returned, she said, 'Dr. Baker is a good Christian Scientist, but like all of us, he forgets that God is by his side all the while. I had to remind him of it just now!'

(Miss Robertson learned afterwards that she had spoken very sharply to him as though to arouse him. The result was that he left in a happy and alert frame of mind.)

Mrs. Sargent asked Mrs. Eddy how she did her marvelous healing in the early days and she replied with a smile, after being silent a moment: 'I just got out of God's way.'

Referring to her sister Victoria who was present, Laura Sargent remarked to Mrs. Eddy, 'Mother, she thinks that if she has anything hard to do and pushes right through it and does it, she will get out of it.' Mrs. Eddy turned to Victoria and said, 'And you will, dear, you will'.

Laura Sargent heard Mrs. Eddy say to Maria Newcomb who had a claim, 'Read *Science and Health* just as you did when you first came into Christian Science, not intellectually, nor as if you were going through the lesson; but praying to be healed as you did when you first read it'.

In the morning of the day when Mrs. Eddy took her last drive Mrs. Sargent opened her Bible and thought, 'I wish I might ask Mother what this means'. As Mrs. Eddy was arranging her bonnet she said, 'Laura, do not bring your questions to me, take them to God. You lose your answer if you take them to me.'

Ella Peck Sweet was asked by Mrs. Eddy in class in 1887 to define animal magnetism. She declared, 'Animal Magnetism is the sum total of all error, and that in itself nothing until you attach belief to it'. The teacher clapped her hands, saying, 'Well answered!' Seventeen years later Mrs. Eddy asked her to repeat this definition, and when the same words were spoken, she again clapped her hands in approval.

Mary Baker Eddy presented her faithful student, John Salchow, with a beautiful scarfpin consisting of a large pearl with a delicate serpent of gold circling around the under side of the pearl. In the head of the serpent was a small diamond.

In presenting this pin Mrs. Eddy unfolded its symbolism as follows: 'Truth is the pearl of great price. Grasp it with selfishness and it has a serpent under it—you may get bitten. But if you handle the serpent with unselfishness it has a diamond in its head.'

One night Miss Shannon was on watch duty at Pleasant View, and Mrs. Eddy saw her in her room very sleepy, She awakened her and said, 'No, that is not a natural sleep. Get up and work.'

(From *Journal,* Vol. IV, p. 94—from item headed 'Strawberry Festival') After due justice had been done to the ices, berries, and cake, Rev. Mary B. G. Eddy made an address from the portico, to the effect that some day Christian Science will enable us to enjoy such a treat without raising the fruit, compounding the cake, freezing the cream, or buying the sugar; just as Jesus fed the multitude, without procuring the loaves and fishes through the usual channels of natural production and supply. She also narrated some incidents about the unusual and seemingly supernatural (but really natural) growth of apple-blossoms in icy winter, and of fresh shoots from dry stems in summer—through the power of Mind. She argued that if belief produces disease, and its removal leaves health to have its perfect work, then false belief may also prevent the perfect fulfilment of Spirit in all our material surroundings, flowers and fruit not excepted.

(From *Journal,* Vol. VII, p. 80—from item on Christian Scientist Association) There was a large attendance at the April meeting of the Association. Our Teacher was present, and spoke at some length on two points, of which her students have need to be watchful. She said error will urge two extremes; the first, to act too far in advance of our understanding, and to strike a blow too soon, and bring on a crisis that we are not fully prepared to meet and master.

We must not mistake self-sufficiency, pride in the letter of Christian Science, and our finite conception of the fitness of things for spiritual intuitions. The other extreme is apathy, inactivity, whereby many who are really good, and might do much for the cause, do little or nothing through a seemingly paralyzed condition of mind, from a false sense of fear. Such individuals must use what they already have, to obtain more. To destroy sin and heal the sick, we must take the sword; sin cannot be healed without. It is the 'sword of the Spirit' we must use, and the sword of the Spirit is Truth and Love; the word of Truth will cut away the belief of pleasure in sin from the human affections, then Love will heal the wounds from both sickness and sin. If, while we are using this sword to the best of our ability, error arouses itself to stop our progress, and we are temporarily in doubt as to what is just the right thing to do, we can stand still and wait on God; and in this waiting, remember what He has done for us in the past, and trust Him to do for us now. We shall thus surely see His salvation, and by these experiences we shall lose the sense of fear; then we gain the spirit of meekness, and in the might of this meekness we go forward and possess (inherit) the earth.

She also showed it to be the positive duty of Christian Scientists to uncover error (as they should a nest of vipers), that the people may see it and be warned of their danger, while they themselves are striving with Divine Science to take away its sting, and destroy its poison.

Short Isolated Recollections of a Miscellaneous Character

Mrs. Eddy said to a student who had a case that was not being healed: 'I would do three things: (1) Rise to a higher sense of the nothingness of matter. (2) Know there is one Mind and it governs you and your patient. (3) Know that no ignorant or malicious malpractice can interfere with you or your patients.'

(6/27/09) In reading the *Sentinel* of the previous day's date, Mrs. Eddy often commented upon someone getting results from declaring his divine sonship, etc. Then she said: 'No such experiences ever come to me. I reach the results without intermediate steps. If anyone was said to be ill in the next room, I wouldn't have to treat, I would just *know* the Truth about them and they would seem to be no more sick or dead than you are. I cannot tell you how I do it, but I have none of the experiences recorded by others, though I enjoy reading them.'

A little boy said to his mother, 'If Mrs. Eddy should say a blossom would come out, wouldn't it? His mother said, 'No, not at this time of the year' (in winter). Some days later Mrs. Eddy said to the boy, 'I will tell you something if you will not tell anyone'. He asked if he could tell his mama. Mrs. Eddy said, 'No, not anyone'. He said, 'Well, I will not'. Then Mrs. Eddy said, 'You see that apple tree?' He said, 'Yes'. She said, 'Now watch that tree every day and you will see a blossom come on it'. He did so and in three days there was a blossom and she had him pick it.

Mrs. Eddy asked the practitioners how many patients they were treating. Some said as many as thirty. She said, 'You cannot do it properly and handle so many. You may do it all right and handle that many now, but you ... cannot do yourself justice, because you are burning your own oil too low. This is the way the enemy robs you.'

At a time when there was a debating club being started in New York City among the Christian Scientists Mrs. Eddy discouraged it. She said, 'Avoid a movement within a movement'.

Mrs. Eddy named her Messages in her own books as follows:
1899. Purification of the church.
1900. What the Spirit saith unto the churches—Revelation.
1901. Infinite personality—My best.

Mrs. Eddy asked one how his branch church was coming along and he replied that everything was running very smoothly. She said, 'That's too bad. If you were making progress, things would not be so harmonious.'

A student went to Mrs. Eddy after having worked on a problem and asked her why she did not receive her results, why she had not had her work rewarded by demonstration. Mrs. Eddy replied, 'You have done everything rightly, but you have failed to do one thing and that is to stick to it. Error has an end, Truth is eternal.'

Mrs. Eddy called the entire household to her one morning and said to them all, 'Take your thought off from me', and then dismissed them. A little later she called them all again and said the same thing. Later she called them all again and asked them one by one what they understood her to mean by taking their thought off from her. Most of them answered thus, 'So you will be more free to do your own work'. Mrs. Eddy replied, 'You have no right to keep your thought on the person of anyone. Your thoughts should always be on God.'

Mrs. Eddy told a student that at first she hurled the Truth into human consciousness, but this caused her to be cast out of her different abodes in the early days. She learned that this was not the way of presenting the Truth and she learned wisdom by the things she suffered.

Mrs. Eddy gave the spiritual senses as follows:
Hearing—discernment;
Seeing—perception;
Smelling—intuition;
Tasting—choice;
Touching—consciousness.[3]

Rule in Mrs. Eddy's household: 'Simplicity, accuracy, and economy. Excuses are intolerable.'

[3] Another student's recollection is given on p. 222.

Mrs. Eddy asked a minister in her class if he thought he always did the best he knew how, and he replied that he thought he did. She replied, 'In Science we do not do the best we know until we do a thing. Science makes demonstration possible, and we all know how to demonstrate the truth in Christian Science.'

Mrs. Eddy once declared that page 275: 6-17 of *Science and Health* was the second scientific statement of being.

In speaking about how she was able to endure so much, Mrs. Eddy said in substance, 'When the foot steps upon me I bend as does the grass, and when it is lifted I come up as naturally'.

A man in the landscaping business who was a student of Christian Science came East from Kansas City. Mrs. Eddy hired him to come to Chestnut Hill with his crew and do some work on her place. The first day he came all prepared and Mrs. Eddy would not permit him to start. This experience was repeated the second day. Since this meant a great expense to him, he was disturbed and spent the entire second day in the study of *Science and Health.* When he arrived at Chestnut Hill the third day his thought was right and Mrs. Eddy permitted him to go to work.

One day a beautifully dressed student called on Mrs. Eddy expecting her to pour out spiritual thought to her. Instead, Mrs. Eddy started talking on her own plane of thought, commenting on her fine clothing and remarking, 'What a beautiful hat you have on!' And that practically ended the conversation.

A student once said to Mrs. Eddy that since coming into Christian Science she had lost fear to such an extent that she did not have the slightest fear of walking down Columbus Avenue alone at eleven o'clock at night. Mrs. Eddy replied, 'Do not tempt the Lord your God'.

Mr. and Mrs. Riley were asked to pay a call on Mrs. Eddy shortly after they had lost both a son and another dear one. Since Mrs. Eddy was having much to meet in the Field at that time, they were determined not to let their own grief appear in the interview and sought to clear their thoughts of the grief entirely. When they went to see her, so far as they knew they had eliminated this from their thoughts; but Mrs. Eddy was keen to read thought and in the midst of the conversation said, 'Now in regard to death: Suppose you were sitting in this chair and I was sitting in that one conversing with you, and suddenly an archer should shoot an arrow into your heart from that window.

'You would experience a sudden shock, a commotion within, nothing more. You would try to continue our conversation, but I, believing the arrow had killed you, could no longer converse with you; so you would arise from your chair, *leaving no body* in the chair, and go among those you could converse with, while I would have to bury my belief of you which was still in the chair.' She declared that death was just like that.

Mrs. Eddy seemed disturbed about something. A student undertook to rebuke her by saying, 'Don't you say in *Science and Health* that it is error to murmur or to be angry over sin?' Mrs. Eddy replied, 'I shall have to take that statement out of *Science and Health*'.

One night the watcher in Mrs. Eddy's room saw her make a convulsive movement in her sleep and the suggestion came into her mind, 'Oh what would I do if Mrs. Eddy passed on in her sleep while I was watching?' Instantly she woke up and dismissed the watcher.

A lady came to Mrs. Eddy in a pregnant condition and told her that she was to have a spiritual child. Mrs. Eddy said, 'Then it will not need to be born of the flesh, will it?'

'Oh! to be nothing', was the line from a hymn that kept going through the thought of a student on the day when a group met with Mrs. Eddy. While our Leader was talking with them she suddenly stopped and asked, 'Where does this thought come from, "Oh! to be nothing. Oh! to be nothing"? I do not want to be nothing.'

After the Next Friends' Suit instigated by the *New York World* Mrs. Eddy said, 'The *New York World* has shown us what an unscrupulous newspaper can do. Now we will show them what a just and kindly newspaper can do for the world'—referring to the *Christian Science Monitor.*

When the Court convened at Mrs. Eddy's home at the time of the Next Friends' Suit, when she was requested to appear, she delayed. The members of the household observed her walking the floor, working, and at times raising her arms as she worked. After a few moments she signified her readiness to go before the Court.

Later, one asked her why she delayed. Her reply was, 'Oh, I could not go in. There was a witness against me.' Judge Aldrich admitted that when the case had been presented to him, it seemed to him that a woman of her age did need the help of her two sons in the conduct of her affairs. Suddenly he awakened to realize that he had formed an opinion of the case—was judging it—before he had heard it.

Was this the witness that Mrs. Eddy felt was against her—that was ruled out?

CHAPTER NINE

INSTRUCTION IN METAPHYSICS

RECORDED BY DR. ALFRED E. BAKER, M.D., C.S.D. DURING HIS ASSOCIATION WITH MRS. EDDY

(Includes several second-hand items gathered then or subsequently)

NOTE. The following pages are complete, except for a few dictionary definitions at the beginning and except for a few items which have already been fully recorded in earlier chapters and seem in place there. Where Dr. Baker has included two versions of the same item, it is the fuller which has been reproduced here.

God sees in man the perfect reflection of Himself. God's thoughts of us are unchanging. To help ourselves or others, we must think God's thoughts after Him. Cast aside sense testimony, accepting only the spiritual facts.

'If God be for us, who can be against us?' Sensuous, wilful malpractice has no power to distract or confuse me so that I cannot perceive the Truth clearly; it can neither make me believe that I am suffering from old beliefs or poisons nor make me see its image, nor fear its mental argument. No danger can befall, for everything is in God's keeping.

To affirm anything is to assert its possibility; to assert it, even in the face of all the contrary evidence. You may not be able to see how by simply affirming a thing to be true, which to human reasoning or sight does not seem true at all, we can bring it to pass, but we can compel yourself to cease all quibbling, and go to work to prove the rule, each one for himself.

This beautiful presence all about us and within us is the substance of every good which we can possibly desire; yea, infinitely more than we are capable of desiring, for, 'Eye hath not seen, nor ear heard, neither hath it entered into the heart of man, the things that God hath prepared for them that love Him.' 'Thou shalt decree a thing and it shall be established unto thee.'

There is but one power in the universe, and that is God. Good is omnipotent. Apparent evils are not entities or things of themselves;

they are simply an apparent absence of good, just as darkness is an apparent absence of light. But God, our good, is omnipresent, therefore, the apparent absence of good—evil—is unreal; it is only an appearance of evil. There is no reality, life nor intelligence in matter for the 'things which are seen are temporal, but the things which are not seen are eternal'.

Pain, sickness, poverty, old age, death, cannot master me, for they are not real. There is nothing in all the universe for me to fear, for greater is He that is within me—true self—than he that is in the world. God says, 'I will contend with him that contendeth with thee'. He says that to every child of His, and every person is His child.

I am the image and likeness of God. No mortal nor mortal opposer of Truth can confine this image in a mortal body to mar or molest it, because divine Mind alone governs it and holds it forever free from mortal touch. I cannot be seen or known or even thought of mortally. I dwell in the spiritual realm of the real....

Do not care who thinks about you nor what they think. All true thoughts are from God and are good. There are no other thoughts for God has no opposite. God's grace is sufficient for every need; and we must know that good thoughts are power, and evil thoughts are powerless when met by Truth.

Our rightful heritage is satisfaction, for God supplies all our needs.

There is no dreaded future and no clouded past. Admit only thoughts that you wish externalized.

Truth does govern our business, and there are no failures nor reverses; God directs our business in Truth and the power of right thought regulates everything.

God has made all provision for us and no legal provisions nor mortal mind limitations can keep us from our God-given heritage. The only God there is can never forsake us. God never fails in His promises, and the only reason we think He does is through faulty consciousness, which is destroyed.

The only satisfaction is in knowing God is with us. It silences grief and exterminates poverty. 'Right alone is irresistible, permanent, and eternal.' 'Human pride forfeits spiritual power.' (*Mis. Writings*)

Whenever you treat a patient, include in your understanding of the case the idea that no ignorant or malicious mind can affect the case and there will be no relapse. Progress is the law of the infinite, and finite views are but suppositions and beliefs. Realize this as a law for every case you treat. A mortal cannot make laws and the real man is not the law-maker.

God gives you daily supplies. Never ask for tomorrow. It is enough that Love is an ever-present help; and if you trust, never doubting, you will have all you need every moment. [1]

Do not doctor the error much, but make yourself so conscious of the opposite Truth that the error will be destroyed.

There is no law that can work against me. The only law does everything for me. The perfection of the divine Mind must be externalized here and now.

There is no unconscious action. All is the action of Mind that is always conscious. All is the voluntary action of Mind and its manifestation; hence there is no disease in process of development in my body.

The fetters that bind me are falling. The fetters that bind my understanding are falling, for the absolute good is guiding me into the land of Truth through Christian Science.

There is no one known to my personality, within my circle or without it, naming the name of Christian Science—loyal or disloyal—that can ignorantly or maliciously malpractice upon me. Neither can malpractice or mesmerism prevent me from recognizing such error and handling it.

Nothing can come to me except that which comes from God, and that is always good.

I am a law unto myself. There is no ignorant, malicious, wilful, superstitious, sympathetic, intentionally directed malpractice from theosophy, palmistry, phrenology, occultism, witchcraft, necromancy, black or white magic, spiritualism, animal magnetism, hypnotism, mental science, free love, malpractitioners, trustees, directors, laymen, occultists, *materia medica,* or from Roman Catholicism, neighbors, friends, enemies, acquaintances or relatives, that can mesmerize me or influence me or confuse my spiritual continuity, or interfere with my spiritual work, or cloud my vision (mental), or darken my consciousness; neither can it impede my progress in my true understanding of God.

[1] See *Mis.* 307:1-10.

Man reflects the wisdom, the intelligence, the ability, the power, and the law of divine Mind. Man is the understanding of God; therefore I do understand God as revealed in Christian Science. I am MAN....

Your joy no man can take from you, and your peace no woman can take from you; the masculine thought (in the mortal) representing sensuality, brutality, animality, etc., etc. Jesus often spoke of his joy and peace, which also should be enjoyed by his followers, and which the world could not give, neither take away.

Mortal mind is to be denied; Spirit overcomes it. We must cease to admit in our thinking the reality and power in themselves of sin, sickness and death, of misery, pain, evil in all forms; and we must steadfastly and persistently think the Truth which stands opposite to them. We do in this way overcome discordant conditions of consciousness now. Everyone who persists in this course many times each day will have signs of the lessening of all evil. (For additional text, see page 282.)

There is no morphine of malice poison that puts to sleep—that is, to your own best interest, and causes dreams and illusions.

There is no strychnine of jealousy poison that contracts and keeps from seeing beyond one's own self—that is, to make us voice error where we should voice truth.

There is no sulphur of hatred poison that always inflames—that is, we must watch this that it does not open the door to the hatred of the world.

There is no arsenic of envy poison to swell and puff up.

There is no cocaine poison to cause depression.

There is no corrosive sublimate of worry poison that eats and gnaws.

Expressions Given at Various Times by Mrs. Eddy

There is no aggressive mental suggestion directed or undirected that can keep me from the love of God, the life of Christ, and the clear light of Christian Science as revealed by the revelator, Mary Baker Eddy.

First, find out what error is trying to do. Second, keep it from doing it, or know that it cannot do it. Third, see that it is not done.

Now Truth hammers error. If you hold to error you get the hammering.

Evil is always zero '0' until you put your unit with it (that is, take it into consciousness).

Truth does mighty things when left to its own vitality.

Supply is continuous, ever-present, available—prove it.

It does not take time to think right.

I thank Thee, dear Father, that there is nothing between Thee and this little child.

According to your spiritual growth, you will hear and see things.

Loving enough to say 'Our Father' we will heal instantly.

Error has no life except the life we give it.

A lie has no voice and no audience.

Disturbed thought needs healing, not nursing.

A demonstration is never made until you see the manifestation.

Mortal material body is human consciousness, Eden—and in reality there is none. Look long enough and you will see perfection

My individual Christ Jesus will go before me and lead me in the work.

By their fruits we shall know them, not by their roots (ancestry).

'A lamb which is the symbol of innocence, is one of the ideas included in the compound idea that expresses God in full. A tree symbol of beauty and aspiration, is another simple idea and portion of man or the compound idea of God, and so of the entire universe.' Taken from 9th edition of S. & H., 1883.

'Mortal thought has never known what God's thought is that we name the sun.' From old edition of S. & H.

'Mesmerism is the error that leaves man at the mercy of matter, will, caprice and mortal mind; God, Spirit, never mesmerized man or matter.' From first edition.

LAW SUIT—Woodbury Case. God governs it. Justice, Truth and Love govern it, and nothing else can or does affect it in the least. I have faith in God. I know that faith as a grain of mustard seed does remove mountains. I have no faith in evil. I know that it cannot do anything. It is nothing. God is All. The wrath of man shall praise Him and the remainder of wrath shalt Thou restrain. All things work together for good to them who love the Lord (given to six students to work with on the Woodbury case).

'God has placed us all in our orbit and, like the stars, we are held there by His power. One cannot interfere with another, and none can fall out.'

Digestion is harmonious action. Assimilation is unity of ideas. Nutrition is life.

Lean on Him (God). Trust Him. Understand Him and He will give you the foresight, wisdom, and capacity to execute His will and benefit His Cause. S1. V. 10.

He who supplies all good will fill all vacancies in His own way; and He will fill them with those who are spiritually equipped to take up the cross and follow whithersoever He leadeth.

Regarding vaccination; there is only the mental vaccination; I would take the point of Spirit which is Truth and prick the human affections, then inoculate with divine Love, circulating the system of thought, and the liability of contagious disease, sin, or sickness will cease.

Instruction

Keep your aim; stick to your text, and have faith in your understanding of the letter of Christian Science: for instance, the claim is paralysis. Your aim is, there is no inaction, there is action. Your text is, God is almighty, and you know it, and error is a lie and is powerless. Your faith is, God is All, and you *know* in whom you trust.

This will win every time; this is the way Jesus healed the man who was healed of blindness, after two trials; stick to it, and *know* we *want* to, and can heal in every case. We know the Truth, and we must be more positive that we know it. We are not hypnotists nor hypnotized.

Always commence and continue ten or fifteen minutes on *no fear,* and if your patient is a Christian Scientist, say, 'You can help yourself'. Argue strong: No laws but the law of Love. Think up no comparison or correspondence with error (as for instance, as to what a leg is in Mind). When treating of bones, e.g., know there are none, hence there are no stiff joints or painful joints or rheumatism, chalky calculus, or other lie. When treating liver, know there is no liver, arsenic, morphine, opium, affecting the belief of liver, no rejection of food, no pain.

The whole matter is covered by knowing that there is no poison nor effects of poison produced through a lie. Here name arsenic and the cyanide of potassium and morphine, and know that neither you nor your patient can be made to believe a lie, also, if either one did not believe it, there would be immediate relief, recovery. It is easier in belief for the practitioner not to believe in disease than for the sufferer. The only proof one has that he does not believe in disease is that his thought of the disease destroys it.

Be not deceived, whatsoever a man soweth, that shall he reap. If one sows a half belief the case will linger; if one sows a whole belief in the understanding the case will show it.

The error is to think one believes what one does not, and understands what one does not, and then to console one's self with this self-deceived state of thought. We have no possible proof that the state of our thought is right unless the effect of the state of thought produces the right result on the patient. Human reason or human imagination is as material as pain. Reasoning or reverie is as erroneous when treating the sick as a sensation of fever would be. The spiritual attitude and altitude gained is the measure of success in healing. Human love can be mistaken; if it is divine, it removes fear and heals quickly. If it is human and yet not at all impure, it does not heal. I name these deep points in metaphysics to show what are wheat and what are tares.

A Correction

In the last *Sentinel* was the following question: 'If all matter is unreal, why do we deny the existence of disease in the material body, and not the body itself?'

We deny first the existence of disease itself, because we can meet this negative more readily than we can negative all that the body affirms. It is written in *Science and Health*, 'There are degrees in the material or human beliefs, and a harmonious step is one step out of error; a belief of health is an improvement upon a belief of sickness'.

Thus it is that our great exemplar, Jesus of Nazareth, first takes up the subject. He does not require the last step to be taken first. He came to the world not to destroy the law of being, but to fulfill it in righteousness. He restored the diseased body to its normal action, functions and organization and in explanation of his deeds he said, 'Suffer these things to be so now, for thus it becometh us to fulfill all righteousness'. Job said, 'In my flesh shall I see God'. Neither the Old nor the New Testament furnishes reasons or examples for the destruction of the material body, but its restoration to life and health as the scientific proof of God with us.

The power and prerogative of Truth are to destroy all disease and to raise the dead—even the self-same Lazarus. The *spiritual* body came with the *ascension*.

Jesus demonstrated the divine Principle of Christian Science when he presented his *material* body absolved from death and the grave. The introduction of pure abstractions in Christian Science without their correlative leaves its divine Principle unexplained, tends to confuse the mind of the reader, and ultimates in what Jesus denounced, namely, straining out gnats and swallowing camels.

A belief of personal sense that is governed by the Truth is a harmonious belief. A harmonious belief governed by Truth is spiritual sense -understanding.

Jesus, in the silent tomb, spiritualized his personal, corporeal body to the extent of presenting it sound, then he ascended, laid off corporeality.

All his mechanism was restored and preserved until the ascension. He ate with the disciples, showing you he could digest his food with the natural functions. I always preserve the actual harmonious being in my thought just as Jesus did.

During parturition your mind can assist your patient, or the prospective mother. At the birth let your mind govern the action, prevent pain and control the presentation of the babe. Mind is master of all the rules and conditions pertaining to obstetrics. Mind governs the results in every respect contingent on delivery and the condition of the infant and mother and treatment thereof. But if you, in certain cases, cannot demonstrate this, then call a surgeon mid-wife, but only as Jesus was baptized, saying, 'Suffer it to be so now'.

I will name, before it slips my memory, that I claim Christian Science admits the personality of God, but calls it infinite Person. Man is the reflection of God, but if God was impersonal, man would be thus. The term infinite Person seems to be a paradox, but in this instance it is scientific sense. All that *is* must be included in the word infinite. And we have in men and things individuality, and this we name in our grammars, persons and things; hence, let us cover the objection that we disbelieve in God as Person after the manner aforesaid....

Remember, Jesus was a carpenter before he was a Savior of men.
Remember, God is the business man.

The Trinity -—To class of seventy

FATHER— is man's divine Principle, Love.

SON—is God's man, His image or spiritual idea.

HOLY GHOST—is divine Science, the Messiah, or Comforter. Jesus in the flesh was the prophet, or way-shower to Life, Truth, Love, and out of the flesh Jesus was the Christ, the spiritual idea, or image and likeness of God.

Evil cannot make an avenue of me to produce a manifestation of error, for there is no evil; and this declaration made every hour makes me invulnerable to evil.

Instantaneous healing—'I and the Father are one'.

ONE WORD—the Word of God, Scriptures and *Science and Health*.
ONE READER—the voice of God. God is All-in-all.
Nothing can go from or come to the Readers but Love.

In the opening of the seals, they shall not buy nor sell unless they have the number of the beast.

Every part of your body is perfect and spiritual, and always at rest.

Mr. Kimball said, 'In a recent conversation with Mrs. Eddy, I said, "Mother, I am telling the people that *no matter* what the error to be overcome is, they must always remember, 'My grace is sufficient for thee'. Am I making this too strong?" "No", she said, "You are not making it strong enough. There is absolutely no cause for failure, or discouragement, or sorrow. Every Scientist must *put absolutely* out of his thought the belief that he must sometime change to another plane of existence. God is Life. There is no other plane of existence, and we must make our plans for immortality—stop talking about death. There is no death to Life." '

Do not say there is no intelligence in food. 'The earth brings forth food for man's use' (*Science and Health*). And we must reflect divine intelligence that enables us to use that food; adhere to the statement that divine intelligence directs man, and governed by it, man eats, sleeps, walks and talks harmoniously.

Depict the real Christ; the man-made is not the image.

Oh, how much we win and lose by taking up the cross, lose self and win Love, lose the pleasure of meeting often our friends, and win the soul of friendship...

Malicious animal magnetism's false claims cannot separate me from God, from Christ, from divine Science, from *Science and Health*, nor from my teacher, Mary Baker Eddy. There is no malice, no hatred, no revenge, no fear, no remorse, and animal magnetism cannot suggest any of these claims as a power to govern me, and cannot make me an avenue through which any of these claims of personality can work evil to myself or any other; cannot suggest through any personality any of these lying claims, nor make a law that I shall in any form manifest them.

Animal magnetism cannot make me restless or dissatisfied; cannot suggest to me any doubt of the absolute Truth of Christian Science; cannot make a law that I cannot heal; that I cannot succeed; that I will not heal my patients; cannot frighten me or prevent me from healing others; cannot darken my thought, nor dim my spiritual perception; cannot produce or bring back a belief with an argument or poison of any kind (name).

'It is our pride that makes another's criticism rankle, our self-will that makes another's deed offensive, our egotism that feels hurt by another's self-assertion.' *Miscellaneous Writings.*

Spare the oil, the balm of repentance; and the wine, the newly inspired love of Christian Science.

Grant, O my God, that neither the joy nor the sorrow of this period shall have visited my heart in vain. Make me wise and strong to the performance of immediate duties and ripen me by whatever means Thou seest best for the performance of those that lie beyond.

Love divine is impersonal, pure, universal and impartial.

Human love is personal, impure, limited and partial.

Love does not fight, but stands, and standing wins.

To a student: 'Do you love yourself?' He hesitated because he did not quite understand.

'Why, you love God, don't you?'

'Yes.'

'And you love God's idea?'

'Yes.'

'Why, you are that idea.'

Substance of What Mother Said from Her Porch to the Students Gathered There in 1900

Beloved Christian Scientists:

I greet you. I thank you and the six thousand. We have had the blessed communion season together. It has been blessed to you all; behold, you have been weighed in the balance and have not been found wanting.

Now, dear children, Christian Scientists ... you are the walls of the earth. This week has been a memorable week to you and to me, coming to commune with our Lord. Carry back the glad tidings to the other six thousand. [2]

[2] Other versions include the following sentence at this point: 'All that I have ever accomplished and all that I ever hope to accomplish for myself or for the Cause has been accomplished through my absolute consecration to God alone.'

Thirty-four years ago, in Boston, I took on myself the cross. I said —

Jesus, I my cross have taken,
All to leave and follow thee.
Naked, poor, despised, forsaken,
Thou from hence my all shalt be.

Perish every fond ambition,
All I've sought or hoped or known,
Yet how rich is my condition,
God and heaven are still my own.

Let the world despise and leave me,
They have left my Saviour too;
Human hearts and looks deceive me
Thou art not like them, untrue.

Oh, while Thou dost smile upon me,
God of wisdom, Love, and might,
Foes may hate and friends disown me,
Show Thy face and all is bright.

When you see the little room upstairs with the swing, think of Mother at twilight, thinking, pondering and praying, I would say to all those who have come from far and near, showing their gratitude to The Mother Church of Christian Science, through me, Good-bye, Good-bye, which in the Saxon means, 'God bless you'.

Do not give life to evil by attaching it to a person or thing; it cannot live without a body; *man is immortal one*. There is but *one infinite manifestation*. No error can attach itself to man, and why deceive ourselves by thinking it can be so?

Rebuke error, keep the standard firm and still, live in the consciousness of good....

Jesus was so good that he had to deny constantly that he was God,

There is no malignant animal magnetism to prevent me from reflecting light. There is no self-mesmerism to hide me from Truth or Truth from me. There is no mental malpractice to harm me, to affright or touch me, for divine Love surrounds me. *Intelligence, substance, power,* are the source of my being. There is no creative power but God, *no universe but Life,* and *Truth,* and *Love.*

If God is the only power (and He is); if God is the only presence (and He is); I am not met by another power and presence to pain, fetter, and befool me.[3]

Man is image, not person—made by the Word, and expresses the Word.

Of two evils, one must always choose the least; and of two evils the wife alone must make the choice, and above all choose the *least* evil. A loss of affection is a great loss. A wife can lead the element of love up higher, from the basement to the upper chamber.

May each day unfold to you the manifold treasures of Christian Science, and may you become the rich partakers thereof Remember that the power to heal is gained through peace, wisdom, Love, dominion over self, and good-will toward men. You possess these graces of Spirit, or Christ-power, only by loving God—good—supremely. After this cometh the recognition of but one Mind, which enables you to know that there is no power or presence that can resist good, or prevent your prayers being effectual. While you remain in this attitude of mind, you are obedient to the Principle of your being, and naught can hinder your healing the sick and the sinner .... [4]

Can the dull pen tell the heart's errand? Can words depict feeling and speak the language of love? If they can then will this tiny shee comfort you, lift you to a realization of a great infinite gain. Never is God so good, so loving, so near to His beloved child, as when she needs Him most. Now you are sharing His benediction, His hand is taking thine, and from the night leading thee swiftly into light. 'Sweet are the uses of adversity.' The gospel of Christ was a Gospel of Glory that could not have been given except through suffering. Let your joy be full; the time has never been before when you were so worthy to bear His cross and prove your loyalty to Him as now. Take His cup, darling, drink and give thanks. 'Tribulation worketh patience, and patience experience, and experience hope, for the love of God is shed abroad in your hearts'. Your husband is not dead; your thought of him is not necessarily sad; he lives and is wiser now than he ever could have been without this lesson. Do not sigh to see him; the evidences of the senses never could, never can, bless him, or you. Be happy, darling, in knowing that he is cared for by infinite Love that is doing more for you both in this seeming affliction than

[3] See *Mis.* 173:21.
[4] See *Christian Science Journal,* July 1936.

Love, altho, boundless, could in any other way. This Love is caring for you in the divine order of progress, and will hide you under His feathers, and under His wing shalt thou trust, rest and rejoice.

Ever tenderly and truly,[5]

Your sweet, sad letter at hand. May the dear Love that wounds to heal bind up the wounds and pour into your life the pure sense of having been tested by chastisement and found legitimate. Yes, you are right that the avenger of Truth stabs us through those we love most, as much as to say, 'You have no moral authority for loving aught but God and His likeness'. What is our remedy? It is to watch, work and pray to make first one's self and then all others into that likeness, patient, meek, loving; then the warfare is comparatively ended and we are saved from a false selfhood. Oh, may the dear Love that knows no lack be so near that you catch the contact and are comforted. My own trials can never be spoken. They are beyond the present sense of mortals. But the one dear Love binds up my bleeding heart, and I lean on its heart till I get breath to stand before the next volley. Let us rejoice that the captain of our salvation is training us for higher service....

Tumor—false action. There is no action opposed to God, no opposite to Truth. Mortal mind is the root, or claim, or claimant, and that root is a sense of personality—my personality—it is a myth. Love reforms and nothing else does. Handle prenatal mesmerism. God is law, and manifests law. Unity of Principle and idea is the only marriage.

Your inquiry—what is the wedding garment?—embraces a long answer, but I can name its hem for you to touch. It is first, the desire above all to be Christ-like, to be tender, merciful, forgetting self, and caring for others' salvation; to be temperate, humble, pure, whereby appetite and passion cease to claim your attention and you are not discouraged to wait on God—to wait for the tests of your sincerity—longing to be good, and seeking through daily prayer for divine teaching. If you continue to ask, you will receive, providing you comply with what you must do for yourself, in order to be thus blessed.

Reading or listening to my teaching the truths of Christian Science will not do for you what the constant seeking and knowing and following will do for you.

[5] Corrected. A letter dated January 2, 1890.

Run, and not be weary. Let our activity in Truth be equal to our sense of running.

God is our source of supply, and supplies every need. He is infinite, and in Him there is no lack, no loss, no want. Mind holds all in position.

In building a church we have the devil to overcome, and he thinks he can stop the work by cutting off the supply. God is our Father and He is rich; His resources are inexhaustible, and whatsoever we ask for we shall receive. The devil tries to make us indifferent and ungrateful.

An effect of animal magnetism is to make you think you have all your old beliefs back again.

The action of error is to tell you that as mortals you have no mind; it says *Science and Health* tells you so. To believe this is to lose your free moral agency. This evil must be met by a counteracting influence of prayer. Let Truth be heard above error and God will bless your efforts.

Handle death and then relapse. Relapse is the result of affection of the mucous membrane. Relapse is mesmerism. Be positive in knowing that there is no animal magnetism. I KNOW THIS.

Three steps: First, original sin. Second, malicious mental inoculation. Third, man's sinless, pure origin.

By these steps we rise from mortal sensuousness and sensitiveness into the true understanding of Life and being, into a realization of freedom and power as the idea of God.

Since malicious animal magnetism knows all the arguments of Christian Science it is necessary to declare that no argument of mental malpractice can make null and void, antidote or reverse, any statement of Christian Science that you make.

Truth and error commingling is the kingdom divided against itself. We must talk more closely to God. Bring Him nearer to us, more like the old style of praying. We must feel and know that God is what we live in—like the atmosphere and sunlight. It is all about us. We must rest more in God. When treating a patient do as well as you can and let God do the healing. If your children need treatment, don't sit up all night, but treat yourself and go to bed, and go to sleep. Give up more to God. Ask for daily bread, enough for today. A child with its mother does not ask all the time for tomorrow and next week, if it will have food and clothing, but runs along happy and trusts its mother's care. So must we do. Have trust in the one Father-Mother God, and without fear. If you suffer, do not fear, suffer it out. The true thought brings the error to the surface, and if we fear not it will pass off. Put physical ailments in the mental. Know they are the result of fear, anger, envy, or some wrong thinking, and do not fear the physical. Just ask for more light, more goodness....

Unless malpractice is exposed by Christian Scientists, the world will be little benefited by Christian Science....

From what appears I fear you did not quite understand my few words of caution, so as to take the wise way of meeting all error, and therefore, I name *this way*: Never address the person who errs by treating (him) mentally or treating yourself against it. Never recognize the person in your argument. You must not. But take it up—the error only—and never doctor the error much, but make yourself so conscious of the opposite Truth, that the error disappears; e.g. know that nothing can come to you, or go from you, but what God sends, and therefore that no mortal mind can influence you, for only one Mind exists, and this is immortal *Love*. Overcome the evil mind with good. Never talk to it, or of it, but hold steadfastly to good. Love—and do not feel that any other power exists.

This will deliver you. If you dwell in thought on any person, it will hinder you from overcoming personality in your healing and casting out sin. There is no *personality*, and this is more important to know than that there is no disease. Your life-long mistake has been your strong sense of personality. Drop it, and remember you can never rid yourself of the seeming effects from a personality while holding in mind this personality. The way is to put it wholly out of mind, and keep before your thought the right model.

Not how much we love one another, but how we love. Passing under the rod of the shepherd means to keep the sheep from jostling one another as they enter the fold....

To sit down and treat yourself and others for animal magnetism is worse than useless. You must find your protection in declaring and living good.

It is not safe to change oars in the current. Courage, stand. When the wind blows the wheat bows its head and does not receive the full blast. It is the empty kernel that keeps its head up and receives the full blow.

Do not take Catholics for patients or students. Leave that problem for future generations.

We are quick to see faults in others and to have the same in ourselves. The only avenue error has to us is our own personal condition of thought.

When you are troubled or disturbed about any matter, that is animal magnetism. God's method of work is quiet, and brings rest and harmony.

In class:

Can our errors be met and overcome other than by crucifixion?

No, there is no other way, else Jesus would not have been crucified. Each one must pass through Gethsemane and up Calvary's height to the cross.

Child's Prayer

Dear Father, I want to love Thee supremely; I want to be unselfish, temperate, pure and good; I want to love and honor my earthly parents, and so be able to uplift humanity. I know that God is good, and that He hath made me in His own likeness, harmonious and immortal; and I will strive daily not to make myself appear otherwise. I thank Thee now and forevermore. Amen....

Oh, God, I ask for Love divine to lead me, not to be tempted or yield to temptation in any way. I ask for wisdom and grace to know and do just what God would have me do....

Benediction:

Thou dost lift the burdens from the overburdened heart.
Thou knowest the ones who rejoice,
And dost comfort such as mourn.
Thou dost waken the sinner from his dream of sin.
Thou dost waken the sick from his dream of sickness.
Thou dost (make) all earth's shadows flee,
And the long night wake,
And the shadows break on the summit of divine Science,
With perpetual beams of Life and Love....

Do you find any difficulty in healing? If so, strike for the higher sense of the *nothingness* of *matter*. Do not care to search into causation there, for there is no cause and no effect in matter; *All is Mind,* perfect and eternal. Whenever you treat a patient, include in your understanding of the case, that no ignorant or malicious mind can affect the case, and there *is no relapse;* Science tells us this in all it manifests. *Progress* is the law of the infinite, and finite views but supposition and belief. Now, *realize* this, and *be a law* to every case when you commence treating it, that there is but *one Mind,* and this one governs your patient, that there are no *minds* to interfere; error is *not mind,* and has *no power* over *you* or the patient. These are the rules for you to work out every hour of your life.

Realize constantly that no mortal mind (so-called) can affect *you* or make you believe you cannot cure your patients. There is no *malice,* no *envy,* no *will-power.* All is Love and Truth. Argue this clearly.

Lovingly yours,[6]

Daily know that mental malpractice cannot cause Christian Scientists or their patients to have return of old beliefs, as this is the argument sent out, also that there is no reversal of the treatment of Christian Science.

To Students Gathered at Pleasant View

My dear students, guard your tongues. When you see sin in others know that you have it in yourselves, and become repentant. If any of you think you are not mortal, you are mistaken.

I find my students either in an apathy or a frenzy. I am astounded at your ignorance of the methods of animal magnetism. Your enemies are working incessantly, while you are not working as you should. They do not knock, they come with a rush. They do not take *me* unawares. I know before they come.

Would that my head were a fountain of waters, and my eyes rivers of tears, that I might weep, because of the apathy of the students and the little they have accomplished.

You have never seen me in my real home, but you may sometime. Come with me into it.

When the New York Scientists presented her with two hundred dollars worth of floral offerings, she looked at the latter sadly, and afterward, with tears in her eyes said, 'But they are not doing the work as I want it.' 'If ye love me keep my commandments.'

[6] Corrected. Written to Mrs. Janette Weller, January 26, 1885.

Answer to the Question in Class—
'What Value do you give to Organization?'

Organization is a method of Mind, and of course a necessity of creation. This is indicated by the perfection of the counterfeit. The form and structure of personality are the crowning work of material sense, and show the effort of error to rival the true and enduring. Ideas body forth Principle in various manifestations. Because mortal sense bodies forth the highly-organized personality, it is an indication that the best success in reaching thought will be along the line of organization. To reflect as perfectly as possible the divine methods, Science chooses the best beliefs of mortal sense to indicate to mortals the perfection of the infinite idea. Of two seemingly necessary evils, always choose the least. Select the best beliefs and methods of mortal mind, and make them serve your highest understanding. The without should reflect the within.

Our organization should show above all things UNITY. There should be but one field. The church in Boston should be the center—The Church of Christ, Scientist—all others tributary to it, not separate organizations. So the thought of many members, but one body, should come into expression. Organization is necessary to meet the banding together of all phases of error.

Mrs. Eddy impressed upon a student the great importance of urging her students to work against mental malpractice in all directions. She said that through the law of malpractice the students have a great deal to meet in themselves physically and also financially, and also in a business way.

The argument is that Scientists are not wanted in business; and because you are a Scientist you will not succeed, etc. All this is evil suggestion. Meet it by knowing and declaring that there is no evil mind, for only one Mind exists—God, good—only one voice, the voice of God, good.

When we get the right idea of father, mother, husband, wife, and child, we will never lose them.

A painless man, a painless God, a painless universe. . .

Mortal mind cannot give us money, nor can it prevent us receiving all the money we need for building up the Cause of Christian Science. Divine Love increases and blesses our supply. It is possible for us to do everything that it is right to do. Do not work for money to come through personality.

In consistency is progression.

Beloved brethren: My heart greets you with Christmas joy. Continue, fellow-worshippers, vigilant in that whereto God calleth thee. Unity imparts the spirit of the trinity. Opinions of men are not substitutes for Science. Be patient with misjudgment. Christ, Truth, overcometh error. Today is tomorrow understood. Love maketh right prosperous. Pure hearts and clean hands upbuild the Cause and Church of Christ, Scientist. Have one God, live in conformity therewith, obedient thereto, governed thereby. (See p. 130.)

No person, no thing, in all the universe, no claim of circumstances, can by any possibility interfere between me and all joy, and all good.

Repeat the following affirmations silently several times each day not with strained anxiety to get something out of them, but trying calmly to realize the meaning of the words:

God is All; there is no evil.
All is harmony; there is no discord.
All is health; there is no sickness.
All is Spirit; there is no matter.
All is joy; there is no sorrow.
All is Truth; there is no falsehood.
All is faith; there is no fear.
All is Life; there is no death.
All is Love; there is no hate.[7]

We must cease quibbling, cease to admit in our thinking the reality and power in themselves, of misery, pain, and evil in all its forms. We must think steadily and persistently the Truth which stands opposite to them. We do in this way overcome our discordant conditions of consciousness.

Now, everyone that persists in this course, several times a day, will have the following, viz.:

1st. Signs of lessening fear of aught that can happen to them.

2d. Signs of mental equilibrium, a self-poise and reliance that faces steadily that which others flee from.

3d. Lack of painful consequences from doing that which is one's duty to do.

4th. Signs of less love for those things which we formerly considered necessary for our happiness, a growing independence of them.

5th. Broadening love and charity, encircling around that which is ours, and including all men.

[7]A letter to Augusta Stetson, July 21, 1904.

6th. Strength sufficient for the demand of each day, when each day's work only is considered.

7th. Signs of peace within which all the tempests of mortal belief cannot destroy—a 'Holy of Holies' with ever-burning lamp; a covenant with God, the All-good; the peace which passeth all understanding; a peace which is above and beyond happiness.

Materia Medica

There is no power, intelligence or principle, mesmeric or hypnotic, *in materia medica* as individual or collective mind. Therefore it cannot blind nor hypnotize mortals through human beliefs or willpower from seeking the true healing as it is in Christ Jesus and Christian Science. There is but one Physician because there is but one Mind; whose medicine is Truth; which destroys all error; whose attraction is Love; which casteth out *all* fear. This is the one Mind which was also in Christ Jesus, and this Mind alone can draw all men unto Him—divine Love.

Materia medica cannot hide under the guise of hygiene, witchcraft, magic, spiritualism, mind-cure, faith-cure, or any other subtle form of carnality, for to be carnally-minded is death.

Man (I) cannot be bewitched or mesmerized by alluring or high sounding phrases or methods, nor by any personality, individual or collective, which substitutes matter and *materia medica* for the healing power of Truth, Christ. The nothingness and impotence of *materia medica* is demonstrated through divine Science by its loyal students who reflect divine intelligence, which destroys any claim of intelligence not in God, good, divine Mind. To enmity's own hell of ignorance, superstition, hypocrisy and hatred, justice consigns the lie which would slay man in order to satisfy its own beliefs in *materia medica* and false theology. God made man immortal and in His image, the image of His own eternity, and to this end gave him dominion over all the earth, over all the works of His hands.

This is the Truth of being, and nothing can change the Truth into a lie. Nothing can wrest man out of the Father's hand, for 'It is He who hath made us, and not we ourselves', and hath given us life everlasting. Therefore health, harmony and immortatity are the everlasting facts of being. *It is so.*

The fullness of the earth belongs to the free circulation of honesty, virtue, and progress in the footsteps of truth.

SAMPLES OF METAPHYSICAL WORK OR WATCHES KEPT BY DR. BAKER

Divine intelligence creates and governs all things in perfect harmony.

The lie and the liar are one: which is the only reversal.

Declaration is demonstration. This is God's law, not a human assertion.

What is true of the claim is not the Truth.

So-called loyal students who read or study Oriental witchcraft cannot cause an unknown chemicalization.

The claim of insufficiency cannot be found in Truth.

Mind is action. No effects from narcotics or opiates, and no aftereffects.

There is no worker working but Love. No mental malpractitioner working. Error has no identity. Error has no justification. There is but one consciousness, Life, Truth and Love.

There is no animal, vegetable or mineral kingdom, there is no poisonous thought or mind. There can be no inflammation from fear, hate, lust or poison, through mental malpractice or mental malpractitioners. There is no mind to transfer or be transferred, telegraphed or transmitted, and no man or woman to operate those claims.

There is no mortal mind to declare. Declaration and demonstration are one.

Error's unreality is for the world.

To instantaneously destroy claim of error know that error will pursue its course to its own destruction—error reversed upon itself.

Christ, declaring in the right way, raised Lazarus, declared Life as God, and admitted no death—the Truth—knowing that enables us to know there are no sick.

DAILY TEST—Always test as to whether a belief of a law of malicious animal magnetism or the law of Love is working, by seeing if the thoughts and actions would unify or divide the workers in the field—ourselves and others.

THE CLAIM—On the stroke of the hour death will come.

TREATMENT FOR MALICIOUS CLAIM—There is no time but God's. No death. No hour for death to strike. Every moment belongs to God, *and is God.*

INSTANTANEOUS DEMONSTRATION—The instantaneous plane achieved in healing and teaching is: Declaration is demonstration. 'The words I speak unto you, *they* are spirit and they are fife.' 'In the beginning was the Word, and the Word *was* God.'

TREATMENT—'You shall know the Truth, and the Truth shall make you free.' The knowing is the thing that counts; not human reasoning, or diagnosis, which is an admission of hundreds of causes, but none of them God or in God or Mind. This knowing the Truth is silent or audible, and is silent or audible declaration.

Results of Treatments—Experiments

The treatment, Love is All, will make the person treated mentally strong and confident, and without fear. Love is All, will destroy lust or sex desires, as sex is lack of mental confidence.

The treatment, God is All, will make the person forget all personal problems.

A mental assassin's treatment of No, which is the thought of a person thinking No to every thought of you, results in a complete nullifying of what you are trying to do. The No treatment is a blanket and results in blankness and thoughtlessness.

Mrs. Eddy said, 'The power of Mind fully understood is the ability to discern whether the thoughts you entertain are your own, or someone else's'.

A thought of Mrs. Eddy's—'Who doth but give me of his earthly wealth, gives to me that which cannot reach the heart and may but serve to stir my neighbor's envy: while he who gives me just a simple thought of Life, or Truth, or Love, gives to me that which I may give again, yet have and keep and use throughout eternity.'

Mrs. Eddy reminded her household of her instruction in one of her classes where she asked what the students would do if they had a case that would not yield in spite of everything. She asked every member. No one knew the answer. Finally, with just a note of exasperation, but with marked emphasis and finality declared, 'Handle animal magnetism'.

Mrs. Eddy instructed me to make a law that my declaration is the only power, the only presence, the only law, the only action, the only thought in the case. 'I know (declare) that Thou hearest me always.'

When Mrs. Eddy dissipated a thunder storm in my presence one day while I was in her study, I asked her how she did it. She replied, 'I saw the face of my Father.' This is an illustration of the Christ. Literally, they are living words, the Word of Life, that is, Words proceeding out of the *mouth of God, which is God.* Nothing to do with terminology.

Mrs. Eddy said God's complete explanation of Himself, at all times, and in all ways, is going on eternally, and nothing else ever was going on, and will go on; and this continuity is God, or one Mind and man.

Students who profess loyalty to their Leader cannot confuse loyalty with superstition or idolatry. Some students, yielding to mesmeric sleep, would put Truth in a bottle and label it with a formula, or drag Truth down to the level of a false concept and use it as a mental- or word-drug.

Hypnotism, mesmerism and theosophy are mindless and powerless because Godless and Christless. God reigns.

PLEASE SEE OVER

FOR ORDERING

ORDER PAGE

To acquire additional copies of *Divinity Course and General Collectanea*, or, to order your copy of *Essays and Other Footprints* (aka the "Red Book") you may order from your local bookstore (have them check in "Books in Print"), Amazon.com, or contact the publisher:

Healing Unlimited
(800) 962-1464
heal@ChristianScience.org
www.ChristianScience.org

The following prices apply to both *Divinity Course and General Collectanea* or *Essays and Other Footprints* and are per copy prices in US dollars.

Hardcover	$25.00 ea.
Paperback	$17.95 ea.
CD of BOTH books in digital searchable format (PDF)	$37.50 ea.
CD of ONE of the above titles (please specify)	$22.50 ea.
Both paperbacks and CD of both books	$70.00 set
Both hardcovers and CD of both books	$80.00 set

Quantity discounts are available. Please check with each distributor for appropriate shipping charges. Contact the above organization for a catalog of their offerings. Prices are as of January, 2006, and subject to change.

Made in the USA